Censoring Hollywood

Censoring Hollywood

Sex and Violence in Film and on the Cutting Room Floor

Aubrey Malone

McFarland & Company, Inc., Publishers
Jefferson, North Carolina, and London

LIBRARY OF CONGRESS CATALOGUING-IN-PUBLICATION DATA

Dillon-Malone, A. (Aubrey)
　　Censoring Hollywood : sex and violence in film and on the cutting room floor / Aubrey Malone.
　　　　p.　　cm.
　　Includes bibliographical references and index.

　　ISBN 978-0-7864-6465-4
　　softcover : 50# alkaline paper ∞

　　1. Motion pictures — Censorship — United States — History — 20th century.　I. Title.
PN1995.62D57　2011
363.310973 — dc23　　　　　　　　　　　　　　2011033394

BRITISH LIBRARY CATALOGUING DATA ARE AVAILABLE

© 2011 Aubrey Malone. All rights reserved

No part of this book may be reproduced or transmitted in any form or by any means, electronic or mechanical, including photocopying or recording, or by any information storage and retrieval system, without permission in writing from the publisher.

On the cover: Sharon Stone and Michael Douglas in the 1992 film *Basic Instinct* (TriStar/Photofest)

Front cover by TG Design

Manufactured in the United States of America

McFarland & Company, Inc., Publishers
　Box 611, Jefferson, North Carolina 28640
　　www.mcfarlandpub.com

Table of Contents

Acknowledgments vi
Preface 1

1. Sinema 7
2. West and the Rest 46
3. Decades of Revolt 75
4. The Liberal Ethos 112
5. Nothing Succeeds Like Excess 151
6. After the Deluge 181

Chapter Notes 193
Bibliography 203
Index 209

Acknowledgments

I wish to thank Jeffrey Taplin for his tireless efforts in putting this text into an electronic format, for chopping and changing it in its various incarnations, for being as patient as he has always been with my demanding requests. Jeffrey has also processed the text, transforming it from the often indecipherable cut-and-paste tangle that technophobes like myself tend to specialize in.

I am exceedingly grateful to my brother Keith for furnishing me with so many books and movies from his inexhaustible library to help me write this, and to my wife Mary for being there for me through all the long hours of its composition. She was, as always, unstinting with her time and practical advice, not to mention those endless cups of tea which kept me awake in the small hours of the morning.

Thank you to the legendary Patrick McGilligan for his much appreciated encouragement when the book was at the teething stage. Also to Jim Burr of the University of Texas Press and Malcolm Henson and Dania Aldeek for their close reading of the text and very astute inputs.

I am indebted to the staff of three libraries in Dublin — Raheny, Coolock and Donaghmede — for locating rare and out-of-print books for me, and to the staff of Easons, Waterstones and Hodges & Figgis for their often thankless labors in similar vein.

A special thank you to Margot Davis for running my book and film reviews in the late lamented *Modern Woman* over the years. Also to Jeremy Addis, Peter Costello, Garry O'Sullivan, Michael Kelly, Paul Keenan, Roisin Fulham, Phil Murphy, Des Duggan and John Low for similar favors. And to my agent Darin Jewell for being as obliging as ever in his exertions.

Last but not least, Roberta Mitchell, the wife of esteemed McFarland author Charles Mitchell, has been a godsend in tracking down a set of all-but-inaccessible movies for me with her especial enthusiasm and good cheer.

Preface

I've been fascinated by the vexed subject of film censorship for almost as long as I've been going to films. In these pages I explore the history of the topic from its heady origins to its virtual invisibility today. I've read over a varied selection of books dealing either directly or indirectly with it, and these are referenced both in my notes and bibliography for any readers wishing to pursue their own research.

My research hasn't been so much the books I've read as the films I've seen. I feel this is where any writer should begin, if not end.

My book, with a first chapter titled "Sinema," begins at the start of the 20th century, at a time when sex and violence were taboo on the screen, and those who engaged in anything to do with either suffered dearly on celluloid. Two decades later an era of gay abandon was ushered in as the Roaring Twenties blew away the cobwebs, notwithstanding the efforts of Will Hays, a former postmaster elevated to the rank of Moral Guardian of the American Nation, to stem the tide of licentiousness in an era that predated the notorious Production Code.

Afterwards came Prohibition, the Depression and the Wall Street crash. In 1934 the erstwhile silent majority of conservative Catholics mobilized themselves to spearhead the formation of the Legion of Decency, a self-regulatory body endorsed by the higher echelons of Hollywood to ensure that its movies would find favor among the prudish and sensitive alike, and thereby guarantee the survival of an industry threatened both by economic meltdown and quasi-religious fervor.

Alongside Hays sat the redoubtable Joseph Breen, a man who seemed to have a personal vendetta against a woman he saw as the greatest threat to public morality, i.e., Mae West, who's the main subject of Chapter 2, "West and the Rest." West was a colorful damsel flying the flag for sexual permissiveness at a time when women weren't supposed to even know about promiscuous behavior, let alone engage in it. A diehard Catholic, Breen cashed the repressive check Hays wrote but couldn't deliver on, waving his big stick in a manner that made sure the liberal flourishes of the pre–Code era were radically curtailed.

Breen and his cohorts Martin Quigley and Geoffrey Shurlock, as well as the clerical duo of Fathers Little and Lord, engaged in a war of attrition with stars and directors who tried to push the envelope, resulting in ruthless deletions of crucial scenes. Their rationale may seem comical to us today but was hardly so at the time the decisions were being made. Their efforts meant that the forties and fifties were decades of ringfencing, horse-trading, and jockeying for position on the Tinseltown totem pole as the definition of what was allowable became ever more tenuous.

The name Will Hays doesn't roll as familiarly off the tongue as that of his arch-nemesis Otto Preminger. We know Billy Wilder better than we do Joseph Breen, and Federico Fellini better than Jason Joy. But the men behind the scenes — in fact, the men *cutting* the scenes — wielded their axes mercilessly, and many directors quaked in their boots when they met them because they knew their livelihood depended on the decisions they made. Releasing a film without a Seal of Approval was at one time tantamount to career suicide.

Chapter 3 discusses the seismic changes of the forties and fifties. In 1951 *The Miracle* created a storm of global proportions, forcing society to re-think its appraisal of what was allowable within the constraints of an outmoded mindset. *The Miracle* was condemned for blasphemy; an appeal by its distributor Joseph Burstyn rendered this short film palatable for general viewing.

The rest, I suppose, is history. Afterwards things could never be the same. For many, the legal reversal was seen as the death knell of Hollywood's "Golden Age."

Many other debates raged during the fifties while the power of the Legion waned, as did the almost fundamentalist *zeitgeist* of its apologists. A brave new world was dawning, and a whole generation of indie directors queuing up to demolish the sacred cows of yore. The very rationale of censorship was now being questioned with a brace of movies that inverted (some would say perverted) what went before.

With this in mind, I pay particular attention in my text to seminal movies like *The Moon Is Blue, Baby Doll, Alfie, The Pawnbroker, Who's Afraid of Virginia Woolf?* and *Bonnie and Clyde* for their groundbreaking contributions to outmoded attitudes and laws.

In Chapter 4 I describe how the whole censorial edifice came tumbling down in 1966 when a mode of classification replaced the old system of films being deemed worthy of being seen or not, depending on whether they received the coveted Seals. Now almost everything was shown, and almost everyone could witness what was formerly regarded as reprehensible, depending on their age or who was accompanying them to the movie theater.

Chapter 5 introduces us to some of the *betes noir* of modern cinema, people like Stanley Kubrick and Ken Russell who gave censors such as John Trevelyan many headaches as he sought to pacify the public and still allow *auteurs* like these men the exposure they deserved, albeit in truncated form. I have used the final chapter to amalgamate many of the themes discussed in previous ones, including the age-old debate of how the actions we see on the screen can influence real-life behavior.

So where does all this leave us now? Today we can go down to our local Wal-Mart and pick up a DVD of something like *9 Songs* — arguably the most sexually explicit mainstream movie of our time — for a few bucks. Is this progress? Hard cases make bad laws, we're told, and if we remove censorship totally from the voyeuristic equation, we're entering an area of moral anarchy. But we still need to raise a toast to the Premingers and Wilders who put their heads above the parapet at a time of national repressiveness, risking their reputations and careers by doing so. If films like *9 Songs* are the legacy of that fight, we can hardly blame these men for it.

Pauline Kael once said that the history of the American cinema could be summed up in two words: "kiss" and "kill." She might have added that many great masterpieces would have gone unmade were it not for the freedoms accorded to the film industry to explore the psychic fall-out occasioned by such urges. It's with this thought in mind that we should relish the freedoms gained by the gallant pioneers who revolted against a sanitized form of life embedded in the heart of an era where every cause had a predictable effect and every crime a predictable punishment. Life was never like that, so why should films be?

Those opposed to that viewpoint would argue that today, "anything goes" in the cinema, which means that subtlety suffers. There aren't many of us old enough to remember when a kiss could only last a few seconds — and then on a closed mouth. Or when married couples had to sleep in separate beds, and live like monks.

As a child I left the cinema during the kissing scenes to get my popcorn, or whatever other substances I ingested to get me through such *longueurs*. In later years such scenes, and what followed them, were probably the *raison d'etre* behind my entering cinemas in the first place. Such are the vicissitudes of adolescence.

There's a scene in Giuseppe Tornatore's *Cinema Paradiso* when the aging projectionist shows a film on the wall of the little village where he lives so all the inhabitants can see it without having to enter the cinema. I had a somewhat similar experience when *Alfie* came to the small town in which I grew up in the west of Ireland. The local cinema was situated less than a hundred yards from my house, which made it into something of a second home for me. You could even say I grew up there. The manager had a red velvet cushion which he placed on the seat to enable me to see the screen when I was, as they say, knee-high to a grasshopper.

In 1966, however, at the age of 13, I was refused admission to *Alfie*. I seem to remember it had the warning "No Under 21s Admitted" appended to it, something I had never seen before (and have never seen since). To help matters, the projectionist (who was a family friend) tried to "bounce" the film's images onto the back wall of his little booth and out onto the street. I viewed the film delightedly with some others of my age from this street. Unfortunately, it all meant little to me. The sauciness was mainly verbal. Neither would I have had any conception (no pun intended) of what the abortion scene entailed.

Fast forward to 1972 and I'm watching *Last Tango in Paris* in a film club in Trinity College University in Dublin because it hasn't been allowed to be shown in the mainstream theaters. Some people suggest clubs like this are used by those who want to see obscene films. Was I there for salaciousness or aesthetics? Whichever, the evening becomes rather comical when the (second-hand) projector breaks down halfway through the screening. Marlon Brando is having sex with Maria Schneider as it happens. The moment seems somehow appropriate, the projector vibrating frantically as if in counterpoint to Brando's pelvic exertions. We don't know whether to be embarrassed or amused. We walk out into the night feeling flat, as if the ghosts of a thousand censors have somehow got their revenge on us.

But this was still forbidden fruit, and forbidden fruit is the subject of the book you are holding. When something is rare it's precious, and any time we can crawl under the wire to see something society warns us against, we tend to do so.

That's the second theme of the book: the manner in which guardians of virtue, far from clamping out illicit desires with their *diktats*, merely succeeded in fanning the flames of fantasies. This applied just as much to the Legion of Decency as it did to the Church, the State, and the censors who took it upon themselves to decide what was palatable viewing for the masses.

Needless to say, these bodies possess little or no power today. As a certain Meir Zarchi propounded in the *Irish Independent* on September 25, 2010: "Since the birth of the Internet, all censor boards around the world have instantly become irrelevant. Anyone anywhere in the universe can simply push a button on any video website store and order it."

I've concentrated mainly on sex and violence in these pages. Related themes like the suppression of political ideas, the McCarthy witch-hunt and the fate of the "Hollywood Ten," etc., are touched on tangentially, insofar as they impact upon my central concerns of motion picture history through a hundred years of infighting, adventurousness, philosophical unrest, vested interests, directorial trickery, xenophobia, racism, sexism, homophobia and cant.

The book ranges from the scatological to the eschatological, from the historical to the hysterical, and from the Ten Commandments to the Men Commandments. In the process, I hope it entertains as well as elucidates.

1

Sinema

Colonial Puritans outlawed theatrical productions in early America in the belief that they poisoned the minds of those who attended them. They had less success imposing such restrictions over literature, but movies (and later television) seemed to inhabit the same un-intellectual framework as theater (with the exception of certain *avant garde* plays staged on Broadway) and thus were easier prey. There was a big difference between smutty nickelodeons and the cerebral sexuality of the post-war era so it was easier for such watchdogs to impose their will here.

America suffered its first moral threat from the movies in 1896 with *The Kiss,* a film that was aptly named as it had a smooch lasting all of a minute between May Irwin and John C. Rice. It was innocent enough, but a foretaste of more erotic things to come. The National Board of Film Censors was established in 1908 and this became the National Board of Review eight years later.

D.W. Griffith's *The Birth of a Nation* was banned in 1915 for presenting the Ku Klux Klan in a heroic light. The United States Supreme Court ruled that the film couldn't claim the constitutional protection of "freedom of speech," a ruling that lasted until Roberto Rossellini's *The Miracle* caused a similar furor three decades later and resulted in a reversal of that decision.

The Birth of a Nation was a huge hit, grossing over $18 million at the box office largely because of its innovative editing. Almost single-handedly it heralded the death knell of the two-reelers. It was even shown in the White House, causing President Woodrow Wilson to remark, "It's like watching history being written in lightning."[1] *The Birth of a Nation* portrayed blacks so negatively that it all but ratified the demonic deeds of the Klan. Its propaganda effect relegated blacks to the back of the bus — both physically and metaphorically — for decades afterwards.

Lois Weber was one of the first directors to come to the attention of censors in Hollywood's early years. In 1916 she dealt with the vexed subject of abortion in *Where Are My Children?* and birth control the following year with *The Hand That Rocks the Cradle*. This was banned in New York. She dealt with religious duplicity in *Hypocrites* in 1915.

Where Are My Children? had an interesting storyline. Richard Walton is a district attorney who wants to have children but can't due to the fact that his wife secretly keeps getting abortions when she becomes pregnant. In the film's central irony, Walton finds himself prosecuting the abortionist for circulating a book about birth control and, later on, for fatally botching an abortion. As he's been led away to prison, he informs Walton of his wife's activities. Walton is distraught.

He returns home to find his wife with her equally childless friends who have also availed themselves of the services of the abortionist. "I should bring you to trial for manslaughter," he tells them, "but I shall content myself with asking you to leave my house." After they go, he turns to his wife and utters the line that gave the film its name. In the following years his "murderous" wife tries to get pregnant but, we're informed, "having perverted nature so often, she found herself physically unable to wear the diadem of motherhood." Everywhere she goes, she gazes longingly at children playing.

In the final scene we see the couple looking bewildered as Weber superimposes an image of a group of children around them, just to hammer home the didactic point more forcibly. We can hardly blame her for this. As somebody once said of a dog wheeling a pram, the surprise wasn't that it was done poorly but that it was done at all. Any other emphasis would have guillotined the film from the outset as far as the censors were concerned.

Weber wasn't the only director to come to the attention of the censors. In 1919 three films were released with equally inflammatory subject matter: *Open Your Eyes*, *Fit to Fight*, and *Damaged Goods*. *Open Your Eyes* dealt with three young men who contract syphilis after respective flings. One of them goes to an unqualified practitioner for a cure which doesn't work. He then marries and has a child born blind. The second man also goes to a bogus doctor and suffers by transmitting the disease to another woman. The third goes to a properly qualified doctor and (surprise surprise) is cured.

Fit to Fight also had the theme of syphilis at its core, featuring some soldiers who are foolish enough to engage in sexual congress with prostitutes before realizing that clean living is the only sure way to guarantee the physical integrity necessary to fight for one's country. In his book *Policing Cinema*, Lee Grieveson informs us that this film was re-titled *Fit to Win* after the war, but was caught up in considerable controversy, "including the emergence of a Catholic-led campaign that foreshadowed the later actions of the Legion of Decency."[2]

Damaged Goods centered on a man who contracts syphilis after casual sex but doesn't inform his fiancée. Their child ends up contracting the disease too, after which his wife leaves him. Reconciliation only takes place when the man consults a "proper" doctor for a cure. (He's consulted with a "quack" earlier on.)

Strong themes presented themselves in some form or other in early American films but the treatment of them was either facile or preachy. Theda Bara was Hollywood's first *femme fatale*— or should I say *femme comique*. In Fox's first film *A Fool There Was* (1915) she trapped men in her web. The following year she played a nymphomaniac in *The Vixen*.

Sexual permissiveness, in Edward De Grazia's phrase, took a "quantum leap" in the 1920s. Bara had more or less "invented" the screen vamp, and Clara Bow made her more alluring. And then there was Cecil B DeMille, who "practically invented the bathroom scene."[3] Bara appeared in *Cleopatra* in 1917, her image of "faintly malignant sexuality" far enough removed from real women not to be considered dangerous by the censors.[4]

Molly Haskell believed that Bara and fellow vamp Nita Naldi were "comic carnivores" intended to represent "demonic forces that, like a cyclone, threaten to uproot man from himself" but ending up "more like storm warnings than the storm itself." Bara especially; her "hypnotic glare of the bird of prey, and eyes smoldering under half-closed lids like shades partly lowered in a whorehouse was more farcical than seductive."[5]

As Marjorie Rosen informs us in her book *Popcorn Venus*, the first major film moguls were Jewish immigrants who generally subscribed to the "South eastern European ethic in which woman was either Madonna or whore, a mother to be revered while she stirred the chicken soup but discarded if she succumbed to an unsanctified libido."[6] One of Bara's lines in *A Fool There Was* is "Kiss me, you fool!" Rosen believed this silent comment "cut through the rubble of Victorian sentiment like a stiletto."[7] She thought Bara also had her roots "firmly founded in Victorian denial. She was an absurd sexual distortion. She was unnatural; therefore she was safe.... There was no confusing Theda Bara with the girl next door, not even the bad girl next door. No woman at the time could have looked like her without being locked up or laughed off the street. If Lillian Gish or Mary Pickford had posed in such outrageously flimsy costumes, the vice squad would have been appalled, but Theda's exaggeration gave her amazing license."[8]

Her achievement, rudimentary as it was, was to act as a sexual pioneer, to bridge the gap between austerity and flamboyance: "Before Freud's theories of behavior had become popularized, she cast that ominous shadow, the vagina with teeth. She sucked the blood from her lovers; she deprived them of self-respect. For her they groveled. And while by the mid-twenties her vamp

Theda Bara, one of Hollywood's first sex symbols, albeit an over-the-top one, in a scene from *Cleopatra* in 1917 with Fritz Leiber.

aroused ridicule, was she not the mother of the *femmes fatales*, the Mysterious Women, the Impenetrable Bitches of later screen generations?"[9]

By 1917, suffragettes were heatedly clamoring for recognition, chaining themselves to government buildings to force the authorities to listen to them. In August of that year, ten of them were arrested for picketing outside the White House, four receiving six-month prison sentences. By November the number arrested and sentenced had risen to forty.

Working for the war effort had driven women into factories by this time, and cars gave them mobility. War widows were forced to become self-reliant. Tragedy forced them to grow up faster than their mothers and to embrace the liberalism the Jazz Age was championing. Movies became an adjunct to this, a celluloid lamp that could light the way to more heady adventures both on and off the screen.

Women owned the twenties. Prohibition was introduced at the beginning of the decade but they still managed to make their spirits soar. The flapper was born. Dress sense became adventurous. Women smoked, danced, cut themselves loose from the shackles of convention. They also became sexually free.

In 1921 Margaret Sanger organized the first American birth control conference in New York. It was shut down by the police upon instructions from Archbishop Hayes but the point had been made: The "gentle" sex was about to take control of its destiny.

Two years later, in *Main Street*, Norma Shearer spoke for a generation when she said, "Solitary dishing isn't enough to satisfy me or many other women. We're going to chuck it. We're going to wash 'em by machinery and come out and play with you men."

Of the ten best-selling books of 1925, eight were written by women. People like Edna Ferber, Willa Cather and Dorothy Parker were household names. By 1929, the number of college-educated women trebled. Marie Stopes was another hot-button scribe. *Maisie's Marriage* (1923), loosely based on Stopes' book *Married Love*, received much abuse for its association with the family planning pioneer. The title character initially refuses to marry her boyfriend because she fears that having a large family will curtail her freedom and economic independence. She's turned out of her home as a result of her decision and undergoes many traumas thereafter, becoming "redeemed" only when she reunites with her boyfriend. It was clearly a propaganda movie but the fact that Maisie had the audacity to contemplate life outside marriage was enough for her to be made to suffer the slings and arrows of spinsterhood.

Her fear of having a large family, as Annette Kuhn outlines in her book *Cinema, Censorship and Sexuality, 1909–1925*, was a sore point for the censors in the early 1920s, a period during which the birth control movement had begun to secure a broader base of support for its objectives than it had hitherto enjoyed: "One of its new goals was to persuade government and local authorities to sponsor clinics dispensing advice and contraceptives."

The first birth control clinics in Britain, which were private, had opened in 1921. Arguments in favor of birth control began to emphasize its benefits in terms of health, welfare and general happiness of mothers and children, a shift away from the earlier, predominantly eugenic emphasis on the quality of the "race."[10]

Stopes' books had been banned in some countries. In 1923 she brought a libel suit against a Catholic doctor, Halliday Sutherland, who'd made uncomplimentary comments about her in one of his own books. Sutherland won the case but the decision was reversed upon appeal, and then reversed again in Sutherland's favor.

Maisie's Marriage was made in just two weeks. It was originally going to be called *Married Love*. Even though Stopes' involvement in it was minimal, the makers wanted to capitalize on the publicity any association with her would create. The censors had other ideas, however; they ordered the title changed and insisted that the promotional material avoid using Stopes' name.[11] Far from being a dangerous film advocating family planning, it ended up as a fairytale espousing the multifarious delights of marriage, with any number of children coming in the wake of that union.

In the 1920s, U.S. movie attendances reached a record of 50 million per week. That worked out at almost a billion dollars being taken at the 14,000 cinemas in the country. The end of World War I and the advent of the Jazz Age meant Americans were ready to party and they could do this vicariously in cinemas. But to some people, this was a sign that the country was going to hell in a handbasket.

When talkies arrived, the doors were blown open as far as what was allowed to be screened. Gregory D. Black summed up the situation: "Now sexy starlets could rationalize their immoral behavior. Criminals using hip slang could brag about flouting law and order. And politicians could talk about bribery and corruption."[12] What was previously implied was now out there plump and plain. It was time for the anally retentive to be very worried.

The talkies heralded a huge leap in what could be shown: "Once on-screen cards of stilted dialogue vanished, audiences found a thrilling intimacy that hadn't existed before. Now they could be seduced by actors' voices — and by the sounds of passion."[13] James M. Skinner saw it like this: "What had been impossible or innocuous in a silent picture — the creak of bedsprings or the mouthing of a curse — now assumed a far greater degree of salaciousness."[14]

Censorship wasn't a major issue in the days of the silent movies. With dialogue came boldness. Even though film is primarily a visual medium, its words seemed much more threatening to the *status quo* than its images. And yet in a strange way, the talkies took away some erotic magic.

It was in 1921 that the film industry got its first major jolt from the moral contingent. That was the year comedy star Fatty Arbuckle was arrested on charges of rape and manslaughter in San Francisco. Arbuckle, a former plumber to Mack Sennett, became famous as a slapstick comedian in Keystone Cops two-reelers but during an infamous party (thrown to celebrate a new contract with Paramount Studios), his life changed forever. It was at this party that Virginia Rappe, a "good time girl" who drank too much and then became flighty, died after her bladder was ruptured. Was Arbuckle responsible? Opinions differed on exactly how complicit he was in her demise but some witnesses testified to her moaning "It was him" before she passed out in his bathroom.

Press stories about Arbuckle's trials — there were three in all before he was finally acquitted — sold more newspapers than the sinking of the *Lusitania*. The public were hungry for scandal and here they had it in spades.

The Moral Majority also had an axe to grind. Mary Pickford had just divorced her husband Owen Moore to marry Douglas Fairbanks — that marriage would also run aground in time — and Charlie Chaplin was embroiled in a scandal with his teenage bride Mildred Harris.

Arbuckle became a sacrificial lamb, the burnt offering upon which Middle America foisted its outrage over the Rabelaisian antics not only of himself, but also others of his thespian ilk. His premature ejection from the film world became a caution to those who would fill their cups to the brim and sup aplenty. David Thomson wrote, "Threatened by its own excesses, haunted by insecurities, the picture business reacted cravenly, as it would later under McCarthyism."[15]

Though Arbuckle walked free from the court, it was a pyrrhic victory because his contract was swiftly cancelled and his unreleased films shelved. (The already released ones played to empty houses on the odd occasions they were shown.) Legal fees ate up his fortune and he started to drink to drown his sorrows. His friend Buster Keaton gave him some work under the ironic pseudonym Will B. Good but nobody saw the joke. He was washed up and he knew it.

Towards the end of his life he lamented ruefully, "I read what they printed about me in the newspapers. After things are printed, whether they're true or not, you can't change people's ideas. But it didn't seem as if it could be me they were talking about."[16] He died at 46 of a broken heart, a salutary reminder to all of those who were given too much too soon and abused the privilege. James Robert Parish suggested that "even in death, Arbuckle received no peace, because the slander still exists."[17]

There was also the drug death of Wallace Reid, a former All-American boy who had succumbed to morphine addiction. This shook Hollywood to its foundations. Up until now there was a concerted effort to airbrush scandal out of stars' lives, giving them identities almost as glamorized as those of the characters they played on screen. But you couldn't argue with an autopsy.

Also in 1921, the director William Desmond Taylor was found murdered. Mabel Normand was the last to have seen him alive and this very fact hurt her career. The love of his life, Mary Miles Minter, whose career was on the rise at the time, was never heard of again after the scandal.

It was as if the lid was suddenly blown open on a hermetically-sealed world. A Pandora's box of scandals erupted within an inordinately short time. Something had to be done to stem the flow.

Arbuckle didn't only cook his own goose by his drunken excesses but also that of a whole colony of fellow-minded hedonists. Pressure was brought to bear on them all from a number of quarters. One writer concluded, "Enough happened in the early twenties to provide adequate ammunition for those who maintained that Hollywood was the Sodom and Gomorrah, to say nothing of the Babylon, of the world."[18]

It wasn't only religious groups that were pressing for stricter control over what they watched in cinemas, but governmental bodies and even the general public themselves. Deciding to act rather than wait for a time when power in this regard could be wrested from them, they set up a self-censorship body. Their attitude was that the seen enemy was preferable to the unseen one. This way they would at least have some autonomy.

Gerald Gardner gave a straightforward explanation for the move: "It is said that democracy is the worst form of government except all the rest. Self-regulated movie censorship was the worst form of control except all the rest — i.e., censorship imposed by the federal government, the states, the church."[19]

It was called the Motion Picture Producers and Distributors of America (MPPDA) and was overseen by former postmaster Will Hays. Hays was an innocuous little man with "ears like the handles of a water pitcher."[20] Within days of Arbuckle's acquittal, Hays saw to it that he would never work in Hollywood again. Barry Norman described Arbuckle as "a scapegoat offered up by Hollywood to appease the forces of moral disapproval."[21]

Hays may have been "an idiot and a humbug"—the view of David Thomson—but his influence was huge.[22] He made sure Arbuckle's films weren't even shown in prisons because they might be a bad influence. In time Hays would come to be regarded as something of a Frankenstein figure, a monster created from within the industry itself. But he was really just the barometer of a moral climate. Anybody less stringent wouldn't have lasted in the job. In fact, if he was more lax he would have been an irrelevance.

Hays could never have got away with what he did unless there was a groundswell of support for his policies from Ordinary Joe, who was really Holy Joe, the man in the street but not of it, and hardly possessing "street cred."

Feeling that the MPPDA was losing its iron grip on the industry, Hays enlisted the help of Martin Quigley, the Catholic publisher of *The Motion Picture Herald,* and Father Daniel Lord, a Jesuit priest with a particular interest in ethics in the cinema. Between them they drew up a Production Code based, they claimed, on the Ten Commandments.

Audience attendance plummeted shortly after the inception of the code in 1930. Part of the drop-off was due to the Depression, which had hit every industry, but part was also due to the fact that films with anemic messages weren't as enticing as those with dangerous ones. "Anemic" was an anagram of "cinema"; it could also be its downfall.

The studios slashed admission prices to try and reverse the downward spiral but they also knew they had to inject more "juice" into their movies. The trick would be to do it without offending those who saw Tinseltown as an open sewer. Since audiences were dwindling on account of the Depression, Hollywood feared they'd be decimated altogether if church groups launched a crusade against them, mobilizing all their various factions in all-out boycotts.

The end of the Depression ushered in a period of bacchanalian frenzy in Hollywood, both on and off the screen. But some people weren't laughing.

Stranded on the outside of a post–Prohibition party that seemed to want to go on forever, the reformers lay in the long grass waiting to pounce on the reckless revelers.

Hays was on a salary of $100,000 a year. As far as the studios were concerned, that was a small price to pay to get him onside in their battle against governmental censorship. They employed him to make them look good. They mightn't have liked what he did but he was the lesser of two evils. They needed him to ward off a bigger threat.

At this time a morality clause was also inserted into actors' contracts, sandwiching them between a rock and a hard place both in their private and public lives in one fell swoop. Woe betide those with Communist sympathies, homosexual leanings or even a large degree of testosterone. The love that dared not speak its name wasn't just homosexual but heterosexual too. The mop-up had begun. Hays took it upon himself to act like some Old Testament God of wrath. He became the unofficial boss of almost everyone in the industry, a man people rarely saw but who wielded a huge stick.

His word, literally, was law. Those who disobeyed him were threatened not only with cancellation of the said contracts but outright blacklisting from any other studio as well. It wasn't long until his "Doom Book" included 117 names of those deemed "unsafe." It was a precursor of the McCarthy witch-hunt in a non-political context. It was only when movie attendances of Catholics in big cities began dropping off that directors really started to get worried, adopting the slogan "Where there's a Will [as in Hays], there's a way."[23]

Kenneth Anger chronicled the phenomenon in his landmark book *Hollywood Babylon*: "The picture people were about to observe a perpetual Lent. Male stars would henceforth be monks and women stars nuns."[24] They joked that they were the only pieces of merchandise allowed to leave the studio at night.

Moral guardians, of course, were nothing new, but in each generation they tended to foist themselves upon a different medium. Leonard Leff remarked in his book *The Dame in the Kimono* (the title is a reference to an excision made in *The Maltese Falcon*) that down through the centuries the "moral guardians of the masses" issued warnings about "cheap amusements." In the seventeenth century it was theater. In the eighteenth it was romance novels. In the nineteenth it was "dime novels and the penny press."[25] The time had now come for films (the latest "penny dreadfuls") to stand up and be counted.

The first headache for Hays was the spate of crime movies that seemed to romanticize violence. This was the era of the speakeasy, the flapper girl, the fast-talking, sharp-shooting hood. An early draft of the Code stipulated that the sympathy of the audience should never be thrown to the side of crime by making it attractive or alluring. John Lyden qualified this: "Even if evil was depicted rather brutally, this might actually *increase* audience interest and fascination, so that the Hays Office not only had to ensure that the criminal was punished in the end, but that the violence not be depicted too explicitly."[26]

At first, Hays merely issued general statements, huffing and puffing about the need for high moral fiber in things cinematic. He listed books and plays which he urged studios not to buy. As time went on, he became more forceful in his demands. After tackling crime, he got onto what he perceived to be a much bigger ethical fish: sex.

Women suffered most under the Code, according to author Mick LaSalle: "It wasn't only crime that didn't pay. Sex outside of marriage didn't pay. Adultery didn't pay. Leaving your husband didn't pay. Getting pregnant outside of wedlock didn't pay. Even having a job often didn't pay. Nothing paid. The Production Code ensured a miserable fate — or at least a chastened one — for any woman who stepped out of line."[27]

Hays believed that the American public was the real censor for the motion picture, just as it was for the press and the pulpit. He overstated their sense of purity: "We must have that sacred thing, the mind of a child, that clean and virgin thing, that unmarked slate."[28] The studios could have been forgiven for thinking that he was joking with this kind of hyperbole; he wasn't.

The clampdown on crime was one thing but the manner in which the expression of emotion was inhibited made movie-going a rather fabricated experience. As John Roeburt phrased it, "The lover's screen kiss was now casual and quick, as personally impersonal as a father's indulgence towards a minor daughter."[29]

Showing the sex organs of animals was utterly taboo at this time. Close-ups of the milking of cows wasn't allowed, streams of milk issuing from their udders being regarded as violating the vulgarity clause. It was recommended for one film that the action of an electric milking machine be suggested rather than shown.

Scenes of childbirth were prohibited, even in silhouette. Neither were a woman's off-screen moans permitted. Labor pains couldn't even be indicated. The showing of toilets in bathroom scenes was also prohibited. Even the off-screen sound of a toilet being flushed was outlawed. In one film, a "Ladies" sign on a door had to be changed to "Ladies Lounge." Not only were stars not allowed to relieve nature; burps and belches were also verboten.

The Hays Code had other strict edicts, among them being a proviso that no double beds were to be shown, even among married couples, and a husband could only sit on his wife's bed with both feet on the floor. Kisses could last no longer than eight seconds and had to end up with the lips sealed. Neither could anybody be kissed in a horizontal position and there was to be no touching of legs under tables unless the people in question were married.

'In the old days," Ronald Reagan reminisced, "kissing on screen was very beautiful. The two people doing it were barely touching sometimes, in order to not push her face out of shape. You were doing it for the audience to see what in their minds they always think a kiss is." Gary Cooper added, "You were allowed to kiss your horse in Westerns, but never your girl." Cooper, one imagines, made up for lost time after shooting finished.[30]

To combat such sexual prudery, Universal-International Studios wrote into its contracts a "cheesecake clause" to allow them to show off their female stars' curves in promotional shots. Such a clause specified that suitably endowed female newcomers would, for the first five years of their contracts, be allowed to display their charms in publicity pictures. As well as being exploitative, this was dishonest to lusty filmgoers as it suggested that such charms would also be visible in the films themselves. As was evidenced by movies like *The Outlaw* (of which more anon), such was clearly not the case.

The Code made it its business to ensure that no audience would sympathize with wrongdoers. To this end, using its own tortured logic, it forbade sex outside marriage, "excessive and lustful kissing," lustful embracing, suggestive postures and gestures, indecent or undue exposure, and sexual perversion or any reference to it.

The authors of the book *Hollywood Be Thy Name* satirized this as they documented a hypothetical conversation between Jack and Harry Warner about it. "It's all due to a bunch of tight-assed Roman Catholic bishops," alleges Jack as he reads the Code out to his brother, adding that from now on, the authority to exhibit films in America will be denied even if there's any "long tongue-involved kissing." This will necessitate studios having to fire actors with long tongues. The idea of a man having to have one foot firmly on the floor if he kisses a woman who's in bed makes him wonder "Why in the hell don't we just have them rub noses?" He finally tells Harry that there's to be no nudity at all, not even on babies, leaving him to conclude, "Good God — are they supposed to be born in Little Lord Fauntleroy suits?"[31]

Other myths to flourish under the Hays Code, according to one writer, were "the belief that divorced couples invariably remarried one another, the conviction that all criminals were punished, that war is a glorious adventure in which American boys are impervious to harm, and that women have no navels, since none could be exposed on the screen."[32]

Miscegenation (i.e., sex relationships between black and white people) was forbidden. Children's sex organs were never to be exposed. Venereal disease wasn't to be shown or discussed. Any film that failed to comply with these guidelines was denied a Seal of Approval, which automatically excluded it from most American cinemas.

There were many organizations Hays was answerable to: The PTA, the American Citizenship Council, the American Association of University Women, the YMCA, the National Council of Jewish Women, the Council of the Methodist Episcopal Church, the Young Ladies Institute, even the Boy Scouts. Clearly, it would have been impossible to satisfy all of them as they had differing agendas, so he was always going to be wearing contradictory hats. It was a question of damage limitation.

Needless to say, prostitutes could never be featured, their occupations euphemized into dancing girls and/or barmaids when plots called for them to appear as romantic sub-leads in Westerns or crime movies. In one film, the MPPDA objected to a scene where a "Do Not Disturb" sign was placed outside the door of a married couple in a hotel. In another, it insisted upon the deletion of a scene where a man buttoned his wife's dress while kissing the nape of her neck, and then pinched her bottom affectionately.

Liquor even had to be presented with "good taste." The mention of adultery was abjectly ruled out. Indecent dances were forbidden, as were flippant references to religion, the family or the law. Needless to say, such topics as rape or abortion were totally forbidden.

Hays was responsible for ushering in a world where, in some instances, a man and a woman weren't even allowed consummate their marriage. In one film, a scene where a soldier had been away for several years and now wanted to sleep with his wife was regarded as overly "intimate."[33]

In his autobiography, Pat O'Brien, as conservative an actor as they come, admitted that films had been wild before Hays: "Moral values were slipping down the girls' sweaters," he wrote, "as the studios tried to recover from the

Great Depression with raw sensation."[34] But the sex, he claimed, was more earthy than perverted: "It was shaking dance steps, Charlestoning knees, necking in the family jalopy while sipping hooch from a flask." He said heroes were made of gangsters to an extent, "but the underdog always got the break" and "only rats shot anyone in the back." An acquaintance of O'Brien's joked, "Hays' 12 Commandments was just like Hollywood — two more than even God felt the world needed."[35]

The motive may have been grand, but adopting an ostrich-like attitude to life's problems wasn't going to make them go away. On the contrary. By avoiding a realistic tackling of issues, one was allowing them to fester. Also, people had to be aware that the antiseptic images they saw on the screen bore so little relation to the world around them as to constitute a monstrous distortion. And when they left the cinema, it made tragedy all the more tragic because the buffer was gone. Somehow, you got the feeling that moviegoing children would have fared better under the old regime. The life they were seeing there, even if it wasn't ideal, was more akin to what they could expect to be confronted with in adulthood.

In June 1922, Montana senator Henry Myers, a speaker in Congress, gave this post–Arbuckle tirade: "Hollywood is a colony of these people where debauchery, drunkenness, ribaldry and free love seem to be conspicuous." Many stars didn't know what to do with their wealth except to spend it in riotous living, dissipation and high rolling. "From these sources our young people gain many of their views of life, inspiration and education. Rather a poor source, is it not? Looks as if censorship is needed, does it not?"[36] Mindsets like this were responsible for the over-compensation.

One day Hays called a meeting of various studio directors to criticize their films' "sexy advertisements," which he thought violated the Code. As he was speaking, a pair of pigeons appeared on a ledge outside one of the windows and began to mate. "What's going on out there?" Hays enquired, only to be met with the response, "They're violating the Production Code."[37]

Many of the films produced under the moral watchdogs of this time were little more than chewing gum for the eyes, forgettable fodder, and/or B-movie double bills made by people who, as the joke went, knew only one word of more than one syllable: "fillum."

The emphasis wasn't so much on the "show" element of show business as the business end. As most people knew, the moguls' hearts were close to their wallets and their cash register brains went into panic mode when attendances fell off. The till was the final arbiter, not the ideology.

Another organization, the International Federation of Catholic Alumnae (IFCA), was established in 1922 for the express purpose of vetting films that might be unsuitable for children. This was a function that had formerly been performed by the National Catholic Welfare Conference, but the IFCA soon eclipsed it in its strenuous opposition to any film that appeared to undermine the parents' role in sex education, claiming that "celluloid teachers" were causing children to become increasingly precocious in such matters.

Writing in *Columbia,* a cautionary Knights of Columbanus journal, Philip Burke emoted, "Until children are no longer children, the best sex education is the forgetting of sex." The "cold shower" remedy championed by the Christian Brothers for hormonal adolescent excitement was still alive and well.[38]

Dorothy Cummings was made painfully aware of the new regimen when she appeared as the Madonna in Cecil B DeMille's silent version of *The King of Kings* in 1926. When she sued her husband for divorce the following year, she was reminded that her contract with DeMille specified that for seven years after the film she was expected to behave in an ethically upright manner, to prevent any degrading of the role she was about to play.

She'd signed her name to this but with her divorce pending she argued that it was an infringement on her personal liberty. Her divorce went ahead but her career options were severely curtailed as a result. (As late as 1965, when George Stevens cast Max von Sydow as Christ in *The Greatest Story Ever Told,* the actor had to agree to cut down on his smoking and drinking until the film was completed, and even forego press interviews for fear of uttering something unseemly.)

"In its support of the holy institution of matrimony," Molly Haskell joked, "the Code was trying to keep the family together and protect the American female from the footloose American male who would obviously flee at the first opportunity unless he was bound by the chains of the sacrament, which Hollywood took upon itself to keep polished and shining."[39]

Offscreen in the same year, the irrepressible Tallulah Bankhead gave a magazine interview in which she said she was perfectly able to have a love affair with any man an hour after meeting him. Hays arranged to have her declaration deleted from what appeared in the published interview. This was a measure of his power.

Clara Bow, the infamous "It" girl, was another bugbear for Hays. The epitome of the flapper era, Bow threw wild parties that were legendary in Tinseltown and, despite repeated warnings from Paramount, she refused to buckle under. Eventually, using a carrot rather than a stick, the studio offered her a bonus of $500,000 if she didn't run wild in public.

More scandals followed and eventually she was sacked by Paramount — but only, as David Shipman emphasized, "after two of her films bombed at the box office."[40] Once again ethics had been sacrificed to expediency, or at least delayed by it. Bow subsequently had a nervous breakdown. She retired at the age of 26, moving to a ranch in Nevada with her husband Rex Bell, where she lived as a recluse for the rest of her life.

In 1927 Hays drafted 25 regulations concerning the screen depiction of religion, sex, crime, violence, profanity and international relations. Such a method of enforcement backfired in the same way Prohibition did. If drinkers had speakeasies, suggestive filmmakers also had evasive tactics. Bow didn't need sexy dialogue to get her oomph across; it was embedded in her very presence. Likewise for stars like Marlene Dietrich and Jean Harlow.

Dietrich always had something of an androgynous persona on screen. In *Morocco* (1930) she dresses in a tuxedo and kisses a woman on the lips in one scene. Three years later Greta Garbo, another actress who was tagged with being a lesbian in some quarters, played a bisexual in *Queen Christina*, though the theme was hardly developed. Bow's *Call Her Savage* (1932) featured a scene in a gay Greenwich Village bar. The Code era sought to drive out all themes like this, unless they were — forgive the pun — coded. (Having said that, William Wyler's *These Three* brought a lesbian theme to the fore in 1936 in a powerful adaptation of Lillian Hellman's play *The Children's Hour*, subsequently to be re-made under that title with Audrey Hepburn and Shirley MacLaine in 1961. MacLaine hangs herself in the final reel in a manner which made the 1936 version look more progressive).

The Roaring Twenties did just that: roar. Almost as an over-reaction against Prohibition, a spirit of wildness took over the nation, leading to all forms of excess. During this decade, many Americans lived in a state of wild abandon: "Millions of people, despite Prohibition, pursued a fast and reckless life. Drugs were a national concern. Drinks were consumed in a thousand illegal speakeasies. Skirt hems went up, and for many a Puritan mentality went out the window."[41]

But then the stock market collapsed and the cavorting came to an end: "People suddenly made poor became severe and intense. Life meant work. The morality of the twenties no longer became applicable in the somber thirties; there seemed to be a grassroots reaction against light-heartedness and frivolity."[42]

After the Wall Street crash of 1929, Jack Vizzard pined, "The Party was over. In the littered debris of confetti and tickertape an enormous sense of guilt set in. In a mood of sobriety a chastened citizenry reacted against the symbols of its great debauch and began to punish them."[43]

But enforcement of the Code was always going to be problematic. Presenting adultery as unexciting, for example, wasn't practical. Leading actresses were usually attractive. If seductresses were plain, audiences wouldn't accept the male lead being tempted by them. But if he *were* tempted, so also might the audience be. And when they left the cinema, they mightn't be thinking so much of his punishment (which would definitely come) as the pleasure that preceded it.

It wasn't the expulsion from the Garden of Eden that stuck in people's minds so much as the eating of the apple. This was the way people thought and it was the way they would always think. There was no way around it.

The Production Code Administration (the PCA) clearly outlined what it wanted to be seen — and not seen — on the screen. Its caveats were ironclad: Sex wasn't to be portrayed in any way at all and the sanctity of marriage was to be adhered to in all its shapes and forms. Sexual intimacy of any form had to be expressed in highly covert fashion. Any time a couple threatened to gravitate anywhere near a double bed, the camera had to cut to a roaring fire or a pair of curtains wafting in the breeze to convey to an audience that things were going on (or, as the case may have been, coming off).

Other disingenuous metaphors of the time included trains entering tunnels at decibel-breaking speed, fountains spurting upwards, oil derricks pumping, cannons roaring, fireworks exploding, volcanoes erupting, champagne corks popping or waves crashing tumultuously onto beaches.

When a film was finished, it had to go through a final check from Hays before release. If it failed this, reshoots could cost a studio a considerable amount of money as the sets might have to be reconstructed, or cast members summoned from other projects.

The humorist Gene Fowler echoed the sentiments of many people when he poked fun at Hays and his Code with these conjectural movie commandments, e.g., "Thou shalt not photograph the wiggling belly, the gleaming thigh or the winking navel, especially to music, as goings-on of this ilk sorely troubleth the little boys of our land and so crammeth the theatre with adolescence that papa cannot find a seat."[44]

Another wit deadpanned, "Hollywood buys a good story about a bad girl and has to change it to a bad story about a good girl."[45]

The anti-war movie *All Quiet on the Western Front* (1930) even ran into trouble with the Studio Relations Committee (the SRC), mainly because of a scene where some soldiers spend the night at a French farmhouse with various girls. No sex is seen or even referred to, but some members of the SRC felt the film gave us to believe it took place — a rather flimsy pretext for wanting the scene out. They were also disturbed by a scene where a soldier has an involuntary bowel movement from fear. Removing this was like cutting out the central axis of the theme but such were the times that it had to go.

Profane language was also outlawed by the PCA, including "hell," "damn," "Jesus Christ," "Lord" and even "God" (used as an expression of surprise). It also stated that ministers of religion ought not be portrayed as comic characters or villains.

Maybe the ultimate sacrilege was to play God, which was a kind of subtext to *Frankenstein* (1931). Here we had Hollywood's first example of what we now regard as second nature, if you'll pardon the pun: the idea of assembling a live creature from the various body parts of others. The surprise is that Henry Frankenstein's creature turns on him. For Boris Karloff, the role of the Monster became a virtual pension for the rest of his life. For the film industry it seemed proof positive that audiences actually enjoyed screaming — though there were also some tender scenes here.

Mary Shelley, who wrote the novel on which the film was based, was an atheist so it was viewed by the censors with this in mind. The novel's subtitle was "The Modern Prometheus," which suggested that Frankenstein, like the mythical thief of God's fire, rebelled not only against social convention but Heaven itself. Bearing this in mind, the film could be viewed not only as a horror story but also an allegory about Luciferean pride.

Martin Quigley hated it and said he couldn't forgive James Whale, the director, for permitting the Monster to drown a little girl. This scene was subsequently cut out by New York censors, as was a line where Frankenstein says, "Now I know what it feels like to be God." The drowning scene wasn't restored until 1986.

Quigley's reaction betrayed a fundamental misunderstanding of the film. The Monster throws the child into the lake not so much from malice but to see if she can float. This is actually one of the most tender scenes in the movie, outlining both his naivety and his need for friendship. He's equally as childish in his ways as the little girl whose life ends so tragically.

Quigley wasn't expected to be aware of details like this, which is perhaps the saddest thing of all about censorship, i.e., the people making the decisions, as well as being right-wing, were often quite dim to boot. They certainly didn't seem to be interested in the cinema as art. The *Frankenstein* example wasn't a subtle nuance. Anybody of average intelligence would have understood it. The scene was played for poignance rather than shock value, but Quigley was only interested in the empirical evidence before his eyes. Child dies at monster's hands, *ergo* "inadmissible."

The main problem besetting Quigley at this time, however, was sex. He was particularly concerned about Jean Harlow. In 1929 she had been scantily clad in, of all things, a Laurel and Hardy short called *Double Whoopee*. The following year she appeared in Howard Hughes' *Hell's Angels*, a World War I aviation drama with a love triangle at its core. In this film Harlow was allowed a line many other actresses of the time wouldn't have gotten away with: "Would you be shocked if I put on something more comfortable?" It became a smash hit and a Harlow craze swept America, women everywhere dyeing their hair platinum in her honor. Her trademark role was in *Red-Headed Woman* in 1932. She played a gold-digging secretary, Lil Andrews, who corrals her (married) boss on her uncompromising way to the top.

Red-Headed Woman was unlike previous films about what were usually dubbed "fallen women." In the past, such a breed usually ended up in the gutter for their sins but vice seems to pay for Lil here and this clearly couldn't be expected to wash with Hays. He condemned the movie unequivocally.

The studio ignored him and started filming it anyway. This was a clear breach of protocol and he didn't take it lying down, dispatching James Wingate, the head of the SRC, to put the brakes on it. Some compromises were made and the film was released amidst much controversy. Thirty-five minutes of this fairly innocuous fare was cut for the British censor, as well as all of Harlow's contribution to Charlie Chaplin's *City Lights* the year before.

Religious groups fumed when *Red-Headed Woman* was given a Seal of Approval by the Hays Office. They sent letters of complaint to MGM but the studio refused to withdraw the film from circulation or re-shoot it. There had, of course, been more reprehensible women than Lil Andrews on the screen before but they had always either repented for their sins or been severely punished for them.

Lil, on the contrary, gloated about her misdeeds right until the end. This meant that a gold-digging bed-hopper had actually got away with it. Hays made it abundantly clear to MGM that this kind of thing couldn't be allowed happen again, for all their sakes. (Lil is taken into custody at the end and her ill-gotten gains confiscated, but what's unique is her unrepentant attitude.)

This is how Molly Haskell accounted for America's obsession with squashing sex out of films as if it was some rabid household bug: "Sex, like dirt, disease and death, is anathema to a country that treasures cleanliness above godliness and innocence above experience. To the number one producer of antiseptics it becomes a matter of both religious and professional honor to sanitize what it cannot dispense with. The terms 'vamp' and 'sex goddess,' like the names of hurricanes or classical deities, are incantations invented by men to explain the inexplicable and, as in the custom of naming hurricanes after women, to locate the source of destruction within the 'mysterious' sex."[46]

One of the most talked-about films of the year was *Blonde Venus*, which featured Marlene Dietrich as a nightclub singer turning to prostitution to help pay for an operation to cure her husband (Herbert Marshall) of radiation poisoning. She subsequently falls in love with Cary Grant. The film struck a deep blow to the "sacred" institution of marriage and also featured a steamy scene of Dietrich in a gorilla suit grooving to the rhythms of "Hot Voodoo." Nonetheless, it managed to find its way into cinemas without being spliced apart by Hays' scissors. Two years later, however, what with the formulation of the PCA, it was withdrawn from circulation by a no-nonsense Irish-American named Joseph Breen.

Most people left the cinema sympathizing with Dietrich rather than reviling her. If she trawled a sewer, it was for a noble intent. In a way, it was hard to believe Marshall was worth it.

As well as *Blonde Venus*, Breen would pull many high-grossing films from circulation in the coming years. Examples included *Baby Face, She Done Him Wrong, Scarface, The Sign of the Cross* and, hardly surprisingly, *Red-Headed Woman*. The latter was never shown in a cinema afterwards, emerging in 1988 in a restored version for the video market. Other films were destroyed rather than locked away so they were never seen anywhere again, even after the veil of censorship was lifted.

All of Dietrich's films were banned in Germany during World War II. Hitler himself appealed to her to return to her home country and work there but she refused. She became a U.S. citizen in 1937 and from 1943 to 1946 made more than 500 appearances before Allied troops.

Ernest Hemingway's much-revered novel *A Farewell to Arms* was also made into a film in 1932, with his good friend Gary Cooper in the lead role of Frederic Henry and Helen Hayes as Catherine, the nurse with whom he falls in love. Wingate was deeply distressed by their premarital sex. The Code's name for this was "impure love."⁴⁷ The fact that Hayes dies in childbirth (an apt punishment for her "sin") might have made it palatable to him but the birth was shown on screen instead of being depicted off it, which broke another Code stipulation, so even this compromise was tainted.

Henry says to Catherine at one point that death was "the price you paid for sleeping together" but then adds, "It would have been the same if we had been married fifty times." The latter line was deleted from the movie for obvious reasons. The thinking was that even though Catherine died, there was still not "sufficiently clear moral compensation for the undue emphasis on illicit love." The film was given a "B" rating, which meant it was deemed to be morally objectionable in part or all."⁴⁸

Hemingway's status as the pre-eminent author of his time cut little ice with Wingate. A *Farewell to Arms* was remade in 1957 with Rock Hudson and Jennifer Jones. In the final scene we have Hudson saying to the dying Jones, "Poor kid. Maybe this is the price you pay for sleeping together," a further bowdlerization of the book but possibly the only way the film could have got itself made. Hemingway was disgusted by producer David O. Selznick's capitulation to such bullyboy tactics, but then he loathed most of Hollywood's versions of his work (with the exception of *The Killers*). He would have agreed with John Le Carré's comment, "Having your book turned into a movie is like seeing your oxen turned into bouillon cubes."⁴⁹

Paramount made an alternate ending to the 1932 version of *A Farewell to Arms* in which the heroine didn't die and offered to send Hemingway both for his perusal. His reply was perhaps expectable: "Use your imagination as to where to put the two prints."⁵⁰

There were also problems with Cooper's desertion of the army because he'd stopped believing in it. This was unacceptable in 1932, an age of jingoism. It would be many years before post-war disenchantment set in. *A Farewell to Arms,* like Erich Maria Remarque's *All Quiet on the Western Front,* were before their time in this regard. Most soldiers adopted an attitude of "Ours not to wonder why." The upshot was that another reason had to be found for Cooper's desertion.

The one they came up with was typical Tinseltown cornball: He ended up deserting because his letters to Hayes weren't answered. This is one of the great aberrations of moviemaking, in any age. Military outrage was trivialized into a moan about the postal system. It was as a result of this that Hemingway lost faith with movies. It was hard to blame him. His novel had been turned into a treacly farce by dint of this ludicrous detail. It was like a knife in the gut to him, as was the weepie finale. Gone was the hardboiled brilliance of his last few pages, which he had reputedly re-written 38 times.

In 1932 there was also *Red Dust,* a steamy jungle romp featuring Clark Gable and Jean Harlow and *Night After Night,* the film that launched Mae West's film career with her suggestive array of naughty one-liners.

Both Universal and RKO went into receivership that year. Paramount was near bankruptcy as well. Much of the fall-off in audiences came about as a result of the fact that the Catholic Church felt that many of the films on show had failed to comply to the Production Code to the letter. As a result, they urged their congregation members to boycott them.

Hollywood now went for the tried and trusted, anxious not to offend any institution that might make movies teeter.

Edward G. Robinson looking mean and moody in the hardboiled *Little Caesar* (1931).

To this extent, wholesome MOR book adaptations with a family appeal unerringly made it to the top of the moguls' lists. Targeting the conservative mass market was much more lucrative than seeking out eclectic "sleepers" for the imaginative. If they found a formula that worked, they ran with it.

Esther Williams used to complain that the only things they changed in her movies were her swimsuits and her male leads. That principle (or lack of it) applied almost across the board. The First Commandment was "Thou Shalt Not Get Up the Backs of the Money Men." Epics, musicals and light comedies usually fitted the bill, with an occasional foray into the thriller genre (provided it wasn't too *noirish,* or dark).

The Church wanted Hays to come down heavier on crime movies but he didn't see these as a priority. This wasn't because he was soft on crime but rather because in this area he felt Hollywood was good at censoring itself, i.e., the "bad guy" always got his just deserts. Evil didn't flourish for thugs, but in the sexual milieu, Hays felt, there was a tacit acceptance of falling standards. It wasn't just what people were doing on screen that bothered him but what the directorial judgment (or lack of it) was.

Somewhat surprisingly, the moralists often argued among themselves about films. Jason Joy, a colleague of Wingate's at the SRC, thought the fact that Edward G. Robinson's past finally caught up with him in *Little Caesar* (1931) made it safe. Wingate, on the contrary, was unimpressed with the fact that his character dies at the end, feeling that a young viewer "unconsciously forms the idea that he will be smarter and get away with it."[51] If we take this argument to its logical (or rather illogical) conclusion, it meant that no studio would be allowed release a film with a criminal at its core, regardless of what happened to him or her.

Little Caesar was followed by *The Public Enemy* (1931), which was shot in just 21 days at a cost of $150,000 and earned over $1 million on its first run. In 1931 alone, over fifty gangster films hit the screen. Father Lord worried about the cumulative effect of these, if not their particular dangers. The criminals in question may have ended badly, but would audiences remember this or their previous opulent lifestyles? Even gallant death had its own charm, making martyrs out of these reprobates.

In 1932 *Scarface,* a gangster movie loosely based on the life of Al Capone, was condemned for glorifying its anti-hero, played by Paul Muni. And yet in *Rain* in the same year Joan Crawford was allowed play a prostitute led astray by a preacher. There seemed to be little consistency in the choices of what went or didn't. *Scarface* was condemned despite the fact that the lead character died violently at the end because it was adjudged to have treated him sympathetically (if not empathetically).

Joy rejected the whole concept behind the film when Howard Hughes first proposed it. He warned: "If you should be foolhardy enough to make *Scarface,* this office will make certain it is never released." Hughes showed the letter containing these words to his co-producer Howard Hawks, causing Hawks to react with a brusque "Screw the Hays Office." Hughes told Hawks to start the picture immediately, and to make it "as grisly as possible."[52]

As time went on, Hughes lost his bravado and ended up acceding to most of the demands of the SRC, including the appending of a subtitle to the film. It eventually went on release as *Scarface: The Shame of a Nation*. More significantly, he was forced to excise any reference to collusion between the gangster and corrupt politicians. (*Scarface* also contained an allegation of incest between Muni's character and his sister, which further fanned the flames of outrage with the Hays Office.)

Gangster films enjoyed their greatest popularity between the Wall Street crash of 1929 and the death of John Dillinger five years later. In that time frame, America needed a drug to lift it from its economic gloom and it found it in Robinson's *Little Caesar*, Cagney's *The Public Enemy* — who can forget him squashing a grapefruit in Mae Clarke's face? — and of course *Scarface*. Prohibition (literally) sucked the juice from the national spirit.

Roosevelt's New Deal was a shift in the right direction but it was on the cinema screens that the fantasies were writ large. Dillinger cocked a snook at convention in the most dastardly way possible and Hollywood's hardchaws seemed to ape his *chutzpah* vicariously. His death in 1934 was like a *carte blanche* for the reformers to tell any wild child that the party was over. It was "Goodbye revolution, hello the censor's shears."

Women also came into their own in these five years. The flapper vamps and fallen women of such films as *Baby Face* and *Ladies They Talk About*, both released in 1933, copper-fastened the freewheeling edge. This was Jonathan Munby's reaction: "In the context of the Depression the sexually empowered woman took on an added edge. In an era of massive unemployment the *laissez-faire* capitalist order had been brought into disrepute. The out-of-work male symbolized not only a collapse in the economic sense but also in patriarchal definitions of agency." The gangster, in such a context, "re-masculinized" him. But he "met his match in the gold-digging woman."[53]

A central precept of the Code, as mentioned, was that the sympathy of the audience never ought to be thrown to the side of crime. As if to underline this point, as Patrick McGilligan reminds us in his fine biography of James Cagney, a postscript narrative to *The Public Enemy* "explicitly warns audiences that Cagney's Tom Powers is an average person, and, further, that crime is not the recommended escape from a dull average existence (a sop to the Hays Office)."[54]

This was fine in theory. One could have the likes of Cagney or Humphrey Bogart going to the chair in the final reel. But did that mean that audience sympathy wouldn't be with him? The more the villain was punished, the more likely audiences would sympathize (if not empathize) with his plight.

At this time, films were practically built on the star system. Actors like

Cagney, Bogart and Robinson were typecast as "heavies" and in a brace of films were seen to flout the law, slap women around, stab their "friends" in the back (either literally or metaphorically) and wallow in all forms of ethical compromises. The fact that they were killed or imprisoned in the end was beside the point. One is reminded of Cecil B DeMille, who titillated a whole generation with his lush orgies before tacking on neat messages to appease the censors.

What people remembered was the sinner, not the sin. They remembered the crime rather than the punishment. Cagney and Bogart etc. became role models. That didn't mean filmgoers left the cinema to become criminals or thieves. But they left admiring the way such criminals conducted their business. Otherwise, how had these stars such lengthy careers? This is why the Catholic system of checks and balances had an inbuilt self-destructive element. Influence-wise, it was doomed from the outset.

People went to films primarily because their heroes, or anti-heroes, were in them. Surely the would-be reformers realized this. If one really disapproved of James Cagney's "crime, wrongdoing, evil or sin," would they go and see him in his next movie? Especially if such morally reprehensible behavior was likely to be replicated here?

In Sarah J. Smith's book *Children, Cinema and Censorship* she quotes two kids reminiscing about their cinema experiences: "When we went to gangster films [my friend started] aping the gangsters. He'd strike a match on the wall. My friend and me, we bought a black shirt and a white tie because one of the gangsters had them."[55]

These children were typical of many filmgoers, at least of that age group. They weren't remembering retribution but rather the gangsters in their heyday. In the end, Stephen Tropiano concluded, "the Hollywood gangsters of the 1930s were defeated not by the cops or the courts, but by the censors."[56]

Alfred Hitchcock once talked to fellow director Peter Bogdanovich about the way audiences are always "rooting for the evildoer to succeed." If a man is robbing a safe in a film, he contended, and the director cuts to somebody coming up the stairs, the audience tends to shout "Hurry up!" at the robber. Apart from murder, Hitchcock suggested, people are on the criminal's side: "They don't care if he's going to steal a million dollars. Robbery isn't immoral to them on the screen. They want him to get away with it."[57] And the same principle (or lack of it) applied to Cagney & Co.

Some filmmakers defied Hays' commandments. Some even used the slogan "Banned by the Hays Office" as a carrot to audiences. They suspected he was out of touch with the actual circumstances of life. In crime films, gangsters were doomed "despite clear evidence that many real villains were doing very nicely."[58]

On one occasion the Hays Office deleted a scene from a musical not because of anything inherently objectionable in what was going on in the scene, but simply because there was a statue of a nude in the background. Murray Schumach sighed, "It had been on display for countless thousands of decades, but was considered erotic for a movie."[59]

"Speaking to the directors," Hays explained, "I appealed to their ingenuity and artistic pride, hinting that it takes vastly more artistry to be interesting while observing decent limits than when being *risqué*." He told them that "instead of seeing how far they could get an actress to lift her skirt and still stay within the law, they might try seeing how she could *leave* her skirt and still maintain audience interest."[60]

This sounds fine in theory but merely by speaking in these terms one imagines he was already breaching his own caveat. Perhaps he would have been better employed not mentioning skirts at all, instead placing his emphasis on the wearer of the skirt. As it was, he left it ambiguous as to what he meant by "audience interest." Did he mean interest in what the skirt was hiding? Obviously not, but merely by bringing up the subject, one can imagine directors trying to work it out that focusing their camera on any skirt, however lengthy, was going to cause certain kinds of thought processes in audiences. The more thigh the skirt hid, the greater the imagination needed to conjure up fantasies.

Mick LaSalle lamented: "By sucking the sex out of romance for the better part of 34 years, the Production Code conditioned at least two generations [of filmgoers] to see romance as bland, chaste and phony."[61]

He added, "A cold-blooded and often depraved cinema that gives us sex with no humanity or tenderness is Joseph Breen's most fitting legacy."[62] One was reminded of Juvenal's rhetorical question, "Who will protect us from the protectors?"

Reformers weren't renowned for their intellectualism or love of art. Neither, for that matter, were the Hollywood moguls. In many ways it was a war between Puritanism and money, the blind leading the blind into a ditch of myopia.

A central issue had to be faced: Did the reformers like movies? Did they even like life? Or were they simply addicted to the wielding of power, to the fact that they could make the creative people feel small? Were their blanket culls the revenge of philistinism on art, though cloaked in the guise of a high-hitting moral imperative? Surely a criterion for someone's appointment to a film board would be that he or she had at least some aesthetic credentials, rather than an overweening desire to purge celluloid of anything smacking of flesh and/or blood.

Archbishop McNicholas, the chairman of the Catholic Episcopal Committee, was in favor of banning films he thought offensive. He was also aware that doing this could make people want to see them more, "thereby making them more successful financially."[63]

Some commentators on this time have seen Hays and Breen as epitomizing H.L. Mencken's definition of a puritan: "Someone who lives in constant fear that someone, somewhere, may be enjoying themselves." This is to miss the point. These men saw themselves in a messianic light, saving the world from a moral Armageddon. They went to work every morning with melodramatic zeal. Each snip of their scissors was like an exorcism to them, the deletion of a pernicious evil. They didn't see their work as work; it was a vocation. They loved morals with the same passion the moguls loved movies. Such passion, needless to say, was all they had in common with the moguls.

The most interesting predicament concerned Cecil B. DeMille. DeMille was a genius at cloaking parables in sensuous sets, thereby satisfying the guardians of morality and also earthy members of audiences. His brother William remarked, "Having attended to the underclothes, bathrooms and matrimonial irregularities of his fellow citizens, he then began to consider their salvation." Darryl F. Zanuck added, "When you get a sex story in Biblical garb you can open your own mint."[64]

DeMille, John Naughton knew, "found he could indulge in sex and debauchery to his heart's content in Biblical epics such as *The Ten Commandments* as long as virtue triumphed in the final reel."[65] In the words of Jeremy Pascall and Clyde Jeavons, "DeMille's magic formula for sex coupled with religious themes — perhaps one of the most blatant hypocrisies ever perpetrated in movies allowed him to bend the Code brilliantly."[66]

Yul Brynner summed DeMille up as "De Phony and De Hypocrite of all time."[67] Howard Hawks claimed he learned a lot off him by doing the opposite of what he asked.[68] For Pauline Kael he made "small-minded pictures on a big scale."[69]

He tabloidized the Bible, making it into a Walt Disney comic strip with grandiose overtones. He used evangelical tabs to conceal Mammon-like puppetry in his characterizations. With his megaphone, his superiority complex and his quasi-messianic directorial style, he acted as if he had a hotline to the Pearly Gates. The reality of the situation was that he worshipped the Golden Calf as much as any of his cinematic sinners. His main conscience was to the box office. He once had ambitions to be a preacher like his father but the studio became his prime pulpit as time went on.

He had an obsession with the Good Book, as is evidenced by Caroline Lejeune's famous clerihew:

> Cecil B. DeMille
> Much against his will
> Was persuaded to leave Moses
> Out of the War of the Roses.[70]

He justified this with the studios by contesting that the Bible had been "a best-seller for centuries. Why should I let 2,000 years of publicity go to waste?"[71] "Give me any two pages of the Bible," he bragged, "and I'll give you a picture." Kevin Brownlow reflected: "He directed as though chosen by God for this one task."[72]

DeMille was able to put himself down occasionally, as with his "Every time I make a picture the critics estimate of public taste goes down 10 percent." He matched that with an apparently contradictory sense of megalomania.[73]

He received a severe shock when his orgiastic parable *The Sign of the Cross* was maligned by the critics in 1932. Daniel Lord had been his technical advisor on *The King of Kings*. For this reason, and his reputation as the movie wing of the Bible, he imagined he was above reproach. But Lord thought the film perverse.

Martin Quigley was also unimpressed, particularly with a scene which contained what he called a "lesbian dance." Quigley got Hays to call DeMille and ask him what he planned to do about the dance. DeMille, as only he could, replied, "Listen carefully to my words because you might want to quote them. Not a damn thing."[74]

In former times, DeMille had Father Lord say Mass on *The King of Kings* set every morning. He referred to this as a "continued benediction on our work," but in Les and Barbara Keyser's view it was more akin to "a good insurance policy against future attacks on the film. Hiring Catholic technical advisors became roughly analogous to obtaining an imprimatur. It didn't assure there would be no controversy, but it did smooth the way to the theater."[75]

DeMille, according to the Keysers, "always protested that *The Sign of the*

Cross was on the side of the angels, and that the Catholics were the heroes, but their sanctity is just too banal to hold a candle to Charles Laughton's Nero. All the juxtapositions in [the film] suggest DeMille's "adoration of the pagan aristocrats, and his very grudging reverence for the deadly dull catechumens."[76]

Where he really shows his pagan colors is during Claudette Colbert's infamous scene where she importunes a friend to join her in a bath *sans* her clothes. The Keysers state: "DeMille's coy focus on glistening bare backs, smooth legs and almost exposed breasts is clearly designated to titillate audiences.... These visual dalliances celebrate the carnality of the Roman Empire most unabashedly, far from providing a paean to Christian modesty."[77] Neither did the censors do anything about a later scene where a naked Elissa Landi is chained to a stake and about to be raped by a gorilla. Once again, the Old Artificer dodged a bullet.

Gerald Gardner argued that, with the exception of Busby Berkeley "who end-ran the censors by relying on leggy chorus girls," DeMille was "the most successful evader of the Hays Office." Normally, Gardner contends, "a scene of orgy, rape, depravity and perversion would send the reformers out shouting for scalps, but when the tale was ostensibly lifted from the Bible, the censors said, 'Amen.'"[78]

Gardner believed that Berkeley brazenly breached "virtually every clause of the Hays Code, yet the Hollywood censors just kept tapping their toes." His camera, according to Gardner, "insinuated itself through the legs of lines of lissome chorus girls. Often they would shed their diaphanous costumes to reveal lace brassieres and gartered panties. Sometimes Berkeley would place his nubile nymphs in pageant-like production numbers: bare-breasted on the wings of airborne planes, or naked in silhouette as a lascivious dwarf looked on, or supporting a line of six-foot bananas from their pelvises, lifting them in improbable erection and then letting them drop, as in some Herculean orgy."[79]

The Sign of the Cross, for one writer, demonstrated how "kinky" DeMille's movies could have been.[80] But he would never admit that fact, or its ramifications. He had too much to lose. In interviews, Theresa Sanders revealed, "DeMille claimed he included scenes of the depraved Roman Empire only in order to highlight the Christians' purity and moral superiority." But when the film was released, "Christians responded to his film with outrage, and their anger was one of the factors that led to the founding of the Legion of Decency in 1934."[81]

It was ironic that the former arch-ally of the church caused such anger amongst its members with his film. Just this once, the Pope of Trash went too far, even by his own extravagant standards. It was picketed by outraged moralists, and his former untouchability by the censors became a thing of the past.

Even though Hays was called "the Czar of all the rushes"[82] the church that felt certain unsavory elements in films were still creeping in, largely due to the arrival of the Talkies, where voices in themselves, regardless of what they were saying, could be deemed suggestive. To this end, Cardinal Mundelein of Chicago convened a group of clerical and secular figures in his archdiocese to draft a document that tightened celluloid strictures even more rigidly.

Hollywood bent the knee, realizing that a large segment of its audiences, about one-third of which were Catholic, might be alienated if it didn't. The "Cardinal's Code" strengthened the limits on what was seen as seemly or not from a sexual point of view (i.e., practically nothing).

The MPPDA empowered the PCA to enforce Lord's Code. To run it, Hays appointed Joe Breen, as mentioned. He stayed there for twenty years. It was Breen who came up with the idea of using the church to force the studio executives to conform to the Code.

From the summer of 1933 onwards, church leaders started turning up the heat on the movie industry. In a speech before the National Conference of Catholic Charities in New York, Archbishop Cicognani declared, "What a massacre of innocent youth is taking place by the hour. How shall the crimes that have their direct source in motion pictures be measured?"[83]

Breen had handled the PR for the Eucharistic Congress in 1926. He'd been working for Hays since 1930 as head administrator of his West Coast operations but these were much bigger potatoes indeed. Hays felt he could do a better job than Wingate because he seemed to have more conviction and drove a harder bargain. He was also, unlike Wingate, a Catholic, which had to help.

In December 1933, Hays made Breen head of SRC. Breen had more mental toughness than Hays. He felt Hays was too lightweight, that Hollywood didn't take him seriously enough. In time Breen would come to be known as "the Hitler of Hollywood," such was his forthrightness.[84]

Also in 1933, the book *Our Movie-Made Children* appeared. Written by one Henry J. Forman, it outlined the catastrophic effects films exerted upon impressionable minds and accelerated the church towards a course of action it had been thinking about taking for a long time. The upshot was that a short time afterwards, a group of bishops convened to organize the national Legion of Decency (LOD) to "spearhead a Catholic attack on the movie industry."[85] In the early days of the LOD, the hierarchy also clung to the hope that Catholics might somehow "transform movies by becoming the directors and screenwriters of tomorrow."[86]

The Legion's ratings comprised four "main categories, ranging from morally objectionable for general patronage" to "positively bad." By 1936 two more categories were added. A "positively bad" film was automatically a condemned one. As far as the studios were concerned, a "C" rating ("C" meaning "Condemned") would significantly limit the number of people seeing a film.

On May 6, 1934, Gerard Donnelly, a Jesuit priest, wrote an article called "The Bishops Rise Against Hollywood." In the course of it he ranted, "The pest hole that infects the country with its obscene and lascivious moving pictures must be cleaned."[87] In the same month, the Detroit branch of the Legion of Decency issued a list of 63 condemned films.

Daniel Lord also began naming five condemned films a month in his magazine *Queen's Work*. As if this wasn't enough, IFCA began listing recommended ones.[88] In addition, the Federal Council of Churches of Christ in America threatened not only to enlist its entire membership of 22 million in the Legion but to campaign vigorously for federal censorship as well.[89]

Members were asked to avoid films which offended decency and Christian morality. There was a threat of mass boycott which was also supported by Protestant and Jewish persuasions. In Philadelphia that year an actual boycott did take place, causing a reported 40 percent drop in box office receipts.

The aforementioned Cardinal Mundelein, one of America's most influential ecclesiastical figures, made it patently clear that members of his flock were to shun "obnoxiousness." Over eight million Catholics took a pledge against watching impurity on the screen as a result. Viewing it was deemed a mortal sin, with eternal damnation the likely punishment. In Chicago, Mundelein's home turf, 70,000 students marched with placards carrying reading, "An admission to an indecent movie is an admission ticket to hell."

The Production Code was enforced more strongly in 1934. Its "brave new world" was one in which "good was equated with conformity and/or sweetness, suicide was never contemplated, drugs simply did not exist, sex was never mentioned, marriages were mostly happy, children called their father 'Sir,' babies were never naked, no one ever went to the toilet, the pains of childbirth were never witnessed, married people never kissed passionately, and when they were married were consigned to separate beds."[90]

When Warner Bros expressed an interest in re-releasing their 1931 version of *The Maltese Falcon* in 1934, they were unequivocally informed that a scene showing Sam Spade dangling a "Do Not Disturb" sign in one hand while fluffing pillows with the other had to go.

Curiously enough, 1934 was also the year in which what Clark Gable referred to as "the walls of Jericho" (i.e. the invisible wall between married couples in bed) came tumbling down because in the aptly titled *It Happened One Night* that year he removed the blanket separating his bed and Claudette Colbert's. Nothing more happened on screen but it didn't take a genius to know that this was a foretaste of marital consummation. The film went on to win all five major Oscars on offer — Best Picture, Best Actor, Best Actress, Best Director and Best Screenplay — the first movie to sweep the boards in this way. So Gable's gesture was forgiven (if not quite forgotten) by the killjoys.

Another seminal event took place in 1934. It was the year that the notorious bank-robbing team of Bonnie Parker and her lover Clyde Barrow were gunned down in Texas by police officers. (How ironic that 33 years later, a romanticization of the death-dealing pair's adventures — in Arthur Penn's *Bonnie and Clyde*—would contribute heavily to breaking the PCA's back).

The excitement many Catholics felt in joining the Legion was unparalleled. For them it became almost like a cause. They saw their mission as the excoriation of evil, with the reformation of society as the inevitable result. Some even displayed signs in their cars saying "We Demand Clean Movies."[91]

The Legion was seen as an alternative to censorship but as Gregory Black maintained, "Using the threat of condemnation, [it] effectively censored films. It called for boycotts of any theatre that dared exhibit a movie that failed to convey the morality espoused by the Legion."[92]

"Freedom of expression," Harold C. Gardiner wrote in his book *Catholic Viewpoint on Censorship*, "is not an absolute freedom."[93] It was against this backdrop that the Legion launched its clampdown on potentially subversive movies.

Breen felt that by the mid-thirties the Code was honored more in the breach than the observance. Many agreed with him in the industry. *Variety* magazine wrote in 1933, "The Code isn't even a joke any more; it's just a memory."[94]

Breen was a small man with a booming voice and a quick wit. One day he visited Harry Cohn at Columbia and handed him his portfolio. Cohn fumed, "What's this shit?" Breen replied, "Mr. Cohn, I take that as a compliment. My friends inform me that if there's any expert in this town on shit, it's you. So if I have to be judged, I'm glad it's by professionals."[95]

Breen had a hands-on approach to what he did. He didn't go into the studio with a hacksaw. This was Thomas Doherty's view: "Unlike most censors, he knew the art he bowdlerized. From story treatments and shooting scripts he spotted early warning signs of trouble and resolved difficulties before more expensive stages of production had proceeded. He made useful suggestions to producers on how to circumvent problem areas, permitting them to abide by the letter of the Code while keeping the spirit of their script."[96]

It wasn't long before he became known as the "supreme pontiff of motion picture morals,"[97] an improvement on the "Hitler" moniker.

He felt that the "dirty" pictures Hollywood was making would only end if people stopped going to see them. He sent a letter to Cardinal Dougherty in Philadelphia to see if he could encourage the Legion to expedite this. Dougherty over-reacted to this request, declaring from the pulpit soon afterwards that Catholics in his diocese were to boycott *all* motion pictures or they would be committing a sin. Box office receipts immediately fell by 40 percent. Harry Warner rang Hays and pleaded, "Will, you've got to save us. We're being ruined by the hour."[98]

There was a potential loss of seven million Catholics in the cinemas and people of other religions were threatening to follow suit. Hays went cap in hand to Martin Quigley and Joe Breen and told them Hollywood would do anything they wanted to save its skin. Breen replied, "You have a Code. Implement it."[99]

Quigley and Breen met the Episcopal Committee to talk strategy. Meanwhile, the Legion held a rally in which a Cleveland bishop, Joseph Schrembs, told the 50,000 strong crowd, "Purify Hollywood or destroy it."[100] One might have been witnessing a revivalist congregation in the Deep South's Bible belt.

After a time the Legion changed its name from the Catholic Legion of Decency to the National Legion, which was felt to be "a more inclusive and appropriate name considering they were encouraging non–Catholics to join, and were getting support from organizations like the Federal Council of the Churches of Christ in America and the Central Conference of American Rabbis."[101]

Cardinal Dougherty took the opportunity to roundly castigate movies for most of the ills of society when he said, "A very great proportion of the silver screen productions deal largely with sex or crime. The usual theme of these pictures moving pictures is divorce, free love, marital infidelity and the exploits of gangsters and racketeers.... This sinister influence is especially devastating among our children and youth. Experience has shown that one hour spent in the darkened recesses of a picture theater will often undo careful training on the part of the school, the church or the home."[102]

These were fighting words, but one has to feel that if the training had been effective in either of the three places it wouldn't have been hanging on such a tenuous string. The cardinal overstated his case and, more importantly, omitted any positive values the cinema possessed. The problem with many (most?) members of the clergy on this issue — if not most members of censorship boards — is that they simply didn't seem to *like* movies. They thereby alienated themselves from the people entering cinemas from the get-go.

A report by the American bishops declared that more than five million people had joined the Legion of Decency by early 1934. By June of that year, the tally had risen to eleven million.[103]

On December 10, 1934, the Legion asked America's 22 million Catholics to pledge their allegiance to it by filling out pledges to "rid the country of its greatest menace — the salacious motion picture."[104] This rhetoric, which reminds one of the kind of language that would be used by Joe McCarthy in his Communist witch-hunts two decades on, must have terrified the parishioners in the pews. They were asked to renew their pledges each year on the first Sunday after the Feast of the Immaculate Conception.

It was nominally a voluntary decision but considering the oath was being taken in public, anybody failing to do so would attract attention to themselves. In the heated climate of the time, this would have taken a lot of courage, and possibly result in one being treated as either a social pariah or an apologist for moral transgressions — or both.

Breen also planned to pull released films from circulation if they failed to meet his demands, and to have films-in-progress re-submitted to him for evaluation if he felt they fell below his redoubtable standards. Tinseltown was about to be whitewashed, with any whiff of cordite snuffed out by the triumphalistic hands of this latter-day savior.

Alexander Walker rhapsodized about him thusly: "A good Roman Catholic, he would appear to have secularized his Church's technique of expiating sin in order to make the utopian morality of the Production Code workable in terms of film-making."[105]

Walker believed the Code presented us with a view of morality "in which sin and punishment are nicely adjusted to each other, yet the link between cause and effect is seldom made convincing."[106] In other words, characters were punished *for* their sins instead of *by* them, their deaths or incarcerations being tacked on willy-nilly in the final reels of films regardless of whether such narrative phenomena fitted the context.

Thomas Doherty explained in *Pre-Code Hollywood*: "Hollywood might show the evil that men do, but only if it were vanquished by the last reel, with the guilty punished and the sinner redeemed. Moral compensation was the only justification for a glimpse of the snake in Paradise."[107]

A common fate for sinners in such circumstances, David Shipman observed, "was suicide; but only after a last-minute realization that they were not good enough for this world."[108]

Was this how "real" people felt? It didn't seem to matter because the Legion's threat, Walker emphasized, "could be clamped on to the box office of any allegedly corrupting film in as short a time as it took for the word to be circulated in a parish."[109]

The speed weapon was "coupled with the psychological advantage that the film industry, one of the most worldly outfits on earth, was unnaturally frightened of incurring the wrath of spiritual bodies."[110] Thirdly, in Walker's view, the Depression helped the Legion: "[F]ilm studios that were already facing a sharp decline were in a low state of morale. To have Mammon desert them and then find God coming up on their flank was too horrid to contemplate."[111]

"There is an irony of sorts," Gerald Gardner reflected, "in the Code's insistence that unbridled ambition and sexual depravity must be punished by death. If such compensation were typical of Movieland, you would hear nothing but gunfire all day long, and the streets of Hollywood would be choked with funeral processions."[112]

It's important to realize that in the censorship wars, there were two distinct factions: on one side the moguls who feared losing their shirts and on the other a fiery self-righteous group of Catholics who understood neither art nor fun. Neither faction was to be admired. Nor did they admit what they represented. The industry fell on its sword to placate the reformers — not because they liked (or even respected) them but because they knew they had to live with them, and abide by their *diktats*.

The reformers, for their part, bathed in the glory of their power. They had Big People where they wanted them and, boy, would they take them suffer. This was the revenge of eunuchs upon the excesses of the harem. It was the ghost of Fatty Arbuckle coming home to roost. Hollywood Babylon would be no more.

So ordinary Joe would hold sway. He'd tell Hollywood what to do with itself. With Will Hays and Joe Breen behind him he would be king, even (especially?) from his cinema seat. He could be as powerful as a censor. He would *be* a censor. At church he could assert himself. He could say, with Breen, that he didn't want this filth any more, that he didn't want to be a part of a diseased cosmos. And thus was the decade of the thirties re-written, on a moral high ground of bad art and truncated passion. Society suffered as a result and films suffered even more. What we were facing into was a decade, or decades, of plastic emotion, half-expressed passion, edited-away sex, and villains who went to the chair not because the law caught them but because Joe Breen did. Hooray for Hollywood.

The sad thing was that filmgoers knew in their hearts that something was seriously wrong with this *zeitgeist*. They knew, even if they couldn't express it, the difference between emotion and emotionalism, between belief and creed.

They were also conflicted in the disjunction between their cinema life and their prayerful one: "The same Americans who crowded the neighborhood bijou for Saturday matinees were filling the pews on Sunday morning at the local church. Yet the pictures they saw on Saturdays and the sermons they heard on Sundays almost always seemed to come from different catechisms."[113]

In some instances, Catholic pressure on certain exhibitions of movies was self-defeating, either because it was "more than made up for by the increased non–Catholic patronage, resulting either from the greater publicity given to the supposedly sensational aspects of the film in question, or from a possible annoyance of non–Catholics with the application of ecclesiastically based pressure."[114]

Barry Norman thought that Breen, in his eagerness not to upset Catholics, over-compensated with a "religious fury that would have turned a Calvin pale, and caused a hellfire preacher to tell them to ease up."[115] He cited an instance where it wouldn't even allow a fallen woman to repent and lead a good life: "She had to be seen to fail to lead a good life, thus denying the very possibility of redemption. Never mind what Christ may have said on the subject."[116]

Moguls like Jack Warner and Harry Cohn weren't used to toadying to people in their normal day but Breen got them into line. Cohn used to say "I don't get ulcers — I give 'em" but now the roles were reversed. Breen claimed he didn't just represent the Code; he *was* the Code. It was a bit like the Louis XIV proclamation, *"L'etat, c'est moi."*

He was also notoriously anti-Semitic. "Those Jews," he declared, "seem to think of nothing but money-making and sexual indulgence. They are probably the scum of the earth."[117] In 1932 he sent a letter to Martin Quigley stating that "damn Jews" were "a dirty filthy lot." Paula Kane believed his anti-Semitism wasn't just a personal prejudice but a "calculated strategy of playing Jewish studio executives and Catholic bishops against each other in order to consolidate his own influence over Hollywood." It was a "divide and conquer" move.[118]

Breen had a thoroughly patronizing attitude to filmgoers as well, believing the lion's share of them to be "nitwits, dolts and imbeciles."[119] He saw it as his mission to save these people from themselves. He would be the unofficial father of the nation, doing a job on America's children that their parents, for one reason or another, were unwilling (or unequipped) to do.

This kind of condescension to audiences was like biting the hand that feeds you, but such were the times that he got away with it. "They'd put fucking in Macy's window," he told an associate once, "and argue till they were blue in the face that it was art."[120]

On another occasion, when a producer told him he was about to see "a brief romantic interlude," he replied, "Listen, friend, fucking's fucking. It's not a romantic interlude. Why don't you say what you mean?"[121] It's possible he was right. What's interesting is the cynicism of a man who saw himself as the guiding light of a generation. One was tempted to enquire who really had the dirty mind: the filmmaker or the would-be censor?

Hollywood played ball with Breen because he usually got his way anyway. It was cheaper to learn that lesson sooner rather than later, when scenes had to be re-shot and/or scripts re-written at enormous expense. Sometimes canny directors shot two versions of the one scene, "trying out" the more offensive one and keeping the other one as a "saver." It was almost like an errant pupil in the classroom trying to put one over on the teacher. David Shipman makes an analogy to the literary world: "Just as euphemism was common in presenting unsavory facts in writing, so movies developed a similar code."[122]

Hays gave final approval to films from New York whereas Breen had a more hands-on influence, liaising with the studios from his West Coast base. It didn't take him long to deduce that studios were often economical with the truth when it came to informing him about the content of their films. They used evasion tactics and downright lies to cut him off at the pass. Once he became alerted to this, he acted, or reacted, accordingly.

In Leonard Leff's view, the Code forced writers "not only to be cleaner, but cleverer."[123] It may have been a "moral straitjacket" for directors, as another writer stated, but "rather like the manufacturers of moonlight gin and whiskey during the Prohibition, Hollywood tackled the challenge of sexual prohibition with humor, style and infinite cunning."[124] Its innuendoes allowed moviegoers to decode what Hays encoded. It was almost like a freemasonry. Breen and his disciples realized sex and violence had to be present in scripts to lasso audiences, but not enough to strangle the industry. It was a delicate balance. Everyone knew how far they could go.

Both factions were engaged in a kind of sophisticated chess game. Frank Walsh wrote in his book *Sin and Censorship*, 'Producers treated each concession as an invitation to bend the regulations a little more. If Joan Crawford could be sexy, self-sacrificing and brave at the same time, then Tallulah Bankhead could take to the street to support her ailing husband in *Faithless*. Marlene Dietrich could sleep her way to the top of the cabaret circuit to save her dying husband in *Blonde Venus,* and Irene Dunne could fruitlessly beg John Boles for a child while waiting twenty years in vain for him to leave his wife in *Back Street*."[125] Vice, in other words, came at a price. Contrary to ethical systems outside the environs of Hollywood, here, in essence, the end could indeed justify the means.

To use a motoring metaphor, directors learned how to spot an amber light and prevent it from turning red by changing gears and thereby convincing the PCA (rightly or wrongly) that it was kowtowing to their edicts. In *Marked Woman* (1937) Bette Davis is clearly a prostitute, despite passing herself off as a "nightclub hostess" like so many fallen women before (and after) her. In the same year Claire Trevor died of consumption in *Dead End* while the audience must have guessed that her disease was syphilis, like the Bette Davis of *Of Human Bondage* some years before. (In the 1964 Kim Novak remake of the latter film, Hollywood was now allowed to call a spade a spade.)

Two years before, Alfred Hitchcock escaped the clause about unmarried couples having to sleep in separate rooms by having Robert Donat and Madeleine Carroll handcuffed together in a bedroom. In *Citizen Kane* (1941), Orson Welles used "Rosebud" to refer to a childhood sledge. Those in the know realized this was a euphemism for the vagina of his central character's mistress.

In the 1933 comedy drama *Dinner at Eight*, Jean Harlow tells an older woman, "I was reading a book the other day, a nutty kind of book. Do you know that machines are going to take the place of every profession?" This draws the retort: "That's something you need never worry about." We know what she means right off. Charles Laughton thought of it like this: "They can't censor the gleam in my eye."[126]

As the directors played games with the Code people, so did the Code people play games with the directors. Geoffrey Shurlock, a censor in charge of enforcing the Production Code, boasted about a trick he often used which was to make a suggestion for a scene that he knew in advance the producer wouldn't go for, merely to get him to contemplate the "idea" of another way of doing the scene in question: "The tactic is to make him offer the suggestion. Any suggestion. It gets him out of a state of shock. They start tearing you to pieces but by the time they've finished with you they've worked up an idea of their own."[127]

The censors were often aware of what was being implied but it didn't bother them because in their view, "only a small minority of the audience would read a film for its deeper implications."[128] This is a generalized opinion and a patronizing one. But it's also a fact that filmgoers of yesteryear were less savvy — and probably more sexually innocent — than today's breed.

2

West and the Rest

Almost from the word go, Mae West was seen as Public Enemy Number One as far as Breen was concerned. The crusade waged against her, as Marybeth Hamilton wrote in *The Queen of Camp,* represents "the last word in puritanical foolishness, led by a group of humorless bluenoses who recoiled in horror from the sight of her swiveling hips."[1] Most of Hollywood's sex symbols were created by the so-called "Dream Machine" but West was self-made.

Her play *Sex* hit the stage in 1926 and was swiftly branded by both church and state as the height of depravity. John Sumner of the New York Society for the Suppression of Vice (NYSSV) believed the public were gullible and didn't know what was best for them, which meant that they needed to be protected from themselves by people like him. This imperious usurping of the conscience of the nation was fairly typical of such spokespeople. One is reminded of the definition of a censor as somebody who "No's" what he likes.

The placards tantalizingly advertised "Sex with Mae West" while her enemies called her one of the devil's daughters. The public, meanwhile, just regarded it all as a bit of a hoot. By making fun of carnality ("Is that a gun in your pocket or are you just glad to see me?") she took the harm out of her own salaciousness. She didn't exude the raw danger of a Tennessee Williams a couple of decades down the line. Instead she chose to poke fun at prudish shibboleths as a kind of precursor to the "Carry On" era of adolescent locker room repartee. Up until now, this had been the sole preserve of men folk.

Sex was originally called *The Albatross.* If she kept that title, it's doubtful it would have created such seismic waves. It took a while to gather steam as it was dismissed by most reviewers as unadulterated tripe. But by the first weekend of its run there were lines three deep around the block outside the theater.

So much for reviews. Many of the people in the lines were sailors. Two days beforehand, the U.S. fleet had dropped anchor in the Hudson. West told the manager who'd advised her against her chosen title, "So it shouldn't have been called *Sex*, eh?"

"I forgot about sailors," he replied.

Before her play, West contended that the word "sex" had never been used in a title before, being confined to medical journals or as a synonym for "gender" as in "the fair sex" or "the gentle sex." She applauded herself for her pioneering efforts in this regard, though many felt it should really have been called *Lust*.

She resolutely refused to have truck with the nudge-wink culture, telling it like it was. She gave a two-fingered salute to Hays and his pards. "When I'm good I'm good," she drawled in that W.C. Fields sneer, "and when I'm bad I'm even better."[2] When somebody looked at her jewelry and said, "Goodness — what beautiful diamonds!" she replied, "Goodness had nothing to do with it, dearie." (That line came from *Night After Night*.) Put another way, women got minks the same way minks got minks.

The success of *Sex* led to a plethora of other playwrights trying to get in on the act with similar *outré* productions. West suddenly took the high moral ground, dismissing these as third-rate drivel. It was all very ironic. She was right about most of them but wrong to condemn a play about lesbians called *The Captive*, which was a serious study of its subject. Maybe she felt threatened by it.

In the 41st week of *Sex*'s run, police raided the theater where it was playing and made multiple arrests. West was delighted with the publicity. She had taken drama from the middle of newspapers to the front. The Supreme Court, no less, adjudged it to be obscene, immoral and indecent, three words West adored. She was fined $500 and sentenced to ten days in jail. As she was led away she unrepentantly told reporters she expected it to be the making of her. And it was.

The court case revolving around *Sex* was farcical in the extreme, the prosecution at one point reduced to castigating her for moving her navel "up and down and from right to left." This perceptive insight was delivered by Irish immigrant Sergeant Patrick Keneally. When cross-examined about this, Keneally, who'd seen the play three times, had to admit that he didn't exactly see West's navel in the alleged decadent motion, but held defiantly to the view that "something" in her middle had done so.[2] The mind boggled as to what that something could be.

Most clear-thinking people realized that West wasn't a threat to public morals any more than a naughty impresario trading mildly suggestive banter might be, but that didn't stop toffee-nosed guardians of morality going through her texts with fine-toothed combs.

She complained that she wasn't allowed say things other actresses did. When they did so they were funny but when West herself did, people read double meanings into them. It was a fair point though she was also well aware that her delivery of the said lines was beefed up with the kind of intonation that fed into such interpretations.

Alexander Walker felt that even though West's view of sex was "healthy post–Freudian," and that she saw it as "a commodity to be enjoyed without guilt," "her code of manners was eminently Victorian on screen and off it she insisted on all the social courtesies due to her sex. Men must take off their hats to her, stand up when she enters a room, never smoke in her presence. When she behaves vulgarly in her films we notice it immediately, for it happens very seldom and then usually with justification."[3] Jean Harlow offered this acidic barb: "She's the kind of girl who climbed the ladder of success wrong by wrong."[4]

John Kobal compared her voice to "a vibrating bed."[5] Dwight Whitney saw her as "a kind of Mount Rushmore of the cosmetician's art."[6] John Mason Brown believed she viewed sex as "an animated cartoon."[7]

West threatened the censors because, as well as being a sex symbol, she was a writer. Before this, vamps mouthed lines other people wrote and weren't noted for having too much upstairs. Neither did she fit the template of your average sex symbol, being more rotund than most of them. She was sometimes referred to as "a plumber's idea of Cleopatra." But she was infinitely more threatening than such sex symbols as far as the censors were concerned.[8]

She came clean on one of the ways she dealt with the breed: "I wrote scenes for them to cut. These scenes were so rough I'd never have used them, but they worked as a decoy. They cut them and left the stuff I wanted. I had these scenes in there about a man's fly and all that, and the censors would be sittin' in the projection room laughin' themselves silly. Then they'd say 'Cut it' and not notice the rest."[9] "In the art of innuendo," Alexander Walker gushed, "West has no equal: She can break the Ten Commandments with every inflection of her voice."[10]

After *Sex,* she wrote a play about homosexuality called *The Drag.* She then appeared in *Diamond Lil* as a nightclub hostess who seduces a policeman investigating her for racketeering. As far as Hollywood morals were concerned, she was an accident waiting to happen.

The film industry didn't need her in 1930, when business was booming, but two years later when the crunch came, her allure proved irresistible. Paramount was undergoing financial difficulties and knew she could pull them out of a hole. She made her screen debut in *Night After Night* opposite George Raft in 1932. In Raft's immortal phrase, "She stole everything but the cameras."[11]

She wasn't sexual in the conventional manner of screen sirens. She didn't specialize in plunging necklines or off-the-shoulder numbers. If anything, she over-dressed. Her image was florid and extravagant, like a female Liberace. Neither did she twitter her eyelashes or give come-hither looks. If one were to go up and see her, some time, one would expect a lot of fun — with sex, of course, very much part of the package. But not the only part.

She took the initiative with men but she never impressed one as a woman who wants to change society. If she craved power, it was only in the war of the sexes. Even then, one felt that her bark was worse than her bite. Her revolution, if such it could be called, didn't extend from the boudoir to the boardroom.

She wasn't a standard advocate for Woman's Liberation because of her sauciness. She liked to think she was *born* liberated. She was, in any case, too eccentric to belong to any group, socio-political or otherwise. She liked to see herself as her own institution, her own legend. Also, while the plots of her plays were ahead of their time in featuring bordellos and whatnot, the plots were often wooden, and the insertion of songs completely irrelevant to them. Perhaps the term "vaudevillian with attitude" captures her best.

The critic George Jean Nathan referred to her as "The Statue of Libido" rather than Liberty, an important distinction. She fought for her own independence but not that of women in general. Her basic cause was the right of everyone to be themselves, in bed and out of it, without any taboos — though she drew the line at sleeping with married men. (She also, incidentally, disliked smoking, drinking and four-letter words.)

She forswore marriage and children because she was so devoted to her career, two areas in which she came closest to feminism. But a true feminist would never have flirted with men in the manner she did. Where she best expressed her pioneering instincts was in alerting the world to the fact that women had as much a need of adventurous sexual activity as men without their respectability being called into question as a result.

In *She Done Him Wrong* (1933), she famously tells Cary Grant, in one of the most misquoted lines of all time, "Come up some time and see me." It was a loose adaptation of her play *Diamond Lil,* which Will Hays had lambasted. The film only cost $200,000 to make but earned ten times that, not including foreign distribution receipts. Some of the lines are vintage West. "I was once so poor I didn't know where my next husband was coming from," she exclaims at one point. Asked if she had ever met a man who could make her happy, she replied, "Sure, lots of times." Breen demanded 25 changes to the script, even the deletion of ostensibly harmless lines like "It takes two to get one in trouble."

"In Mae's hands," Maurice Leonard proclaimed, "sin made the world go round. Her philosophy — 'I'm a girl who lost her reputation and never missed it' — was underlined with every undulation of her hips."[12]

In *The Hollywood Citizen News*, Elizabeth Yeaman described *She Done Him Wrong* as "the most flagrant and utterly abandoned morsel of sin ever attempted on the screen. I must confess that I enjoyed it enormously."[13]

Mick LaSalle wrote at length about West and how she gave off the aura of someone who had had sex with hundreds, if not thousands of men, "[but] in America such a woman could not exist."[14] He concluded: "To see West is to come away energized, as if touched by the wand of some weird and wonderful mother goddess."[15] He believed she would probably have been treated even more harshly by Hollywood if her sexual innuendos were backed up by an equally alluring appearance. "Had West looked like Garbo," he surmised, "they would have burned her at the stake."[16]

She was well aware that notoriety made for good publicity. "I was better known than Einstein, Shaw or Picasso," she bragged in her autobiography.[17] On the other hand, she had certain conservative traits. She disapproved of nudity, for instance, feeling something should be left to the imagination. (Such an attitude made her an unlikely opponent of permissiveness in her old age.)

West made a second film with Grant that year, *I'm No Angel*. She played a circus entertainer chasing her playboy co-star and finally suing him for breach of promise in a hilarious courtroom scene. It got the same line-by-line scrutiny as *She Done Him Wrong* but was eventually released. James Wingate found nothing particularly objectionable in it but Martin Quigley thought it was outrageous. Civic groups protested loudly about it and the Legion of Decency condemned it. The Legion, in fact, was formed just six months after West's *She Done Him Wrong* hit the cinemas. This led some historians to conclude that it was established "primarily to remove her from the screen."[18]

Gerald Gardner believed that what most upset the censors about West was her implication that a woman's sexual appetite was as great as a man's. It wasn't until 1948, with the publication of Alfred Kinsey's research on this subject, that such a belief was taken seriously by the general public.[19]

Ireland was so conservative that *She Done Him Wrong* wasn't even submitted to the censor there. Nearly twenty minutes was cut from *I'm No Angel* before it was dispatched to the Irish film censor but it was still banned.[20] The previous year, even the Marx Brothers' *Horse Feathers* was cut in thirteen places because of Groucho's puns and Harpo's "silent lechery."[21]

West sympathized with Groucho. She was a friend of his since his vaudeville days. The Marx Brothers' *Monkey Business* was also banned in Ireland in 1931 for fear it would "provoke the Irish to anarchy."[22] (Some people would contend the Irish already *were* anarchic.)

A Night at the Opera (1935) ran into trouble with, of all people, the Latvian censors. For reasons best known to themselves, they cut a scene where Harpo made a sandwich from Groucho's cigar. Less surprisingly, the dialogue was cut where Groucho is informed that it will cost him $1,000 a night to employ an opera impresario and raged, "$1,000 a night? You can get a record of Minnie the Moocher for 75 cents. For a buck and a quarter you can get Minnie!"[23]

Gardner, like most viewers, was aghast at the censors' treatment of Groucho. His comic routines, he suggested, were more a sign of impotence than virility: "He's incessantly talking about women but when one appears and seems willing, he invariably throttles his sexual urge."[24]

West and Groucho were both hugely successful at the box office. In 1933, a year in which a quarter of the U.S. workforce was unemployed due to the Depression, West earned over $200,000. The following year that figure swelled to almost $350,000, and in 1935 to $480,000. It was obvious to Breen that, whatever about his own reservations, she was hitting the public smack bang in the solar plexus. Cinema owners outlined the prevalent doublethink: The church people clamored for clean pictures but they still came out to see West whenever she wiggled those famous hips.

West wasn't the only actress to give Hays and Breen headaches. *Baby Face* came out in 1933 as well, with Barbara Stanwyck playing a saloon girl, Lily Powers, who sleeps around. Lily is a woman who performs erotic dances — and also more intimate sexual favors — for money. Egged on by her father, who owns the speakeasy she works in, she eventually moves from the small town of her birth to Manhattan, where she becomes the mistress of a bank official.

Ecstasy, another 1933 film, showcased Hedy Lamarr's career. In it she was allowed to skinny-dip, her breasts exposed for all to see. Another scene has her apparently having an orgasm as she canoodles with her lover in a cottage. All we see is her face but one doesn't have to be a genius to imagine what's going on "downstairs." Director Gustav Machaty roused her passion, she revealed in her autobiography, by jabbing pins into her body "until it was vibrating in every nerve."[25] The New York Censorship Committee rejected the film for immorality as a result of this scene. (It was officially banned until 1940.) In 1935 the U.S. Marshal actually burned the print but Eureka, the production company, took the case to the Circuit Court of Appeal and won its case. But over the next twenty years only 400 American cinemas dared show it.[26]

Lamarr went on to marry a wealthy Austrian munitions maker. He tried to buy every existing print of the movie so that he could burn them but his plan was unsuccessful as laboratory technicians had copied the negative by that point.[27] In Italy, no less a luminary than Benito Mussolini campaigned for its screening at the Venice Film Festival. This was achieved, but not even Il Duce could prevent the Vatican from being enraged by it.

A harder line was taken on Mae West, probably because of her prolific output. Also, no matter how many times she was rapped on the knuckles, somehow she seemed to be winning the war.

Many of Hays' detractors cited West's enduring popularity as a testament to his inefficiency. In February 1933, Father Lord sent him a letter saying that *She Done Him Wrong* was no more than a re-packaging of *Diamond Lil* which she'd been clever enough to slip through the net with only cosmetic changes. The wily lass had pulled the wool over his eyes with some judicious editing.

West changed Diamond Lil's name to Lady Lou. She cut the lyrics of some of the objectionable songs in the play, as well as all references to white slavery. But this was still very much old wine in a thinly disguised wineskin.

To be fair to Hays, on paper the script looked innocuous enough. It was her playing of it that made it suggestive. One critic remarked, "Mae couldn't sing a lullaby without making it sexy."[28] It was like Alfred Hitchcock claiming that if he directed a film version of *Cinderella*, people would be looking for the body in the coach. (If West made *Cinderella*, they'd probably have been looking for a *nude* body in it.)

Hays got his way with her by causing her to excise parts of her writing where steam rose from the pages. But by forcing her to dig deeper into her penchant for nuance, he caused her to write a script that was even more potent than the one it replaced.

As if to counteract such stratagems, or to at least gauge their impact on audiences, an organization called the Payne Fund was set up in late 1933. This granted $200,000 to the Motion Picture Research Council to study the influence of films on high school children. The conclusions it reached were quite startling. It held films responsible for everything from moral decay to lower academic grades—and even sleep patterns. In such a context, cinemas showing lewd films became little more than "universities of crime."

Many people disagreed with the conclusions of the researchers. Were films mirrors or lamps? Did they reflect social trends or give rise to them? Were children growing up too fast or was it the moral laxity of the stars they watched misbehaving on screen that was causing them to do so?

Father Lord believed the latter. This was why, after Wingate passed *She Done Him Wrong*—a film that turned his stomach—with only minor cuts, he said he was resigning from the Hays Office for keeps. His departure was a seminal moment in the division between clerical and secular vetting of films after a decade or so of relative harmony. The Payne Fund report also contended that *Little Caesar* had "inspired" the murder of a young boy named Winslow Eliot, a killing that outraged America at the time.

The report concluded that children had uncanny memories of what they saw in cinemas, being able to recount scenes verbatim even weeks later. Movies made them tense, and often insomniac. Their pulse rates increased, and also their empathy with undesirable figures, even if those figures met sorry ends. Children would have been much better employed, it advised, working off their tensions in athletic activities rather than sitting huddled in darkened theaters forming vicarious alliances with the wrong kinds of role models.

We can't generalize. To give one example from our own time, Japan has a relatively low rate of assaults against women, despite being a country where some of the most violent pornography is freely available. On the other hand, the serial killer Ted Bundy said a diet of porn was his catalyst. The Payne Report couldn't be dismissed but it shouldn't have been regarded as gospel.

Ann Vickers was released that year as well. Dawn B. Sova says that RKO were well aware even before filming began that it was going to be trouble because the novel had been "attacked in the Catholic press and was forbidden reading for American Catholics."[29] The Jesuit publication *America* dubbed it "obscene" while *Catholic World* warned readers to stay at a safe distance from it, accusing Lewis of delighting in "the garbage, the dumps, the cesspools."[30]

In the Sinclair Lewis book upon which the film is based, the title character was a married woman who had a passionate affair and a subsequent abortion. In the film, in which she's played by Irene Dunne, this became a miscarriage. Dunne portrays her as a strong liberal who becomes excited by penal reform after witnessing the horrendous conditions under which women are incarcerated. She seems more energized by this than her romantic encounters.

Maybe Vickers could be credited with pioneering what we now call "casual sex," as her love life definitely seems to play second fiddle to her career. In the two instances in which she discovers she's pregnant, she barely flickers an eyelid. Remember, this was no saloon singer or cabaret siren, rather an idealist and social reformer. That made it even more dangerous as far as the SRC was concerned. RKO had to oversee a number of changes to render it palatable to that organization. Vickers is now single when she has her affair (thereby preserving the sanctity of marriage). She also has to suffer for her "sins" by being ostracized by her friends and losing her job.

Vickers falls pregnant the first time after a fling with a Great War soldier (Bruce Cabot). The love scene is handled very delicately by director James Cromwell. All we see is his coat falling to the floor during an embrace. The camera then pans to a hotel window from which we see a cinema advertising the film *Joan the Woman* in a blinking neon sign. The shot dissolves into another one of the same cinema advertising a new film, *Shoulder Arms*. A week has passed, in other words — and Ann is still with her soldier.

After she becomes involved in a second relationship with an about-to-be-divorced judge (Walter Huston), Breen and Wingate ensured that RKO made Vickers suffer after she becomes pregnant by him. She lives in humble circumstances and he's sentenced to six years penal servitude for consorting with some shady characters in the legal world.

The idea of an unmarried woman becoming pregnant twice by different lovers was pretty racy in 1933. But it all ends tamely after Huston gets released early from prison with a pardon and the couple settle down to an old-fashioned marriage with their little boy, thereby diluting the bite of the early scenes. Even so, the film was condemned by the Legion of Decency. It became the victim of a rather nasty campaign by outraged Catholics all over the U.S. The fact that Vickers had a highly attuned social conscience, combined with a deep interest in prison reform, mattered little to those in the PCA. Especially if her extracurricular activities included having abortions and affairs.

The "way out" West, however, remained the main butt of the church leaders. Not that she was unduly perturbed by her pariah status. "At this stage," she joked, "I'd be insulted if a picture I did *didn't* get an X-rating."[31]

West beamed, "I believe in censorship. After all, I made a fortune out of it."[32] Claude Binyon knew what she meant. "Hollywood," he opined, "must never allow censorship to collapse — it's far too good for the box office."[33]

The public couldn't get enough of her, queuing round the clock to listen to her barbed witticisms, her debunking of sacred cows. "The whole country is going West," the Paramount officials punned. West merrily trilled, "Whenever I go wrong, men go right after me."

Breen was intent on reversing this trend, both with regard to West and other divas, and set about tightening the leash anew. He sent down over 30,000 directives in the following three years. The average length of a screen kiss dropped from four seconds to one and a half. References to breast-feeding, pregnancy, and other natural functions continued to be rigorously censored. *King Kong* was withdrawn from cinemas because in one scene the gentle giant tore off a few pieces of Fay Wray's clothing.

Any reference to homosexuality in such movies was a strict no-no, though effeminate heterosexual men were allowed to flounce across studio sets in semi-comedic mode. Lesbians were a different kettle of fish and remained strictly taboo. With the advent of Marlene Dietrich, the phenomenon of cross-dressing appeared. Definitions of what exactly constituted gender-bending became looser. Actresses like Greta Garbo and Katharine Hepburn, fellow members of the so-called "Sewing Circle," followed her lead.

It wasn't long before Breen got his claws round a West script called *It Ain't No Sin*. He believed it was a glorification of prostitution and violent crime. She offered to listen to his concerns and try to abide by them. She wasn't too fussy about deletions if it meant preserving the unity of her work but she added that she'd be keeping her innuendoes. Breen said this was out of the question, seeing her as the doyenne of the *single entendre*.

While West appeared to be toning down her naughtiness, what she was really doing was engaging in send-ups that owed as much "to subtlety as burlesque."[34] She'd learned the art of timing during her early days in front of live audiences. This meant she could wring a laugh from little or nothing. There was no way you could censor a pause — as people like Harold Pinter would prove in the decades to come.

A lot of the time she was genuinely unaware of what Breen's problems were. "I'd hate to have his mind," she said once. "If I sit on a guy's lap he takes something out of it." Though she admitted she'd been on "more laps than a napkin."[35]

Breen sometimes took his markers from audiences. In *Destry Rides Again*

(1939), there's a line where a nightclub singer played by Marlene Dietrich puts a bank note into her bosom with a line West would have been proud of: "There's gold in them there hills." Breen passed it on the page but when he heard a preview audience guffawing heartily at it he changed tack and ordered its removal. Joe Pasternak, the film's producer, thought it was the best line in the film.[36] The one that replaced it, "I'd rather have money in the bank," was a pale reflection.

Apart from this, a blind eye was turned to much of Dietrich's misbehavior on screen. According to Alexander Walker, she got away with things other actresses of her era didn't. Because of her versatility, the plotlines of her films seemed to pass by Breen & Co: "Censorship meant that she had to go on playing the *femme fatale* at prudently remote periods of history, or else in vague and unlocalized settings like an oriental express or a desert garrison."[37]

Sometimes it all became a bit like a Rorschach test. There's a story that tells of a psychiatrist who shows a series of drawings to a patient. As he flips each one over and asks what it conveys to him, the patient invariably replies "Sex." The psychiatrist diagnoses eventually that he has an obsession with sex. "Me?" the man protests, "But it's you who's drawing all the dirty pictures." George Bernard Shaw put it another way when he suggested that it wasn't possible to discuss obscenity without being obscene.[38]

In the same way, too many people of certain proclivities poking around a film looking for something to castigate, and then shout "Eureka!" would certainly find it in time. Whether it was there or not was another question — or whether it could do any damage even if it was.

So was it West or Breen who was making the "dirty" pictures? Or both of them in their unique manner? We might say West was guilty until proven innocent for Breen, whereas Breen, for West, was a challenge she set out to have fun with — at both of their expenses. Maybe a film dealing with their cat-and-mouse games would have been more tantalizing than all her scripts put together. I doubt that the Legion of Decency would have passed it, though. Anyway, she would have balked at cutting him in for a share of the profits.

West reworked *It Ain't No Sin* to placate Hays and Breen by deleting all references to crime and prostitution. Breen even put a spy on the set to ensure that nothing was added to the script. When the film was released, however, priests from the Legion paraded on Broadway with placards saying "It *is*" — i.e., a sin.[39] When Catholic leaders saw the preview, they dismissed it out of hand, resulting in red faces for Hays and Breen and a disavowal of their credibility. The film wended its way back to them and they watched it again, this time with a sterner eye. The result? More cuts were demanded by them. It also had to be re-titled, the *It* being a bone of contention for the Legion of Decency. It was now called *Belle of the Nineties*; once again the tail of the church was wagging the dog of the state. Breen also insisted that West had to marry in the final scene.

These protracted negotiations took their toll on her energy level and her enthusiasm for what she was doing. "By the end of 1934," Alexander Walker summarized, "not quite three years after she had arrived in Hollywood, West was well on the way to becoming a ruined woman."[40]

West wasn't the only actress Breen was concerned about. Greta Garbo portrayed Tolstoy's doomed heroine in *Anna Karenina* in 1935. (She'd already essayed the same role in the silent movie *Love* eight years previously.) She's unfaithful to her unfeeling husband (Basil Rathbone) and having an affair with a cavalry officer played by Fredric March, which means giving up her son to be with March. This kind of material was only acceptable to Breen because she commits suicide at the end, in effect punishing herself for her adultery. Even so, it was still condemned by the Chicago Legion of Decency. What Breen didn't realize was that most audience sympathies rested with Garbo, particularly from women. Few saw her as deserving of her eventual fate in the same way he did.

New York City cleric John Haynes-Holmes informed his flock that year that there seemed to be nothing too sacred to be defiled by Hollywood. It's surprising to learn that the Reverend Holmes, though prudish sexually, was a political liberal who lent avid support to the American Civil Liberties Union. He felt the real problem of the Hollywood ethos wasn't sex but commercialization. He might have said, as David Mamet did a generation later, "I always felt the real evil in films wasn't what people do on the screen, but what we do to raise the money."[41] As Jane Fonda surmised *à propos* her role as a hooker in *Klute:* "Working in Hollywood gives you a certain expertise in the field of prostitution."[42]

West made *Goin' to Town,* the tale of a widow schmoozing her way into high society, not long after Holmes' onslaught. Breen hadn't seen a problem with it but E. Robb Zaring of Indiana's Episcopal church wrote to him accusing him of having his radar on the blink. He saw it as yet another example of a lecherous actress foisting unacceptable values on the people of America. Audiences were also unimpressed with it, as were the critics. It failed to measure up on all scores.

Mae West, an almost permanent headache for the censors by dint of her loaded innuendos and ubiquitous swagger, here pictured in *Belle of the Nineties* (1934).

In 1936 West took on a role that was decidedly out of character. *Klondike Annie* tells the story of a lady of dubious virtue who accidentally kills a man after he makes unwanted sexual advances on her. She flees to San Francisco, meeting an evangelist on board a ship. The evangelist falls into bad health and dies, whereupon Annie (West) assumes her identity. Such a role change affects her mind as well because she now takes upon herself the proselytizing duties of the dead woman with some fervor, reforming various Klondike miners before coming clean about her secret identity and the crime of her past.

The film contained the famous line "Between two evils, I always pick the one I never tried before" and the song "I'm an Occidental Woman in an Oriental Mood for Love" but the film in general, as Frank Nugent wrote in *The New York Times,* was neither as "healthily rowdy nor as vulgarly suggestive" as her earlier work.[43] Graham Greene didn't find the satire on religious revivalists in bad taste at all, he stated, simply because he didn't take it seriously for a second.[44] It's a pity others hadn't the same lackadaisical attitude.

Breen couldn't accept it and ordered all references to both religion and prostitution to be removed, feeling the mix was rabidly combustible. He also felt that Annie's reformation was too contrived. (All too well aware of her talent for inserting levity into the most unlikely quarters, Breen was somewhat like W.C. Fields at the end of his life. At this point Fields was rumored to be reading the Bible "for loopholes.") At the end of the day, the film was little more than a fairytale laced with lewd undertones.

At no point, Breen stressed, could it be implied that West had any connection to religion, be that in the capacity of preacher, revivalist or minister. With this in mind, she wasn't to wear religious garb, carry a Bible, or even utter the word "religion" in any scene. It was as if anything even vaguely spiritual would forever be tarnished by its association with her. She was to be portrayed instead as a social worker.

He insisted on major surgery of the script and West obliged. He passed the second draft but once again was misguided in his laxity as the film opened to almost the same excitement as attended her previous excursions. The first man to attack it was the magnate William Randolph Hearst, though his problems could have been personal, West having recently made a disparaging remark about his mistress Marion Davies some time before. Hearst tried to get West kicked out of Hollywood altogether, using the Legion of Decency as a wedge for his own private grudge on the Davies matter.

Klondike Annie was screened for Breen on New Year's Eve 1935. He immediately granted it the Seal of Approval, seeing nothing lewd or objectionable in it. Afterwards he learned that what he'd been shown was a watered-down version. This made him livid. He forced the studio to re-work it. This delayed its release for two months.

Breen was fed up with her manipulations at this point. It wasn't the first time he'd been duped by her but he was adamant that it would be the last.

He knew now that Mae West would never reform. His anger at her, publicly expressed, resulted in Paramount canceling her contract. The moguls knew she'd made them pots of money but in a sense it was fool's gold because of all the negative publicity her antics generated. And thus a career that had begun so controversially fizzled out on a whimper.

In *Every Day's a Holiday* (1937) she played a con artist trying to expose a bent cop but the film was bled dry of any of her old trademark wit and bombed. By this stage of her career there were so many preconditions to a West screenplay, she might as well not have bothered putting anything of herself into it at all. Breen even had problems with the line "I don't know a lot about politics, but I know a good party man when I see one." She fought to keep this in and won — a late and minuscule concession from an organization that tried to suck the life-blood out of her.

Later came *My Little Chickadee* with W.C. Fields, another star who'd had censorship issues. It didn't sizzle. Perhaps too many disapproving eyes were on the script. It ended up as a languid piece of fluff.

West also did some radio work at this time. She returned to the theater in the 1940s with her play *Catherine Was Great*. "She made love to dozens of men," she quipped, "I did the best I could in a few hours." In the fifties she appeared in cabaret in Las Vegas, often opposite musclemen in a parody of her past.

She made a film comeback in 1970 with *Myra Breckenridge,* a John Huston production based on Gore Vidal's steamy play about a transsexual, here played by Raquel Welch. It was one of Huston's worst films and an embarrassing pseudo-revival for the sometime queen of camp. She and Welch crossed swords off-set, which was hardly surprising considering Welch never looked quite as alluring as here. West never exactly relished this kind of competition, even in old age.

Eight years later she was back on screen to appear in an adaptation of *Sex,* retitled *Sextette*. She would end as she began, in a wry necklace of suggestiveness. She was 85 by now and, as one might have expected, not totally with it.

When I interviewed Tony Curtis, I asked him how it felt to share the screen with a legend. "Terrific," he beamed. "All my life I'd wanted to appear with two people: Marilyn Monroe and Mae West. That's because Cary Grant was the only other star who had done that and he was my idol. I appeared with Marilyn in *Some Like It Hot* but I left it late to catch up with Mae."

Would he see any comparison between the two sirens? "Of course. Mae

West was the Marilyn of the 1930s. If it wasn't for her, there mightn't have been a Marilyn Monroe. She came along at a time when you couldn't do very much without incurring the wrath of the big guns. She took them all on. And with such pizzazz. It was easier for the rest of us to push the boat out a bit further but she was the first. She made sex funny at a time when it was supposed to be this big taboo subject. I'd love to have worked with her in her prime."

The experience of working with the two sex symbols had some unsavory parallels. "Marilyn kept us all waiting for an eternity when she was getting ready for her scenes in *Some Like It Hot.* So did Mae in *Sextette,* but for different reasons. Marilyn suffered from nerves but with Mae it was her enema. She had to have one every morning before shooting began. I tried to work in my arrival on set around that."

This wasn't her only biological irregularity. "Her sight had failed and her hearing was almost gone as well. She wore a hearing aid which had too high a frequency so it picked up police calls as well as the director's instructions. One day instead of the line she was supposed to feed me, she came out with something like 'Pile up on Madison and Fairfax — proceed with caution!' The whole set broke up. But it was a once-in-a-lifetime experience sharing a set with her. Even at 85 she still wielded some of that old magic. I'm proud to have been a part of that movie, the last hurrah of a siren. She was adorable."

Did she look 85? "She could have been more! Some reports put her in her nineties when she made that movie. You never knew with Mae. I just took her as I found her. I'm no spring chicken myself and I admire anyone who keeps at it. You can't be ageist. It broke me up listening to her speaking her lines out of her hair, where the hearing aid was. She was also wearing these six-inch lifts, and being wheeled around by crew members because she couldn't walk properly. People were lying on the floor turning her. She kept missing the chalk marks on the floor and going out of camera range because her sight was so bad. It was funnier than anything in the script. They should have made a film about *that.* And then you had Ken Hughes — the director — in a booth with a loudspeaker and a bottle of Jack Daniels. Suddenly, Billy Wilder's problems with Marilyn were like a breeze. Ken said directing her was like trying to talk a plane down in a snowstorm."

With West gone for her tea, those who'd been irked by her now felt free to flex their reactionary muscles still further, at times making changes to scripts that rendered them suspiciously close to pre-pubescent idylls.

Walt Disney even fell prey to Hays' scissors. Hays insisted he excise from

Snow White and the Seven Dwarfs (1937) a scene in which the dwarfs make up a bed for Snow White. Hays felt an innuendo of cohabitation could be drawn. (Hollywood's first animated orgy? Not.) The Legion of Decency even tinkered with the idea of recruiting screenwriters and directors from their own ranks to, as it were, reform the industry from within. If those running the show were infidels and atheists, the thinking went, the corrective would be to have avid believers outwrite them.

With this in mind, the idea of launching screenwriting courses in Catholic colleges was mooted in 1936, the sanctity of marriage being a particular priority. The magazine *America* suggested making a film where the wedding scene would be one with a white-veiled bride rather than a ten-minute affair signing on the dotted line before a justice of the peace.

Katharine Hepburn was "allowed" to be a single mother in *A Woman Rebels* (1936), and also a suffragette, because she gets married in the finale. Even Clara Bow was tamed by matrimony in *It* in 1927. The hand that rocked the system, it was made clear to all and sundry, must also rock the cradle. As Elinor Glyn put it in *Harper's Bazaar*, "Marriage is the aim of all sensible girls because it is the meaning of life." Glyn also wrote the screenplay for *It*.[45]

Robert K. Johnston made a different kind of point about the sociology of sex. "With the advent of World War II," he argued, "two-piece swimsuits were justified on the patriotic grounds of saving fabric. Women became common in the workplace, and pin-up calendars were everywhere. Standards with regard to sexuality in the movies seemed hopelessly dated.[46] The Hays Office rowed back on its demands for these and other reasons, but wouldn't be steered off-course with regard to its main core points.

In 1938 the Institute for Propaganda Analysis outlined the main shortcomings of both the League of Decency and the Production Code *apropos* four simplistic assumptions they made in their choice of films suitable for mass market consumption. They were as follows:

1. That the successful culmination of a romance will solve most of the dilemmas of the hero and heroine.
2. Catch the criminal and you will solve the crime problem.
3. War and preparation for war are thrilling, heroic and glamorous.
4. The good life is the acquisitive life, with its emphasis on luxury, fine homes, automobiles, evening dress, swank and suavity.

Phrased like this, it makes one more than aware of the intellectually-challenged dross that passed for art in a society terrified of rocking any boats, be they social, sexual, religious or political. In such dross the bad guys (pinkos?) got their eventual comeuppance, banner-waving military heroes kept the world safe for democracy, and Joe Blow had his nuclear family, his pet dog and his white picket fence. Lovers walked into the sunset in the last reel (or maybe followed the Yellow Brick Road) and lived happily ever after.

Breen had a problem with the scene in *Gone with the Wind* (1939) where Rhett Butler (Clark Gable) appears to rape his wife Scarlett O'Hara (Vivien Leigh), with Scarlett eventually enjoying such an act, at least if her next-morning jubilance is to be taken into account. Joan Crawford said she found suggestion "a hell of a lot more provocative" than explicit detail. You didn't see Clark and Vivien rolling around in bed, but you saw that "shit-eating" grin on her face the next morning and you knew damned well "she'd gotten properly laid."

Another problem was posed by Butler's use of the word "damn" in the film's closing scene. This was a word that cost David O. Selznick, the film's producer, more than he cared to remember. Selznick claimed he fought harder over that four-letter word than any of his soldiers did in the Civil War. It became an even bigger bone of contention than the fact that Butler consorted with prostitute Belle Watling (Ona Munson). It was eventually allowed into the script, but only because of the context in which it occurred, towards the end of the movie. And Gable had to put the emphasis on the verb "give" to deflect attention from it.

Selznick shot another version of the scene with Gable saying "darn" instead of "damn" in case Hays refused to budge, a "belt and braces" strategy that ultimately proved unnecessary.[47] In retrospect the whole episode seems like a tempest in a teapot. As one wag joked, the real surprise wasn't that Butler cursed Scarlett, but rather that he "took so long to do so."[48]

Hays actually overruled Breen regarding the offensive epithet, allowing Gable to say "damn" but covering his tracks by simultaneously fining Selznick $5,000 for violating the Code. It was a concession of sorts, considering the fact that, as Warren Harris observes in his biography of Gable, it was the first time the word had been used since the Code's inception in 1933.[49] The Legion of Decency gave the film a B rating which meant that it was, in their view, guilty of having a "low moral character." But "the tens of millions who've seen it since have," as Edward De Grazia wryly commented, "apparently felt otherwise."[50]

Nineteen thirty-nine was also the year that Denver cinema manager Robert Allen was sentenced to 120 days in jail for showing D.W. Griffith's

The Birth of a Nation, on the grounds that he flouted a city ordinance prohibiting the exhibition of motion pictures that were calculated to either stir up racial prejudice or disturb the peace.

Towards the end of the decade, as one author observed, "spiritual redemption" had even become a concern in gangster films: "In the early part of the decade their major preoccupation was whether the gangster hero would die game or turn yellow before the end. But by 1938, social concerns pulled for the gangsters' immortal soul, and *Angels with Dirty Faces* and *The Roaring Twenties,* which followed in 1939, ended with both a bang and a prayer."[51]

Tom Dewe Mathews agreed, especially with regard to the plight of Jean Harlow. When she made her last film (*Saratoga*) he noticed she wasn't allowed to seduce her co-star Clark Gable. With her platinum blonde hair darkened, she merely tempts him in a clearly enunciated accent "more redolent of the sweet tones of a debutante than the wisecracking slang of a woman who wants to claim her man for sin and sex." Because she died in the thirties, Mathews concluded, Hays shifted his disdain (and scissors) towards the "fuller figure" of Mae West instead.[52]

Graham Greene didn't think Harlow's death changed anything in movies: "There's no sign that her acting would ever have progressed beyond the scope of the restless shoulders and protuberant breasts. Her technique was the gangster's technique — she toted a breast like a man totes a gun."[53]

Harlow died of kidney failure at the tender age of 26 in 1937. Cynics would have had us believe that her mother stood over the dying young girl with ill-concealed glee, viewing her pain as some kind of purgative rite she had to undergo to earn her eternal reward. The truth of the mat-

Jean Harlow set pulses racing in *The Public Enemy* (1931).

ter was that her mother wasn't a Christian Scientist at all, and had a doctor attending her right through her final illness. (A further rumor, that the beating she received from her husband Paul Bern on their wedding night in 1932, brought on her kidney failure, was also found to be medically impossible.)

The following decade was characterized by as much insanity as the one just gone, reminding one of Yeats' dictum: "The best lack all conviction while the worst Are full of passionate intensity." One of its most controversial films was *The Outlaw* in 1943. This was the film for which Jane Russell will forever be remembered ... for most of the wrong reasons.

It was justifiably mauled by the critics but still did huge business, making more money in Atlanta than even *Gone with the Wind* had done. Some government censors banned it, a Maryland judge announcing in language that was much juicier than anything in the script that Russell's breasts "hung over the picture like a thunderstorm spread over a landscape."[54] Church protests caused cancellations of the film in Philadelphia, Minnesota and St. Paul, while in New York the police warned cinema owners that they'd lose their distribution license if they screened it. The owners gave in, but United Artists countered by suing one of the cinemas concerned for breach of contract. The PCA had denied the film a Seal but ultimately realized the folly of their ways and quietly restored it. After Howard Hughes, the director, removed some of the more offensive scenes, the Legion of Decency gave it a B rating.

It was a film more noteworthy for its advertising poster, which featured Russell looking so bosomy it was said her breasts had two separate zip codes. Such was the interest in her cleavage that in one three-week period during the making of the film, she was splashed on the covers of no less than eleven national magazines, while stories about her were featured in 532 dailies and 448 Sunday papers. (Mammaries were made of this.)

Hughes wasn't shy about exploiting her estimable assets in his pre-release publicity. This outraged Breen, who didn't need any special insights to know what he was at. The lady in question was pictured in the hay — a different kind of Hay Code than Breen was accustomed to — in a cantilevered bra which enlarged her breasts no matter what angle they were shot from. A voyeur's nirvana! Hughes recycled a gag widely on the go at the time: "There are two good reasons men will go to see her."[55]

Years after the film was made, Russell came clean about the motive behind the angles: "Sometimes the photographers would pose me in a low-necked nightgown and tell me to bend down and pick up a couple of pails. They were not shooting the pails."[56] She lay provocatively in a barn with her blouse hanging off her shoulder and her breasts doing their best to try and stay inside it — no mean achievement. (The outfit never appeared in the film, underlining the exploitative nature of the poster.)

Things got slightly ridiculous when Hughes actually had a mathematician liaise with the Hays Office, arguing that Russell actually showed less of her breasts than other actresses in films that had already been approved by the PCA.

Breen afterwards sent letters to most of the main studios ordering all cleavage shots to be eliminated from their films. Women wearing angora sweaters were especial no-nos because of the revealing nature of that particular fabric. Was this moral guidance or sartorial insanity? Maybe Breen wouldn't have been totally happy unless the collective female population of Hollywood had multiple mastectomies.

The ensuing altercation between Hughes and Breen led to Breen turning in his resignation to the PCA. This was ironic as Hughes had produced the film independently and only submitted it to him as a courtesy. It was a traumatic move for Breen as he had an almost Napoleonic sense of self-importance when it came to the kind of work he did. Without him, he felt the temple of censorship would come tumbling down as the amoral Samsons inside it ran amok.

His health was suffering, though. As far back as 1937 he had told Martin Quigley, "My digestion has gone to pot. I frequently vomit without any seeming cause at all." (Watching too many Mae West films, one was tempted to comment, wouldn't have helped either of these problems.) Three years later he confessed to being "near insanity."[57] He felt let down by everyone: journalists, Hays, even the Legion of Decency. But he shouldn't have looked for scapegoats. The real reason for his depression was much more obvious: The times had simply overtaken him. He was yesterday's man.

After his resignation, he went on to become head of production at RKO. The following year he returned to his old post. One of his first duties here, ironically, was to censor some of the very films he had passed at RKO.

With or without Breen, the censorial axe continued to be wielded in a manner that was frequently ludicrous. After Fritz Lang made *Man Hunt* in 1940 he complained, "The Hays Office warned us that we couldn't show the heroine as a prostitute. We had to put a sewing machine in her apartment so in that way she was not a whore but a seamstress."[58]

Some decisions were so stupid they were funny. In the 1942 espionage film *Invisible Agent*, for instance, a shower scene was banned even though it wasn't shown. All that could be seen were drops of water sticking to the eponymous character's skin, but not the skin itself. The problem was that the bathroom door was open and there was a woman next door.[59]

Japan cut a scene from *Madame Butterfly* as it showed Sylvia Sidney's left elbow as she was being kissed by Cary Grant.[60] RKO were advised to delete a scene from *From This Day Forward* when a character says he didn't sleep well because of drinking two cups of coffee; the censors felt it might offend Brazilian coffee-makers.[61] So not all of the censors' cuts were sexual or violent.

In 1941 the Legion condemned *Two-Faced Woman*, a film which had already been given a seal. It was the first time the Legion overruled the PCA since 1934. Its reasons were that it felt the film exhibited an "immoral and unChristian attitude to marriage" and also that there were too many suggestive scenes in it.[62]

Archbishop Spellman slammed it from his New York pulpit while the Legion's secretary, the Rev. John McClafferty, warned Hollywood not to let "the wartime trend away from God to creep into movies."[63]

In the forties, the censor-free bandwagon every studio wanted to jump on was the war effort. It was safe, it was heroic and, most importantly of all, it wasn't sexual. The typical soldier was more likely to have Betty Grable pictures in his locker than ones of Mae West. Marilyn Monroe wiggled for the troops but there it ended.

Many of the stars went to join the war themselves. James Stewart became a bomber pilot. Robert Montgomery joined the navy. Robert Taylor went into the navy and Tyrone Power joined the Marines. Those who stayed behind made films with jingoism, not sexual danger, at their core. When GI Joe came home, society again moved formerly feisty ladies to the kitchen sink.

Rebellious dames, meanwhile, were relegated to the realms of *film noir* as dangerous specimens you tampered with at your peril. In a word, the trenches replaced the boudoir as the focus of attention, which made Mr. Hays and his clerical cronies breathe a sigh of relief. Adolf Hitler, the little man from Austria with the toothbrush moustache — who had once decreed that any woman who broke up a marriage in a film must die at the end — had indirectly sharpened the moral fiber of Hollywood. As for the genocide of six million Jews, well, that was another matter. It was an ill wind.

Not everything was simple, though. The church was nervous about the film version of Ernest Hemingway's *For Whom the Bell Tolls* (1943), both on moral and political grounds. There's a tacit assumption that Gary Cooper and Ingrid Bergman share a sleeping bag together. (The novel was much more explicit with dialogue like "Did the earth move for you?") The political dimension proved more sensitive but director Sam Wood agreed to delete all references to Franco and the Republican movement that the guerrillas belonged to.

Joe Breen even had problems with *The Song of Bernadette* in the same year. He took umbrage at Bernadette's father getting drunk and uttering innocuous phrases like "What in God's name." His pettiness rachetted up another level when he suggested that the term "Ecclesiasticals" be replaced with "Ecclesiastics."[64] Jones' separation from her first husband Robert Walker was hushed up during the making of the film for fear it would tarnish the image of the young heroine.

Adultery occurred in Billy Wilder's adaptation of James M. Cain's hard-boiled murder story *Double Indemnity* (1944) but it was given the green light due to its undeniable brilliance. It hasn't dated a jot and its razor-sharp dialogue and incredible performances (particularly from the ankle-braceleted Barbara Stanwyck as the *femme fatale* who lures insurance salesman Fred MacMurray into her web) confirm it as the most stylish *film noir* of the decade — if not any decade.

There was a lot of sexual innuendo in the early verbal exchanges between MacMurray and Stanwyck, and one supposes the pair are sleeping together as they hatch a plan to kill Stanwyck's husband, but the film largely escaped the censor's scissors, partly because we don't actually see anything more alluring than that ankle bracelet. And of course the plotting duo both go to the end of the line (i.e., the cemetery) in the final reel. Which always helped.

One writer felt that Stanwyck's feelings for MacMurray were "sexual or sexual-homicidal (sex being the equivalent of evil, evil the metaphor for sex) until the moment when, having just shot him in the shoulder, she drops the gun." And we get the perfect mix of sex and death — mutually, because he shoots her too.[65] Al Diorio believed the scenes between the pair were "infused with sexual anxieties almost never before seen on film.... The eroticism can almost be touched."[66]

Wilder originally intended to have MacMurray electrocuted in the prison death house in the last scene but instead had him dying at Edward G. Robinson's feet as he attempted to light a cigarette. This was infinitely more effective. It was more practical as well as the Code forbade the exhibition of electrocutions.

Tidings, a Los Angeles newspaper, admired the film, believing that its point was that there was "no perfect crime," that "those of criminal tendencies

Publicity poster for James M. Cain's steamy thriller *Double Indemnity* (1944) which breathed new life into the careers of Fred MacMurray and Barbara Stanwyck as the tragic lovers hellbent on self-destruction.

who might have been tempted to try out the formula for murder which this plot propounds might now may reflect what happened to the characters."[67]

It's a pity that magazines like this had pre-conceived notions about plots. There was no "point" to the film. It was a story, pure and simple — or maybe we should say impure and complex. It went where it went because of the dynamics of the plot. The main characters had to die because of the dictates of the time, not because Billy Wilder wanted them to. Which isn't to say he was condoning murder. His brief was to portray real people in real situations, their lives spiraling out of control as events overtook them and they became undone by greed, lust and duplicity. In a sense it *was* the perfect crime. MacMurray's main mistake was in not realizing he was being set up to commit it. Wilder confessed, "My pictures aren't intended to reform people. Hopefully they're sufficiently intriguing to make them forget the popcorn."[68]

Aesthetics beat ethics, in other words. Or was aesthetics a higher form of ethics? Nobody could say they weren't emotionally uplifted after coming out of a Wilder thriller, or laughing after seeing one of his better comedies. Can one give higher praise than that?

Noël Coward's *In Which We Serve* (1942) gave Hays various problems because of its racy language. It was found to contain ten "damns," two "hells," two "Gods," two "bastards" and one "lousy." Most of these were judiciously winnowed out but a few "damns" were preserved, much to Hays' eventual chagrin as other directors cited his laxity with Coward as an "open sesame" for themselves. After this lapse, Hays decided he had to be brutally consistent.

In September of 1945 Hays resigned as president of the MPPDA. By this time he had suffered a heart attack, perhaps brought on by the tensions of the job. He would live for nine more years but wrote disconsolately in his memoirs, "I find that my fundamental convictions have changed little."[69]

The following year, David O. Selznick produced a Western that would extend the boundaries of the genre almost to the breaking point. *Duel in the Sun* (1946) was a film that caused a major crisis among the ecclesiastical fraternity. A kind of *Wuthering Heights* with Stetsons, it chronicled the love-hate relationship between Lewt McCanless (Gregory Peck) and Pearl Chavez (Jennifer Jones) against the backdrop of cattle wars, sibling rivalry and filial treachery. The two main leads were never better, shooting one another on a clifftop at the end and then dying in one another's arms, their debauched union finally complete.

At the beginning, Pearl wards off Lewt's caveman-like advances but gradually succumbs, attracted to his animal charm. She spits at him and he spits back at her, their wild interplay far ahead of its time.

For both performers, it was a huge stretch in character portrayals. Peck had never played a villain before, and Jones had carved out a reputation as a girl-next-door type or romantic lead. Three years earlier she'd made *The Song of Bernadette*, playing a young girl who sees a vision of Our Lady. In 1944, Peck had played a priest in *The Keys of the Kingdom*.

The Legion of Decency accused Selznick of turning the "dignity and loveliness of Saint Bernadette [Jones] into a wholly immoral subject of the flesh" with *Duel in the Sun*. He demanded 32 cuts made to prevent it getting a Condemned rating.[70] One newspaper commented before its release, "It will be quite a sight to see the erstwhile Father Chisholm leering at the onetime Saint Bernadette.[71]

For producer Selznick (Jones' lover at the time) this made their earthy commingling all the sweeter. He intended the film to be on the epic scale of his previous *Gone with the Wind*, idealistically imagining that he could simply let the cameras roll and that would be that.

William Mooring, film critic for the aforementioned journal *Tidings*, found the film little more than "plush pornography."[72] He felt it was overly sympathetic to the two leading characters and he couldn't condone the allowance of Peck's seduction scene. He also felt the character of Walter Huston, the Bible-thumper who tries to save Jones' soul, was rendered farcical. The Archbishop of Los Angeles, John Cantwell, derided the film from the pulpit. At a *Duel* test screening there were loud guffaws during the scenes where Huston tried to reform Ms Jones. These were very worrying signs for Hays & Co.

Selznick took umbrage at what he deemed to be a personal attack on his inamorata, shooting a missive back to the editor of *Tidings*, stating that Jones was a highly respected actress and a convent girl to boot. (One wonders at the relevance of this in the context.)

The fact that the film had received approval from the PCA didn't cut much ice with Selznick as by now the Legion of Decency had more or less parted company with it. The upshot was that the studio forced him to have large chunks of the film re-shot and a huge dollop of dialogue cut from the script.

The early scene in which Lewt rapes Pearl was the first casualty, though not in total as its complete excision would have rendered their subsequent liaison well-nigh incomprehensible. Her Salomé-like dance in front of him was also edited down to the point of blandness. This annoyed Selznick intensely as Breen had actually passed it as it was being shot. Other scenes featuring Pearl in skimpy apparel also got the chop, as did a reference to her being like a mare in heat as she watched a stallion on the rampage with Lewt.

None of this was too surprising in a film that had commonly come to be known as *Lust in the Dust*. Selznick made 31 cuts to placate the Legion but drew a line at stopping the doomed lovers dying in each other's arms. Martin Quigley felt two such depraved souls didn't deserve this momentary solace even as they breathed their last but by now Selznick's patience was at an end and he held firm. Every time he folded over on a point, he complained, more concessions were demanded. It had to stop somewhere. At times it seemed like horse-trading. He didn't want to be left with a shell of a movie after so much sweat.

At the end of the film, in a final humiliation, Selznick was forced to append an Afterword condemning both Jones and Peck for "moral weakness" and "Godlessness" respectively. His only consolation was that most people had probably left the cinema before they read this anodyne wrap-up. But it left him with a sick aftertaste regarding the whole imbroglio — as did the $5 million that the protracted negotiations with Breen and his cohorts purportedly cost him.

Jones had become so closely identified with St. Bernadette that her transmogrification to the hot-blooded Pearl was a source of great outrage among Catholics. Jones commented: "I was never Bernadette, nor was I Pearl Chavez. Each was simply a role I tried to interpret as an actress."[73] Peck came in for less rebuke for his sea-change from priest to rapist in a classic example of Hollywood's double standards, being held to a "much less strict code of subsequent moral conduct."[74]

Selznick, anxious to reprise the success of his earlier *Gone with the Wind*, marketed the film with unashamed (and undisguised) vulgarity. His ploy paid off and despite some critical sandblasting it went on to earn over $17 million.

He suffered a lot under the censors during the shooting of the movie but he had the last laugh on them because he instructed his composer, Dimitri Tiomkin, to create various themes for it, including "a love theme, a desire theme and an orgasm theme." How did he get away with this? It was easy: "The Production Code failed to cover music."[75]

Claiming, as it did, that *Duel in the Sun* was an "occasion of sin," the Church showed an incredible patronization of its flock, imagining they might be so easily corruptible. To portray a less than solid citizen isn't to glamorize him, still less to imagine his (mis)behavior will be replicated by the people in the theaters. *Duel in the Sun*, like *Double Indemnity*, was a story and, as in the former film, the pair died for their sins in the end. Was this not enough to placate the moral banner-weavers? The film was also before its time in its depiction of the love-hate parameters in the relationship between this shop-soiled Romeo and Juliet.

The doomed pair kill each other but "carnal attraction will not be denied and in the final sequence they painfully crawl across the desert to unite in death's embrace." Since when had a western contained so many sexual convolutions? Probably never.[76]

Another film of that year which raised the censors' temperatures was the adaptation of James M. Cain's steamy thriller *The Postman Always Rings Twice*, starring John Garfield and Lana Turner. Cain had also written *Double Indemnity*, as mentioned. It bore many resemblances to that film in its depiction of a couple anxious to bump off the husband of the woman in question.

Breen wanted physical contact between the main leads to be cut to a minimum while Turner's husband was alive. The director, Tay Garnett, appeased him further by having Turner wear an antiseptic white throughout. For Garnett, this made "everything she did less sensuous. And it somehow took the stigma off everything."[77]

Is this to suggest that it's okay to kill somebody if one is wearing white? In a way it makes it worse. Years later in *Psycho*, Alfred Hitchcock would dress Janet Leigh in a black bra when she was having extramarital sex with John Gavin, and a white one when she decided to give back money she stole later on in the film. The symbolism was allowable in this context, and less stark.

A few other films of the forties created less major hiccups. *Forever Amber* (1947) depicted the life of a prostitute during the Restoration. Darryl F. Zanuck promised the censor that the leading character would suffer for her sins at the end to pacify them but she didn't. The upshot was that the Legion was aghast. Zanuck caved in, tacking on a hamfisted prologue and epilogue that, Murray Schumach concluded, "reduced an already mediocre film to soap-opera."[78]

Bitter Rice (1948), an Italian film about sexually charged rice-pickers and their criminal love interests, caused more ripples with the censors, largely due to the considerable sexual appeal of Silvana Mangano and her figure-hugging wardrobe. The *Times-Herald* critic described her succinctly as having "the robust proportions of the Venus de Milo and the personality of a Sherman tank."[79] The film also contained scenes of suggestive dancing and a reference to abortion. This made it, as far as the Legion of Decency was concerned, a serious threat to Christian decency. It had to be trimmed accordingly to secure its Seal.

The Seal situation became even more asinine at the end of the decade. Vittorio de Sica's *The Bicycle Thief* (1948) didn't get one because in one scene the central character wanders into a brothel. The fact that this had absolutely nothing to do with the story didn't seem to affect the decision.

In another scene in *The Bicycle Thief*, the son of the man whose bicycle is stolen urinates against a building with his back to the camera. The Breen Office insisted this be cut but Joseph Burstyn, who would cause a firestorm a few years later with *The Miracle*, refused and distributed the film anyway, without a seal. The New York censors ruled that the scene was unacceptable but Burstyn appealed on the grounds that the censors "would appear ridiculous were it to be known that they believed the average New Yorker would be aroused or offended by the sight of a boy urinating." His lawyer, Ephraim London, who would become famous for contesting such rulings, won the appeal for him.[80]

The decade ended with *White Heat* in 1949. James Cagney was never better as the psychopathic killer who, despite everything, loved his mother. Virginia Graham summed it up best of all in the *Evening Standard*: "This film glorifies violence. The terrible thing is its excellence."[81]

3

Decades of Revolt

The films of this time didn't exist in a vacuum. Society was changing outside cinemas as well. In 1946 Alfred Kinsey shocked many with his book *Sexual Behavior in the Human Male,* a distillation of over 1,800 interviews on matters once deemed taboo, like masturbation, fellatio, cunnilingus, infidelity, prostitution, and so on. (His wife famously remarked, "Ever since Alfred got so interested in sex, I haven't seen much of him.")

The church, predictably, was shocked. Monsignor Maurice Sheeny of Washington's Catholic Union of America declared that Kinsey had written the most anti-religious book of our times. (Kinsey, no great lover of religion, took this almost as a compliment.) His revolutionary research had repercussions for the cinema, which took their lead from him and grew more audacious. *Confidential* magazine also started running stories concerning the secret sex lives of the stars.

As with everything else about this time, though, there were still barriers to be overcome, and gross inconsistencies in the decisions that were made about film scripts. The only constant seemed to be that credibility always had to bow to preordained rules. This was both patronizing to audiences and insulting to directors. Square pegs had to be squeezed into round holes with little deference to the nuances of plot and character development.

In his autobiography *An Open Book,* John Huston chronicles an incident that typified the draconian nature of censorship procedures at this time: "There was a picture in which a young soldier returned from the war to find that his wife had been unfaithful. The scriptwriter's only way out of the tangle was to have the soldier kill his wife. She had been punished. Then he, of course, had to be executed. Now he had been punished. This was the result of a twisted logic that had little to do with protecting morals and much to do with following the letter of the law laid down by the censorship office."[1]

In Huston's *The Asphalt Jungle* (1950) there was a scene in which a crooked lawyer (Louis Calhern) commits suicide. According to the script he was to write a short, moving note to his wife, then shoot himself. The censors refused to allow the suicide unless Huston made Calhern out to be of unsound mind. Huston argued that the act in itself proved that he wasn't in his right mind but they didn't agree. He had to have the man write a number of notes and crumple them all up to indicate unhingement. It turned out to be a better scene for the change but Huston didn't recommend trying to outfox the Code as a way to achieve storytelling success.

At this time, as Sam Kashner makes clear in his book *The Bad and the Beautiful*, film magazines took great delight in advising readers of the spiritual lives of stars, in particular one named Colleen Townsend. Townsend eventually left Hollywood to attend a Presbyterian Theological Seminary where she trained to be a missionary. She had only been in films three years when she made the decision to devote herself fully to "spreading the teachings of Christ."[2] After finishing John Ford's *When Willie Comes Marching Home* that year she told *Modern Screen* magazine she felt it was God's will that she leave films. She related a story about driving along Sunset Boulevard in her car one night. She was speeding, but felt some presence urging her to slow down. When she did, her tire blew out. She felt it was a sign from above.

She didn't fully leave films, but confined herself to roles with a spiritual import. She appeared in *Oiltown U.S.A.* (1954), the story of a greedy man who's reformed by his daughter (Townsend). It was made by none other than the evangelist Billy Graham, who was at this point of his life engaged in what he called a "film ministry." Graham had also made *Mr. Texas* (1951), a cowboy film with embarrassingly trite lines like "All my life I've been riding the wrong trail. I'm turning back, going God's way. I think it's going to be a wonderful ride."

Graham probably wouldn't have known what film art was if it jumped up and bit him on the nose. But he realized that films could bring a huge amount of publicity to his crusade — and even more if he managed to use stars like Townsend to bolster it. Admittedly she was small potatoes but people like Cecil B. DeMille and John Wayne attended his films, as well as his public appearances in places like Madison Square Garden. These always had the atmosphere of prize fights. (Many people would draw parallels between Graham and the title character of *Elmer Gantry*, played with such relish by Burt Lancaster in 1960.)

The year 1951 also saw the release of a work that was as different from *Mr. Texas* as could possibly be: *The Miracle*.

3. Decades of Revolt 77

This Roberto Rossellini film features Anna Magnani as a simple peasant who minds goats on a hillside and sleeps on a pile of rags outside the local church. One day she meets a mysterious stranger whom she imagines to be St. Joseph, for reasons best known to herself. He doesn't speak but persuades her to drink wine. She falls asleep and then, we have to assume, he has sex with her as afterwards she's pregnant. Scorned by the local populace for having had sex outside marriage, she denies this took place. She hides in the mountains until it comes to the time when her baby is due. She then makes her way to the church. After the baby is born, she rings the church bells triumphantly as if to serenade the new messiah.

The stranger was played by none other than Federico Fellini, who also wrote the story upon which the film was based. It was actually shot in 1948 but a couple of years elapsed before a print found its way into the U.S.

At different stages of the film there are motifs aligning Magnani's character to Eve, the Virgin Mary, and even Jesus, as when she says of the disparaging villagers, "Lord, forgive them." Is she mentally defective or merely holy, or both? In one of the scenes, some of the villagers mock her by putting a washbasin on her head to mimic a halo.

Rossellini wanted to keep interpretations of her character as open-ended as possible. He contrasts her pagan innocence with the staid religiosity of the other villagers. When she's about to have her baby, she approaches the church for shelter but there's "no room at the inn." She gives birth in the open, breastfeeding it as the film ends. It's an affirmation of life in all senses, a gesture of defiance on her part against the narrow-mindedness of those around her. In her own quiet way she's shown them all up for what they are, refusing to be bound by their tidy conventions.

The film may be little more than a fragment, an extended short, but it still packs a punch all those decades on. Neither is it strident, which would have detracted from its raw sweetness. Rossellini isn't attacking religion as much as its zealots, its Sunday morning Catholics who look the other way when a lost sheep, or goatherdess, appears.

It was first shown at the Venice Film Festival. It didn't attract an undue amount of attention there but the Vatican condemned it for profanity. It was greeted with howls of protest by the Legion of Decency. On January 7, 1951, Cardinal Spellman, head of the New York archdiocese, read a statement at Mass in St. Patrick's Cathedral urging all Catholics to boycott it.

A month later it was withdrawn from circulation on grounds of sacrilege, despite the fact that the film critic of *Il Popolo,* the official newspaper of Italy's pro-Catholic Christian Democratic Party, described it as "a beautiful thing, humanly felt, alive, true and without religious profanation."[3]

Spellman was unambiguous in his comments. He spoke of the film as a vicious insult to Italian womanhood, adding that only a perverted mind could represent it in such a manner. This was probably a sideswipe at the personal life of Rossellini. He had outraged Hollywood by having an extramarital affair with Ingrid Bergman (she left her husband and daughter for him). After she had his child, churches and schools called for her films to be boycotted. For almost a decade afterwards, she was *persona non grata* in the U.S.

When she became pregnant by Rossellini, Joe Breen wrote to her to tell her that she couldn't divorce her husband to marry him as such a "breach of decorum" could cost her her career.[4] Producer Walter Wanger also wrote to her emphasizing that such a scandal could kill the earning power of her last movie *Joan of Arc* which was already doing poorly at the box office.

In Indianapolis the owner of a group of movie theaters called for a boycott of Bergman's movies. In Annapolis a legislator tried to push through the Maryland State Assembly a resolution condemning her latest one, *Stromboli*. General theater proprietors, as Bergman's biographer Laurence Leamer observed, "took a position of rare moral subtlety: they decided to ban *Stromboli* after its first few days' showing if it didn't make money."[5] It was vaguely reminiscent of Jennifer Jones going from *The Song of Bernadette* to *Duel in the Sun*, except in this instance the scandal overflowed from the screen onto a maternity ward. Rossellini had two women in his life giving birth in blasphemous fashion, one in a cinema and the other outside it. Both were landing him in hot water with the clergy.

Spellman's appraisal of *The Miracle* was totally askew. Not by any stretch of the imagination could one construe that Rossellini was trying to make Magnani symbolic of a nation. She was too idiosyncratic for that. Spellman also saw the film as Communistic, another rabid misreading of its basically simple message.

The public, in any case, turned out in droves and despite bomb threats cinemas continued to show it as long as people wanted to see it. The picketers outside such cinemas only served to swell the numbers who wondered what all the anger was about.

The Vatican newspaper *Observatore Romano* admitted that *The Miracle* had scenes of "undoubted screen value" even if it had reservations about its central plotline. Neither did the Catholic Church blacklist Rossellini over the movie. The following year he made *The Flowers of St. Francis*, a biopic of the saint.[6]

3. Decades of Revolt

Rossellini always claimed that the film was "an absolutely Catholic work."[7] He wrote to Spellman, trying to explain it as he saw it: "In *The Miracle* men are without pity because they have not gone back to God. But God is already present in the faith, however confused, of the poor, persecuted woman. The 'miracle' occurs when, with the birth of the child, the poor demented woman regains sanity in her maternal love. These were my intentions and I hope Your Eminence will deign to consider them with paternal benevolence."[8] Unfortunately, he didn't.

Gregory Black outlined the main bones of contention surrounding the film: "Was *The Miracle* an open attack on the Christian belief in the Immaculate Conception and the Virgin Birth or was it merely a stinging comment on intolerance in modern society? Did Rossellini mean that if the events in Bethlehem were repeated in modern Italy, Mary would be mocked and banished? Or was he saying that the institutional church was no longer capable of recognizing the basic fundamentals of Christianity: Love thy neighbor, care for the sick and the weak, be tolerant and understanding?"[9] I'm inclined to think that the latter parts of these contentions are truer than the former.

The film was a flop in Italy but not in the U.S., where the media flap surrounding it no doubt bumped up public interest. Some priests in Spellman's own diocese held diametrically opposed views of it. They prevailed upon him to tone down his abuse but he was intransigent. Joseph Burstyn, the distributor who had imported it into the country, went to New York's Supreme Court to file a claim for his right to exhibit the film, insisting its removal had violated the First and Fourth Amendments. He lost here, but a further appeal overturned the original verdict.

A film that was only 41 minutes long was about to change cinematic freedom forever. Things could hardly get more ironic than this.

The Supreme Court decreed that to censor a film on a charge of sacrilege would be tantamount to leaving every film open to censorship. "After all," it argued, "there are thousands of religious sects and cults in the United States and some film is bound to offend someone somewhere."[10]

In 1952 the Supreme Court ruled that New York State's Court ban on it violated the First Amendment to the American Constitution because sacrilege wasn't a valid basis for censorship. A long war of attrition was finally ended. But James C. Robertson grunted, "Once the issue had been fought to a decisive conclusion, the American public—even in New York—seemed to lose interest."[11]

The Miracle resulted in many Catholics losing faith in the Legion of

Decency. They couldn't see what was problematic about the film and felt that if the Legion's judgment was "off" on this score, maybe it was untrustworthy on other films as well. The following year, censorship of films in general was ruled unconstitutional by the Supreme Court, thereby giving directors a huge amount of leverage in what they chose to depict.

One writer believed the media buzz was a massive blow to the PCA, "though it would take more than a decade before all state and local censorship boards would be completely dismantled and the Production Code replaced by the current ratings system."[12]

Catholics nominally took the pledge at Sunday Mass to avoid condemned films but they didn't honor such pledges as time went on, and neither did they imagine they were endangering their souls by doing so.

Protestants didn't find *The Miracle* as offensive as Catholics because Protestant theology placed less reverence on the Virgin Mary than did the Catholic Church. "In practice this meant there were effectively less people lobbying for its removal from the screen."[13]

The film was finally distributed after both the Legion and Cardinal Spellman were roundly ignored by the cinema-going public, but tongues continued to wag over the fact that Rossellini had impregnated a married woman. The fact that Bergman decided to have her baby in front of the world's gaze gave the story much more of a profile than it would otherwise have had. The *Joan of Arc* star became so vilified as a scarlet woman that it wasn't only Joseph Breen who imagined her career could be over. Bergman didn't make another American film until *Anastasia* (1956), and didn't return to Hollywood for a further thirteen years, to make a forgettable comedy called *Cactus Flower* with Goldie Hawn.

Fellini told Charlotte Chandler, the author of *I, Fellini*, that he based the story of *The Miracle* on a real event he remembered from his childhood. He didn't think Rossellini would be captivated by the tale if he knew he himself made it up so he pretended it had actually been written by a famous Russian novelist. He made up a fictitious Russian's name to increase credibility. Everybody at the studio was impressed, not willing to admit they'd never heard of him.

After a while they got to like Fellini's story so much they asked him if he could refer them to any more of this great Russian's works. By now he had forgotten the name he'd made up and decided to come clean and tell the truth. Undeterred, Rossellini decided to go ahead with it. His only proviso was that Fellini should dye his hair a light golden color. The dye actually

3. Decades of Revolt

turned it "a hideous shade of golden blonde," Fellini told Chandler. When he came out of the hairdressing salon, people on the street started calling him "Rita" after Rita Hayworth, which mortified him. Since the film was in black and white this didn't show up.[14]

The background to the story is interesting. Fellini wrote it about a gypsy who came to a place called Gambettola, in Romagna, where Fellini had spent childhood summers with his grandmother. Everyone was terrified of him but also fascinated. He had a belt with knives hanging from it and all the pigs in the village squealed when he came near. Fellini was warned to stay away from him or something terrible would happen. He imagined him spearing him with one of his knives, spinning him in the air and roasting him on a spit for dinner.

A simple-minded woman in the village fell madly in love with him and had his son, but denied having had sex with him. Nobody believed her. She was scorned by all and sundry for her so-called "miracle" birth. Two years later, Fellini went back to the village and saw the little boy, "a beautiful child, with long eyelashes and piercing eyes" playing by himself. The villagers called him "the son of the Devil."[15]

The film paved the way for other pioneering vehicles. It was followed by *A Streetcar Named Desire*, which was another huge embarrassment for Breen. Here, in one steamy package, was rape, homosexuality, insanity, infidelity, and even the suggestion that the leading female character, Blanche Du Bois (Vivien Leigh), had seduced a young boy.

Was this streetcar a redeemable vehicle? Marlon

Marlon Brando brought all of his animal magnetism to the screen at Vivien Leigh's expense in Elia Kazan's masterly adaptation of Tennessee Williams' *A Streetcar Named Desire* in 1951.

Brando had blitzed Broadway with it and was set to do the same with Elia Kazan's film version, but it had to be "cleaned up" before the public could be allowed to see it, for fear of their immortal souls. Tennessee Williams, who'd written the part of Stanley Kowalski for Brando, shook his head in bewilderment.

"Tennessee Williams equals Blanche," Kazan said rather startlingly in an interview. "Blanche wants the very thing that's going to crush her"—i.e., the piggish Kowalski. "And that's the way Williams was. Like [Andre] Gide, he was attracted to trash. Part of the sexuality he wrote into the play is the nuance of it. So I had to get that quality from Brando."[16]

Kazan was leery of making the movie from the outset. *Streetcar* had been such an astounding theatrical success, he felt a film version was bound to be anticlimactic, even with Brando reprising the role that made his name. "It would be like marrying the same woman twice," he complained. But he was eventually won round.[17]

Kowalski's rape of Blanche is the pivotal point of the movie. This was a bit more brutal than the last time Leigh was forced into a sexual act on screen against her will, in *Gone with the Wind* thirteen years before. Breen at first wanted the rape eliminated; he suggested that it be replaced by a punch from Kowalski (a ludicrous notion) or else be made a figment of Blanche's imagination. This was hardly a runner either.

Breen also had a problem with the fact that Blanche's husband, tortured by homosexual leanings, had committed suicide some time before. Suicide and homosexuality were two no-no themes for Breen in this context. Their combination made a lethal brew. Kazan eventually compromised, changing Williams' line about Blanche's husband's sexual proclivities to a vague "He wasn't like other men."[18]

As for the rape scene, Kazan agreed to remove Kowalski's line "We've had this date together from the beginning," to appease Breen.[19] In fact the film is shot in such a way that we don't even know if Stanley did indeed rape Blanche as the scene fades out with a mirror cracking. We're not too far removed here from the "swirling curtains in the window" ploy used a decade before, or a camera cutting from a commingling couple to a blazing hearth.

Kazan was also forced to "punish" Kowalski for his actions "in terms of the loss of his wife's love."[20] Thus we get Stella saying to him at the end, "Don't you ever touch me again!" which is distinctly out of character. On the other hand, as Rudy Behlmer remarked, the film forced censors to "broaden their interpretation of the Code and to consider the realities of American behavior."[21] Breen originally wanted to give it a C rating, which would have meant that Catholics would have been formally instructed not to see it, thereby decimating its box office receipts and possibly even leading to a boycott in certain cinemas. Further, the C rating might have been seen as an invitation for every local censor to make further cuts in the film, or ban it altogether.[22]

Kazan was disgusted by the whole business. He told Murray Schumach of *The New York Times*: "Warners just wanted a Seal. They didn't give a damn about the beauty or art. They wanted to get the entire family to see it but at the same time they wanted it to be dirty enough to pull people in."[23] Such an attitude fed into the hands of Breen, whom Kazan referred to as "the gluttonous Pope of Fiftieth Street."[24]

Kazan threatened to walk off the picture if the suggested rape scene was taken out. He'd made many compromises already but this was the last straw. It was like an emasculation. Breen grudgingly allowed him to keep it in but only if it was shot in the manner mentioned. This was good enough for Kazan. "I shot the scene in such a way that grown-ups will know what happened," he told *The Los Angeles Times,* "while children will only sense that Stanley did the woman some wrong."[25]

Amazingly enough, the Legion of Decency's main problem wasn't Blanche's sexuality but that of Stella, played by Kim Hunter. Once Kazan agreed to highlight Blanche's neurotic edge, an over-sexed nature suddenly became acceptable. But Stella was, quote unquote, "normal." So how did she put up with such a brute as Stanley? She couldn't be shown to enjoy his animal vigor even in small doses. Various cuts were made in this regard, which robbed Hunter of some of her best moments. Leigh was the beneficiary of such excisions, which means that even today, most viewers' eyes are only on one actress in this tousled triangle of sweaty passion. Either way, as one writer commented, its release marked "the beginning of the end" for the PCA.[26]

Though compromises were reached on most of the key issues, I agree with Charles Higham that the film was "handicapped by the moral restrictions required in Hollywood at the time."[27] Martin Quigley didn't know what to make of it, finding it both "sordid and morbid."[28] He concluded bewilderingly, "I tell you, this fellow Kazan is the type who will one day blow his brains out?"[29] One can only wonder what he would have made of a director less balanced than this man.

No less than 27 cuts were demanded by the Irish film censor. Despite (or because of?) this, what viewers remembered was Brando's almost animalistic sexual charge, his volcanic eruptions, his simmering rages. Brando himself thought the censors "sapped Tennessee's story of some of its sting," but that it was still better than the play.[30]

Richard Schickel, Brando's biographer, begged to differ, expressing this viewpoint: "The complicated (and ambiguous) things villains wanted to say about the ways we confront and evade our sexuality are built into every line and situation of the play. The vividness of [Williams'] characters and the force of his language could not be blurred or blunted by the censor's scissors either. In other words, we got it."[31]

Streetcar became a sensation. Julian Petley observed that it was the first time the PCA had passed a film which was "clearly not family entertainment." Petley felt that a part of the reason for this might have been that at the time "television was eating into the family audience."[32]

Apart from television, other developments were also taking place in society in general that would bleed into the film world....

Playboy was founded in 1953 by Hugh Hefner, who ushered in the idea of casual sex for clean-cut bachelors. No longer was it regarded as a guilt-ridden activity; indeed, it almost became an athletic accessory of the urban male's lifestyle. Five years later *Playboy* was selling a million copies a month. Neither did people have to queue up in mackintosh coats to purchase it in back alleys ... though those who claimed they bought it for the articles rather than the centerfolds had their credibility questioned.

Back in Hollywood there were still ludicrous scenarios. The following year in *The Four Poster,* a film starring Rex Harrison, there's a scene where Harrison is getting into bed with his wife on their wedding night and she confides to him that she's never seen a naked man before. Harrison jokes, "You haven't missed much." The line was excised by the censors not because it was deemed to be immoral but, even more spuriously, was seen as sacrilegious because "man is made in God's image."[33] Kazan, needless to say, was amused.

The Moon Is Blue (1953), was another objectionable movie which, like *Streetcar,* went on to do enormous business. Directed by Otto Preminger, it was condemned by a number of naysayers despite the fact that little of a sexual nature actually transpired. Cardinal Spellman dubbed it a "near" occasion of sin, a phrase that left a lot to the imagination — as did the film itself.

Maggie McNamara, in the main role, has lines like "Will you try to seduce me?" and "Men are usually bored with virgins." William Holden was a good choice as her foil because he didn't carry overtones of rebelliousness like a Brando or a Montgomery Clift. He made the film palatable to the masses, thereby allowing the *risqué* script to fly over people's heads, as it were. As Billy Wilder remarked, he doesn't bite women's thighs but he's a hot rodder at heart. David Niven starred as another suitor.

McNamara plays a character who delights in flaunting her virginity tantalizingly. She doesn't relinquish it outside marriage but suggests that other girls do, which was like a red flag to a bull to Breen. Geoffrey Shurlock, Breen's aide at the PCA, thought it harmless enough but Breen himself was incandescent with rage that terms like "mistress," "virgin" and "seduce" could be bandied around in such commonplace fashion.[34]

The media hype over the film was really much ado about very little. Admittedly terms like "mistress," and even "sex," weren't commonplace in films of the time, still less the discussions of seduction that spring up at every turn, but nothing actually happens in this lighthearted piece so it's surprising that so many people got into a frazzle about it.

It was originally a Broadway play and had its run there without any controversy. "Since the play had proved to be uncontroversial," Anthony Aldgate opined, "Preminger almost certainly did not anticipate the rejection of his film by the Production Code."[35] David Niven was mystified by the arguments raging back and forth about its suitability for the public. "Why," he inquired, "didn't the Cardinal complain when it opened as a play on Broadway? It has been running there long enough. It's true that in the film I keep chasing the girl in the flat downstairs but she's an inexperienced girl in Reel 1 and she's still inexperienced 14 reels later. I can't see any 'occasion of sin' in that."[36]

Breen felt the film would be offensive to parents who viewed their daughters' virginity as a topic not to be treated lightly. Further, he thought it was improper for an unmarried woman to visit the apartment of a man she'd just met, as McNamara does in an early scene. One can imagine what Preminger thought of these objections.

He was up for a fight with the Legion, well aware that it had suffered a severe body blow with *The Miracle* not so long before. Darryl F. Zanuck warned, "Without the Seal there won't be five theaters in the United States that will show your film." Preminger was willing to gamble on that.[37]

In another scene, Holden accuses McNamara of being "a professional virgin." When she asks him what that means, he tells her that she's always advertising her virginity and, in his experience, those who advertise usually have something to sell.

Legion members fumed at what they saw as its trivialization of sex. Gregory Black outlined the moral goalposts: "Sex, in the Catholic view, was sacred and serious and, as Father Lord wrote in the Code, must not be the subject of comedy or farce, or treated as material for laughter. Sex was a marital duty solely for the purpose of procreation. Impure love was lust."[38]

The studios capitulated to the Legion not because they believed in its ethos but because they were afraid of the consequences if they didn't. It was a matter of pragmatics rather than guilt. Lip service was paid to values they felt were outmoded to help sell their pictures. Compromise meant dollars. But Preminger never bent the knee. His challenge was to the point: "The Legion of Decency has assumed an undue position of power because of the cowardice of some major motion picture companies. They're scared of losing money."[39]

He defended his film, claiming there were "no scenes of passion" in it, and "no scenes of crime and vice."[40] He conceded there was much sexual discussion but the bottom line was that McNamara kept her virginity. This made it, in one writer's opinion, "a sex comedy minus the sex."[41]

Preminger thought Breen's reaction wildly over-the-top and refused to take out the coy banter that underlies much of the dialogue. Breen refused to give it a Seal as a result, which meant that United Artists had to resign from the MPAA to release it. It appeared without a Seal but — in Tony Bilbow's phrase — "the sky did not fall."[42] Slowly but surely, markers were being laid down and bitter divisions being formed. This might have been significant for a watershed film but *The Moon Is Blue* looks dated today, its supposedly progressive script more yawnful than shocking.

In the end McNamara retains her virginity and still gets her man. This narrative convenience wasn't good enough for Breen, who was increasingly irritated by the naughty interplay. The average viewer was more likely to have been irritated by a script that seems to enjoy promising us what it knows all along that it's not going to deliver. It's like a celluloid form of *coitus interruptus*—or rather *coitus non-existus*.

Though Spellman warned Catholics not to attend the film, magazines like *Life* and *Newsweek* praised it. Suddenly, these organs seemed to have more sway. Over 10,000 cinemas screened it, which must have made Spellman feel that his days of belting people over the head with metaphorical croziers were numbered.

Some cities were more courageous than others. Memphis, for instance, prohibited it. (Clearly they weren't ready for the emergence of Elvis Presley yet.) But "hundreds of interested filmgoers drove to see it at a theater some thirty miles away in Holly Springs, Mississippi."[43]

Preminger admitted the hue and cry about the Seal's refusal helped the picture in some places but added that there were "small towns where the people stood in front of the theater and put down the names of the people who went in."[44]

Julian Petley suggested that part of the reason for its commercial success may have been the fact that, with it, Preminger defied the Legion. Whatever, it was 15th in the top movie earning bracket for 1953.[45] It did good business in the U.K. as well as the U.S., though reviewers were as discombobulated by the media storm surrounding it as were the cast and director. In *The Star* Roy Nash declared it to be "as innocent a piece of obscenity as I've ever come across."[46]

Another line of dialogue that Breen objected to was the Groucho-like "You are shallow, cynical, selfish and immoral ... and I like you." Preminger objected to the assertion that he was being deliberately rebellious with lines like this. He denied he was a crusader but held firm on the fact that he had "not only the right, but the duty to defend free expression, because if this right deteriorates, it's the first step to dictatorship, to totalitarian government."[47] These were fighting words. They were listened to by some government censors, like those of New York and Pennsylvania, who licensed the film, though censors in Ohio and Kansas banned it.

In New Jersey a cinema manager showing it was arrested at the order of the mayor but when the Milwaukee Motion Picture Commission banned it, suburban drive-in cinemas beyond the city's jurisdiction played it to capacity audiences. It grossed over $6 million for United Artists. The Legion eventually admitted that it had condemned it not because of its immoral nature but for "extrinsic considerations — namely to support the Code and prevent the seamless garment from being rent," an extraordinary admission from an organization ostensibly formed to guard against a lessening of the nation's moral fiber.[48]

A cinema proprietor named Nicholas Schenck spoke for much of Middle America when he fumed, "I wouldn't let my daughter see it. It's true that the girl isn't seduced in the time she spends with the boy but other girls in a similar situation might get closer to the flame."[49]

By autumn of 1954, the Legion had to admit that it suffered a resounding setback. By now the film had been seen in over 8,000 cinemas, with nearly 4,000 more having booked it. The weight of numbers rather than ethical discourse had finally made the legion buckle.

The success of *The Moon Is Blue* and the failure of the PCA to prevent such popularity, as Anthony Slide observed, "meant that for the first time independent producers might consider adult stories and themes without fear of internal censorship."[50] A few years earlier, Preminger's decision would have spelled "economic suicide" to a director but now the Legion was on the ropes.[51] *Variety* summed the situation up: "Moon Is Blue. Face Is Red."[52]

Preminger's contract with United Artists gave him free rein in editing his films. The studio couldn't over-rule him. It was forced to pay the Motion Picture Association of America (MPAA) a fine of $25,000 for releasing the film without a Seal. This was minimal in comparison to the amount of money the studio would have lost if the film bombed. The fact that it didn't gave him the last laugh on the Legion, which had put further pressure on United Artists by threatening to boycott other UA films if Preminger continued to play the scamp. No doubt he would have been amused by Bob Hope's quip, "Nowadays when a film is awarded the Production Code Seal the producer cries, 'Where have we failed?'"[53]

Another movie of that year, *The Bigamist,* dealt with just that subject. It portrayed the dual husband (Edmond O'Brien) as a decent man who, alienated from his careerist wife Joan Fontaine, has an affair with another woman, Ida Lupino, who then becomes pregnant. He marries Lupino to give her child legitimacy and goes back to Fontaine. When he and Fontaine decide to adopt a child, however, his double life is uncovered.

The film is narrated in flashback like O'Brien's other voiceover role, *D.O.A.* As his defending counsel points out in the last scene, many men have affairs without going to the altar a second time. O'Brien did so for basically altruistic motives. He loved both women but wasn't a "bad" man, merely one who was trapped in a highly unorthodox quandary. The lawyer asks that his punishment be tempered on this account.

We don't get to hear what sentence he gets but the judge points out that his main one will be served outside prison, not inside, because of the fix he's landed himself in: It could mean that neither woman will have him back. This doesn't look to be the case from the film's closing shots, which show each of them as being kindly disposed to the man who cheated on them both. Lupino departs the courtroom with a slight smile (almost of gratitude) playing about her lips. Fontaine, meanwhile, hovers, leaving us in little doubt that she'll forgive him — and probably give up all those silly careerist notions in favor of their big bouncing adopted baby so they can finally call themselves a family after all.

How sad that a work like this with such a brave manifesto should descend to slop at the end, particularly since it was one of the few films of its time to be directed by a woman — Lupino herself. She should have flown the flag for equal marital rights with a touch more conviction. Instead she fudges the issues she raises in the interests of down-home domesticity. Of course if she'd been more daring, the film would have been cut off at the knees without a Seal.

It was a case of half a loaf being better than no bread. In a sense it was more interesting in its portrayal of Fontaine as a woman who didn't want or need children than in the bigamy theme. This was ironically its most daring conceit but it got sandwiched in the middle of the other proceedings and ultimately sidelined.

The Moon Is Blue and *The Bigamist* were both tame, but other events that occurred around this time were anything but. Towards the end of 1953, Marilyn Monroe posed nude for *Playboy*. The incandescent Monroe didn't exude the aura of a *femme fatale*. Hers was a new kind of sexuality, a more user-friendly type. As Norman Mailer proclaimed, sex was like ice cream to her; she was Everyman's love affair with America. This was a different kind of bugbear for puritans because this lady brought sex away from the *film noir* boudoir and into the cotton candy living-room. She made it all look like fun, like children playing with sandcastles on the beach. How could anybody censor this?

Two other people on a beach that year, though with each other rather than sandcastles, were Burt Lancaster and Deborah Kerr in Fred Zinnemann's *From Here to Eternity*. The scene where the pair embrace in their bathing suits has almost become talismanic. Breen wanted Zinnemann to put robes on them. He refused because it would have made the scene look nonsensical. As it was, it looked steamier than it had a right to because it isn't much more than a lingering kiss. But the waves swishing around them, and the context — Kerr being married to someone else in the movie — gave it all an added edge for Breen.

Breen wrote to Harry Cohn, the film's producer, to say he felt the adulterous relationship between Lancaster and Kerr was being handled "without any recognition of its immorality."[54] Daniel Taradash, the screenwriter, snarled back, "What do you want me to do — have her walk around with a sign saying, 'I Have Sinned'?"[55] Breen also wanted the brothel where Donna Reed worked changed into a "club." Cohn was hardly surprised at this. The profusion of such "clubs" in films of the time was nothing short of astounding.

"The censors," Gerald Gardner commented in nudge-wink fashion, "invited moviegoers to believe that soldiers would pay money to young women for the privilege of chatting with them in private rooms." An unnamed wit added, "If you believe that, there's a bridge in Brooklyn I want to show you."[56]

Another film that gave the censors problems around this time was *Blackboard Jungle* (1955) with Glenn Ford as a kind-hearted schoolteacher trying to tame the juvenile delinquents of New York. It was banned in Britain. Julian Petley believed one of the reasons for this was that it had as its theme music Bill Haley's groundbreaking "Rock Around the Clock," a song that had already become synonymous in Britain with teenage depravity and irredeemable Americanization."[57] As it was played, it became a ritual in many British cinemas for "teddyboys" to rip up the cinema seats in accompaniment.[58]

In that same year, Kinsey wrote a sequel to his book. It was called, perhaps predictably, *Sexual Behavior in the Human Female*. Again there were more outrageous revelations about loss of virginity, premarital sex, better orgasms and whatever you're having yourself. Billy Graham said it was impossible to estimate the damage the book would do to the already deteriorating morals of America. Henry Pitney Van Dusen, head of the Union of Theological Seminaries, accused Kinsey of having a "strictly animalistic" view of sex, which depicted a "prevailing degradation in American morality approximating to the worst decadence of the Roman Empire."[59]

What these people failed to realize was that Kinsey was holding a mirror up to what people were already doing, not trying to *make* it happen. To this extent his detractors were always going to be on the losing side in the debate.

The famous shot of Burt Lancaster and Deborah Kerr locked in a passionate embrace on the beach in *From Here to Eternity* (1953) as war rages around them.

Hugh Hefner seemed to speak for a generation by asserting, "When Alfred Kinsey dared to suggest, in statistical detail no less, that women were as sexually active as men, society attempted to kill the messenger."[60]

On October 15, 1954, Joseph Breen "finally reached out with his Sistine finger and touched the fingertips of his alter ego and successor, Geoffrey Shurlock." His sometime colleague Jack Vizzard wondered if he'd been "Hollywood's benevolent conscience," as Sam Goldwyn dubbed him, or "the ass of the universe"? Probably a dash of both, Vizzard concluded, "with a small twist of shamrock."[61] After his retirement, Colleen McDannell reflected, "Enthusiasm for censorship waned. Younger Americans were challenging the values of their parents. What was once hailed as respectability was now defined as prudery."[62]

A naturist film called *The Garden of Eden* had become something of a landmark earlier in 1955. Baxter Philips described it as "inoffensive and unerotic."[63] However, featuring as it did a bevy of nubile females cavorting around a Florida nudist colony, few people were surprised that it was banned in New York. The decision was based on the fact that the activities of this particular nudist colony were, let us say, somewhat beyond the simple celebration of naturism.

The producer, Walter Bibo, contested the decision on the grounds that the film had "educational value"![64] Amazingly, he won his appeal in 1957, thereby opening the door to similarly "educational" films that would allow sexy women to disrobe for the edification of salivating males celebrating the joys of going *au naturel*.

Alfred Hitchcock's *Rear Window* (1954) wasn't exactly a steamy movie but he still managed to irritate the PCA when a minor female character referred to as "Miss Torso" was adjudged to be wearing clothes that were too skimpy in an early scene. Grace Kelly's nightgown was also too "unconventional." Hitchcock predicted these stipulations so shot what he called "protection" footage of Miss Torso, fully clothed, to satisfy the PCA. He also promised to make Kelly less "unconventional." This was good thinking on his part because he had another agenda. He used the clothing debate as a smokescreen to distract Breen from some dialogue he had found objectionable in the screenplay the previous year.

The Man with the Golden Arm (1955) dealt with drug addiction and therefore automatically fell foul of the PCA. Otto Preminger, the director, was again outraged at the narrow-mindedness. United Artists, the studio behind the movie, backed him and withdrew from the PCA in disgust. They knew they'd made a serious movie. Far from advocating drug use, it was really a disincentive to it. Nonetheless, this wasn't an age where exceptions were made. (It would be all of eight years later before the PCA rescinded its decision, the film finally being granted a Seal in July 1962.)

After the initial denial, Preminger attacked the MPAA as "the private club of the major studios." He claimed the movie carried "a very strong moral lesson" and that, if anything, it was "a warning against the consequences of taking narcotics."[65] To satisfy the Legion he deleted a scene showing Frank Sinatra preparing heroin in a spoon.

The Man with the Golden Arm is interesting in that, while it was rejected by the Hays Office (which was almost always stricter than the Legion), the Legion didn't condemn it. Gerald Gardner thinks this was because "the moral climate" of the Catholic Church was changing but I imagine it was more to do with the fact that the old enemy of sex wasn't involved.[66] Whatever the reason, the film starring Frank Sinatra resulted in a revision of the Code to allow narcotics to be mentioned in movies.

Sinatra expected to win an Oscar for the role but he was thwarted by Ernest Borgnine, who scooped it for his performance in *Marty*. In a way it was poetic justice. Borgnine had helped Sinatra to win one for *From Here to Eternity*, his cruelty to him in that film drumming up audience support for Sinatra's Maggio. "He won me one and lost me one," Sinatra commented philosophically as Borgnine went up to collect his statuette.

The fact that Preminger had now released two movies without Seals was regarded as doubly arrogant by his colleagues but Preminger was buoyed up by the fact that he had already taken on the big guns with *The Moon Is Blue*, as we saw, and came away smiling. In both cases a fine of $25,000 was levied on him for releasing non-approved films. More significantly, this was never collected.

Preminger "not only found theaters to exhibit his films, but each attracted a large audience."[67] *The Man with the Golden Arm* went on to gross a cool $5.5 million. What this proved, to quote Harry Shapiro in *Shooting Stars,* was that "[i]t wasn't just the art-house crowd watching new-wave Italian neorealism who could make their own minds up about whether or not to go and see a non-seal movie."[68] Preminger showed everyone that both the PCA and the Legion of Decency could be defied successfully if the film was good enough, and played to audiences' sensitivities.

To expedite the latter ambition he revised the script. Nelson Algren's novel, on which the film was based, wasn't overly sympathetic to the main character. Preminger changed this around. He darkened the character of his wife to throw all the emotion his way. He then got Sinatra, the bobbysoxer king, to play the lead role. Marlon Brando had also been in the running for it but Brando vacillated, as Brando was wont to do, and Sinatra stepped into the breach. The year before, Brando had snatched the part of Terry Malloy in *On the Waterfront* from under Sinatra's nose so this was sweet revenge. The score was now one-all. (The fact that both of them appeared together in *Guys and Dolls* in the same year merely fanned the flames of their rivalry. Brando said Sinatra couldn't act and Sinatra said Brando couldn't sing. The egos had landed.)

Sinatra pushed the envelope of what was deemed acceptable viewing by taking on a subject that had been heretofore taboo in mainstream cinema, "The system's crazy," he complained. "Every manner of things have been seen in the movies, but about drugs everybody's supposed to stick his head in the ground." He went on to talk about drug addicts he'd encountered in his past in Hoboken: "There were a couple of older guys on the block who acted kinda funny and later I found out they were on junk. In poor, tough neighborhoods like that, one peddler can ruin a lot of lives."[69]

This slant, delivered by an icon, made sure that the public knew they were going to see an anti-drug movie, albeit one that was on the side of its main character. The fact that Geoffrey Shurlock (who had, incidentally, thought the brouhaha over *The Moon Is Blue* was a storm in a teacup) threw it out suddenly meant very little to America's viewing public. Once again the curse of *The Miracle* was coming back to haunt the PCA and the Legion of Decency. Preminger scored a double whammy and Sinatra solidified his position on the Tinseltown tree. Still high from the Oscar he received for *From Here to Eternity*, he proved to the world — if not to Brando — that there was more to him than a smoothie with a tilted hat who sang "Songs for Swingin' Lovers." *The Man with the Golden Arm* did for drug addiction what *The Lost Weekend* (1945) had done for alcoholism. It gave it a window, bringing it out into the open as a topic for discussion. We never see a needle entering Sinatra's arm in the film but Preminger shows him using a tie as a tourniquet, and also the look of euphoria on his face as he gets his hit.

There was more trouble ahead for the PCA and the Legion of Decency in 1956 when they differed radically in their views on Elia Kazan's *Baby Doll*. The public contretemps that resulted did neither of them any favors.

Based on a Tennessee Williams play, *Baby Doll* concerns a dispute between a backwoods Mississippi family and a con man, but the main bone of contention was the eponymous nymphet played by the alluringly feline Carroll Baker, pictured sucking her thumb in the film's infamous poster. Baker is a 19-year-old who marries the much older Karl Malden with the understanding that they won't have sex until she turns twenty. But there's a suggestion that she sleeps with Malden's rival Eli Wallach.

It took Kazan three years to get the film off the ground. It was this long before agreement was reached on controversial scenes like Wallach's implied seduction of Baker, and another erotically-charged scene where Baker sits on a swing. A further one where he puts his foot on her stomach was kept in, but inflamed many viewers who were unaccustomed to such bawdy overtures. Wallach's lecherous leering over the thumb-sucking Baker is indeed the stuff of Lolita-like desire, but today it's likely to provoke more laughter than lust.

The film became a *succès de scandal*. Cardinal Spellman ordered a boycott on cinemas that defied him by showing it. In time, the argument spilled over

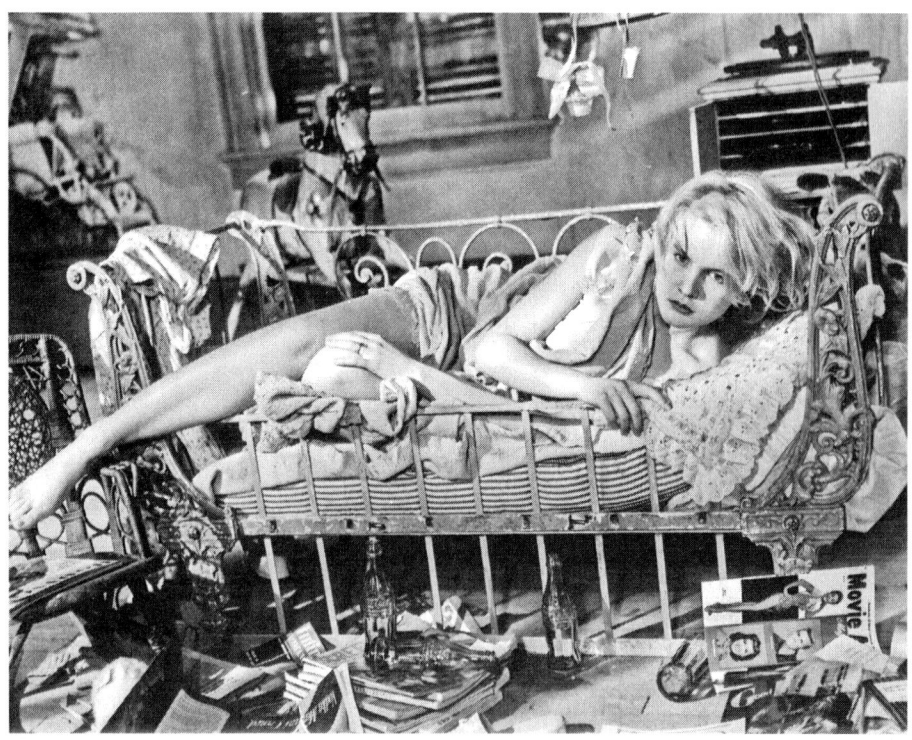

Carroll Baker looks suitably dissolute in *Baby Doll* (1956), which caused enormous problems for the Legion of Decency in the 1950s, but history would see it as a rather ordinary movie elevated way beyond its status.

into an inter-church debate. Some Protestant ministers accused Spellman of adopting the tactics of a bully. Cinema owners pointed out that they were entitled to screen it since it had been approved by the PCA.

Spellman gave a homily in St. Patrick's Cathedral on Fifth Avenue in which he said, "I exhort Catholic people from patronizing this film under pain of sin."[70] Kazan was livid, blurting out in response, "Spellman had the filthiest mind of anybody. He made a dirty picture out of it."[71] Kazan also pointed out that there was "no indication of actual sex" in the film. [72] He said he doubted that Spellman had even seen it, considering his comments were so off-kilter.

The cardinal didn't feel he had to see it to know that it was filth, any more than he felt he had to go to Alaska to know that it snowed there. Kazan was outraged that a film would be condemned sight unseen but Spellman countered that Kazan's reputation had preceded him. Aghast that it was a commercial success, he placed priests in the lobbies of many cinemas and they took down the names of people going in and out. The fear factor kept many folks away but just as many people probably went to see it for its notoriety value. The attendance evened itself out like that. Kazan subsequently called the Cardinal "a dunce."[73]

Apart from Cardinal Spellman's "name and shame" policy, he warned that "anyone seeing it was actually committing a sin and would go to hell," incendiary words even by his terms.[74] Tennessee Williams groaned, "I cannot believe that an ancient and august branch of the Christian faith is not larger in heart and mind."[75] In Britain a Reverend John Burke gave the film a cautious thumbs-up, adjudging it to be "a brilliant piece of work on a decadent subject."[76] His words weren't appreciated, however, and he ended up losing his post as head of the U.K. branch of the Legion of Decency. European Catholics had a much more liberal attitude to the film, as had certain members of American churches.

Dr James Pike, dean of the Protestant Episcopal Cathedral of St. John the Divine, doubted that he had sinned by seeing it. "Those who do not want the sexual aspect of life included in the portrayal of a real life situation," he contended, "had better burn their Bibles as well as abstain from the movies."[77] Cecil B. DeMille would no doubt have concurred with the sentiments, but he wouldn't have liked the dean's next comment, which alleged that *The Ten Commandments* had more carnal scenes than this film, and yet received the church's blessing.[78]

Time claimed it was "just possibly the dirtiest American-made picture that has ever been legally exhibited, with Priapean detail that might well have embarrassed Boccaccio."[79] Today it looks almost quaint, like many films condemned at the time they were released.

After perusing the *Time* review, Wallach had to go to the dictionary to find out what "Priapean" meant. In the days following he sulked around New York imagining people were looking at him and thinking, "Here comes that pornographic, pedophile Priapean!"[80] Then he saw a huge queue of people waiting in line to see the movie on Broadway and his spirits lifted. When he went in to see it himself with his wife, all she said, *apropos* her husband's and Karl Malden's appearance, was "Never have two noses filled the screen so completely."[81]

Not everyone, it appeared, was being corrupted by Baker's thumb-sucking, or living in fear of Cardinal Spellman's denunciations. Some people were just watching a movie. And a pair of noses. Judith Crist was underwhelmed by it, dismissing Baker as "more bomb than bombshell."[82]

The Legion of Decency demanded that cinemas showing it be boycotted for six months, at which point the American Civil Liberties Union became involved. A major row ensued, the liberals winning the day. *Baby Doll* may not be Kazan's best film, or near it, but it was one of the lynchpins of a changing of the guard. Five years earlier a discussion about its exhibition in movie theaters wouldn't even have been a possibility.

Kazan thought the publicity surrounding it said more about the critics than the film itself. Referring to the vexed question of the thumb-sucking, which to many people had overtones of oral sex, he remarked, "If you watch the film carefully, I never even show Silva [Wallach] put his hand on her. He threatens to, but the act is entirely in the minds of the Catholic priests and bishops and cardinals. The fact that she sucks her thumb doesn't mean she wants a penis in her mouth. All babies suck their thumbs."[83]

Baker believed the nub of the issue lay in the fact that the Breen Office had passed the film without consulting the Legion of Decency, to the latter's chagrin. She claimed they went, "Okay, this is it. Now we're going to make an example of this picture."[84] The fact that they manifestly failed to carry out this threat was another nail in the Legion of Decency's coffin.

But there's no such thing as bad publicity, as we've seen. Any time members of the Legion picketed a cinema, box receipts went up. Kazan chirped, "It took a cardinal to make *Baby Doll* a household name."[85] For Spellman the episode was "an own goal."[86]

The greatest crime the film committed wasn't raising the hackles of the

Legion but being boring and obscure. It didn't have a male lead that was strong enough to make the sexual element take fire and its early success at the box office didn't last. The Legion took some satisfaction from this. It felt itself validated, albeit for the wrong reasons. If nothing else, the fact that it did little business proved that "controversy in itself wasn't enough to sell it."[87] Tennessee Williams thought the script had a "wanton hilarity" to it, but he believed this wasn't used in the film version.[88]

Baby Doll was the first film condemned by the Legion of Decency but passed by the PCA. As such it signaled dissension within the ranks of the reformers, surely a promising sign for progressive directors, if not the movie industry in general.

The film, Jon Lewis notes in his book *Hollywood V. Hard Core,* presented cinema-owners with a thorny situation: "First there was the Legion, and the very real possibility of a boycott. Business was bad enough without picketers and priests on the sidewalk in front of the theater."[89]

It finally won its Seal in September 1956, but Cardinal Spellman still denounced it from the altar in New York, asking not just Catholics but "every loyal citizen" to boycott it.[90] In his memoirs, Kazan described Spellman as "a bag of sanctified wind."[91] He still couldn't understand how a man could condemn a film he hadn't seen, hardly being impressed with Spellman's "Must you have a disease to know what it is?" by way of rationalization.[92]

As for *Baby Doll* itself, he wondered what all the fuss had been about. "If you look at the film now," he mused, "you'll see a rather amusing comedy."[93]

Karl Malden spoke of Cardinal Spellman being the film's unwitting PR man. He was amused by the irony of the cardinal condemning it not for sex but rather the absence of sex: "He declared that the film went against natural law since Baby Doll's marriage was never consummated." Malden felt this was just an excuse, that the real reason for Spellman's disapproval was the movie's advertising billboard "which covered damn near one full block over Broadway" showing Baker with her hair disheveled as she lay in an "antique crib not big enough to contain her, sucking her thumb and staring out of vacant, somnambulistic eyes."[94]

Joseph Kennedy, who would soon become the father of a president — JFK — refused to show it in his chain of New England cinemas, proclaiming, "I have been in business 45 years and I think this is the worst thing that has ever been done to the people and to the industry. I think it should be banned everywhere."[95] I agree with Edward De Grazia that there had to be a political motive behind this similar over-reaction.

Another 1956 film caused almost as much consternation as *Baby Doll*, although for somewhat different reasons. In *Tea and Sympathy*, Laura Reynolds, a married woman played by Deborah Kerr, offers herself sexually to Tom Lee (John Kerr), an 18-year-old prep school student, to save himself from the fear that he's gay. Such, at least, was the plot of the play. In the film she gives herself to him "so that he'll know he's a man," a different matter entirely. Gerald Gardner rightly stated that this was "somewhat like producing *Macbeth* without the murder."[96]

As if this wasn't bad enough, Kerr, being married, had to suffer for her "sin" (even though she probably saved the young boy from killing himself) so playwright Robert Anderson was prevailed upon to tack on a scene where Laura writes to Tom to inform him that her adultery has ruined her life. This coda resulted in a New York critic advising his readers to leave the cinema before the scene in question played itself out.[97]

There were other issues in the film besides sexuality, like the fact that, throughout it, Tom refuses to play society's game. He does sewing at a beach, oblivious to the fact that this will inevitably lead to taunts from the classmates playing football nearby. Even after they start calling him "Sister Boy" he still tinkers with the idea of dressing up in girl's clothes for a school play. Laura tries to talk him out of this but it's only when his father, a hardline jock type, lays down the law that the female garments get tossed aside. "Do you spend all your allowance money on curtains?" he asks his son as he surveys his overly neat room. Tom replies rather pathetically, "I wanted to make it look like home."

The truth is, there was no home worth speaking of as his mother left when he was a boy. He was begat, he tells Laura after she starts to take a special interest in him, to try and fix the problems between his mother and father. He adds that it's kind of lousy when you fail at your first job in life.

Laura becomes a sort of surrogate mother to him, more a maternal figure than a sexual one, even if a sexual act closes the movie. This isn't shown, but strongly suggested by Laura's "Years from now when you think about this, you will be kind."

Is it, as the common parlance would have it, a "pity fuck"? Yes and no. She clearly likes Tom for himself, and her own marriage (to housemaster Bill, played by Leif Erickson) is no great shakes. Bill is like Tom's father, a man unable (or unwilling) to understand emotion. Neither of them can take the idea of a boy wanting to play the guitar or read books instead of "hanging out" with the peer group.

The film gave problems to the censors because of the undertone of homo-

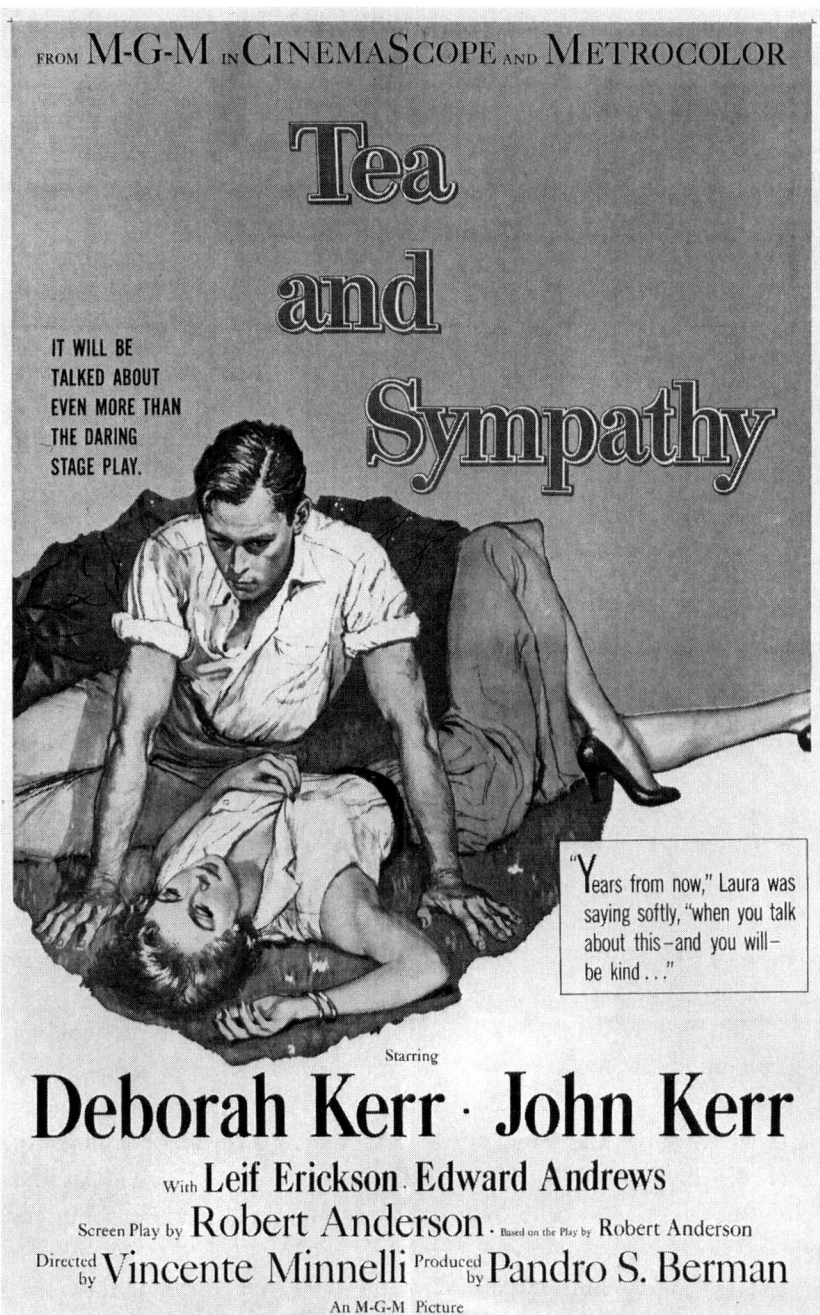

Vincente Minnelli's *Tea and Sympathy* (1956) was a watered-down version of Robert Anderson's gay-themed play but its introduction of a marital infidelity theme still raised eyebrows.

sexuality but it's really a film about individuality, about stereotyping and breaking away from the pack. Tom tries to "normalize" himself by visiting a lady of easy virtue late on in the movie, but when she humiliates him after a botched attempt at teaching him to dance (Laura was much more compassionate in an earlier attempt at this) he tries to slash his wrists with a bread knife. Afterwards he's expelled from the college.

This suits Bill down to the ground. His problem has been removed. Now the college can run again on well-oiled wheels. But what he doesn't bargain on is the fact Laura will relieve Tom of his virginity. It's this act that results in their marriage falling apart. Her letter to Tom outlining the details of this development is the one false note in a fine film. She basically tells him she ruined her marriage to save him. This is in contravention to something we already knew: that her marriage was more or less on the rocks even before she met Tom. So once again the censors managed to bowdlerize two hours of authenticity with two minutes of sanitization.

Laura had actually been married before in the film, to somebody Tom resembles. He died in the Second World War, trying to prove to the world he was a man, but really ending his life as a boy. Laura learns from this not to let the same thing happen to Tom. After he leaves her, he can now be himself. He doesn't become a folk singer but rather a writer — another "effeminate" pursuit, as it were. But by the end of the film there's nobody to jeer him — only to write him "Dear John" letters that betray both of them with fatuous regret.

In the play version of *Tea and Sympathy*, Tom is reputed to have sunbathed in the nude with another man of dubious sexuality but when it got to the screen he does nothing more daring than sew the button on the garment to demonstrate he's not quite a full-blooded male.

Transmuting his homosexual leanings into vague demonstrations of sissiness finally caused Anderson to explode in exasperation at a meeting with Quigley and his clerical compadres, after which he walked out, washing his hands of the movie and leaving its ultimate fate to the tender mercies of the studio distributing it, MGM.[98] Nonetheless, the fact that a film with an adulterous theme was allowed into the public domain spoke volumes about how taboos were being steadily eroded.

The changing climate wasn't only in movies. As stated already, the cinema tended to follow other art forms, like literature. Or rather not follow them. Joseph Mankiewicz explained to Ben Hecht just as the latter was about to begin his screenwriting career, "In a novel a hero can lay ten girls and marry a virgin. In a movie this is not allowed. The hero as well as the heroine has to be a virgin in movies. The villain can lay anyone he wants, have as much fun as he wants, cheating and stealing, getting rich and cheating the servants, but you have to shoot him in the end." Mankiewicz added, even more trenchantly, "When he falls with a bullet in his forehead, it is advisable that he clutch at the Gobelin tapestry on the library wall and bring it down over his head like a symbolic shroud."[99]

In contravention to this punitive mindset, in 1957 Pope Pius XII wrote that movies were "a noble art" that could potentially benefit mankind. His words were taken on board by a new generation of Catholic university students who were exposed to freethinking authors: "Their economic stability enabled them to be more independent of both parish and family pressures. Increasingly, American Catholics were asking their church for a more nuanced understanding of modern arts and society."[100]

Even educated Catholics, however, had problems with somebody as steamy as D.H. Lawrence, and a French production of his novel *Lady Chatterley's Lover* was denied a license in New York in 1957 on the grounds that it seemed to encourage adultery. The decision was appealed and two years later the court ruled that a government couldn't interfere with the exhibition of a film because it disapproved of an idea behind it, even a sexual idea.[101]

Clearly, church and state were in line for a head-on collision. This time the catalysts were the young generation.

Marjorie Rosen painted in the sociological tapestry: "In the early fifties, youth voiced the single dissenting wail against corruption of a politically trembling, morally anaesthetized post-war society. Shattering complacency were the Hell's Angels, the urban teen gangs and the Beat Generation. Desiring only to drift and sate their sense of adventure, bohemians dropped out long before the acid culture came along, and Allen Ginsberg's *Howl* and Jack Kerouac's *On the Road* popularized the movement as more than a metaphysical search for mystical Beatitude."[102]

James Dean more than anyone else crystallized the alienation of the time. "You don't understand me!" he screamed at his parents in *Rebel Without a Cause*. Marlon Brando's rebellion was more macho, whereas Dean's was twisted up like a pretzel inside him. It manifested itself in his slouched shoulders, his shambling walk, his tentative delivery of lines. But that sensitive face showed great poignance. Men wanted to be him and women wanted to bed him; "At once timid and gentle, yet smoldering with bewilderment, good intentions and self-destructiveness, he surpassed Holden Caulfield, the Beats and the Angels as the sullen, mute center of the anti-authoritarian youth subculture."[103]

When "The Hillbilly Cat" first emerged onto the music scene, his image was that of a rebel. Only in time — after he went to Hollywood, in fact — was he really seen for what he was: a man who lived with his mother and honed his trade in church, listening to jiving preachers spread the gospel in Deep South revivalist mode. He was blasted from the pulpits as being yet another nail in America's moral coffin.

Presley was filmed from the waist up when he appeared on *The Ed Sullivan Show* in 1956 but the TV censorship backfired as audiences became even more excited by what they didn't see as what they did.

Two years later, Presley was drafted into the army. It was during this hiatus in his career that his mother died and the fire seemed to go out of his belly. He feared his rock career would be guillotined by Uncle Sam. Whether as a result of this or a combination of other factors, after he was de-mobbed he allowed himself to be shoehorned into a raft of forgettable beach-and-song movies that made a lot of money but ended his push against the establishment.

John Lennon claimed Elvis died the day he went into the army. Just as Marlon Brando "owned" the fifties with a string of Oscar-worthy performances and then let his radar go on the blink in the sixties where, like Elvis, he seemed to make movies solely for money, society suddenly witnessed two rebels going fat and bland before reinventing themselves in the seventies.

The Irish film censor Liam O'Hora ordered eight cuts to be made in Elvis' rather inoffensive drama *King Creole* in 1958. "This picture is a tough one for me," he growled, "because it features the controversial Presley who has such an appeal for uneducated adolescents." It happens to be Elvis' best performance, which isn't saying much, granted, but that was hardly to be a factor in O'Hora's estimation judging by his attitude. He found Elvis' "abdominal" dancing unacceptable.[104]

Marilyn Monroe was also sending men's blood pressure soaring at this time. She affected both moviegoers and censors alike, though for dramatically different reasons, as she embarked on a raft of frivolous sex comedies that insulted both her intelligence and her acting ability.

John Springer disagreed about the lazy "dumb blonde" tag: "They treated her as a bubblehead but she was very bright, very sharp."[105] Mae West conceded that she was "the only gal who came near to me in the sex appeal department.... All the others had were big boobs."[106] Monroe herself thought of it simply like this: "Sex is a part of nature. I go along with nature."[107]

Monroe wasn't your classic sex symbol, more a child in a woman's body, seemingly unaware of the vibe she was sending out, as much in search of a

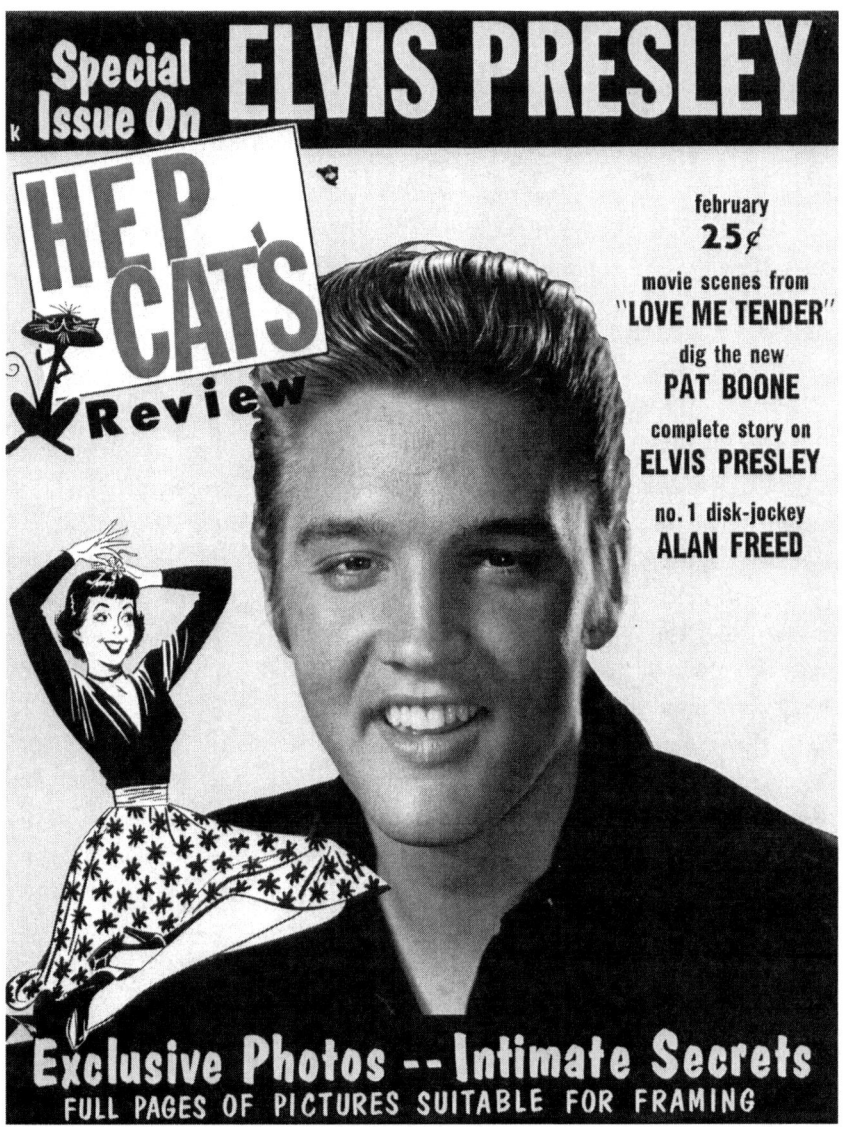

Elvis Presley, shown here on the cover of *Hep Cat's Review* (February 1957), had to be filmed from the waist up in the fifties to keep the female population from overheating due to his pelvic gyrations.

father figure as a bed partner. Her hootchie-coochie walk and baby voice accentuated this, as did her choice of cheesecake roles. It was only in her last (completed) movie, *The Misfits* (appropriately titled), that she became an adult woman. By then, unfortunately, she was too far embedded in her myth to be able to save herself. She was also losing her face and her figure, the two things by which she measured her worth, and a series of failed pregnancies meant there was no child to save her from herself after the men in her life had taken leave of her. The great sex icon died alone, as her male counterpart, Mr. Presley, would 15 years on. What price irony?

In the fifties, though, it was all very different for Tinseltown's twin sex symbols (who, incidentally, never met). Elvis was busy releasing the pent-up sexual frustrations of a nation of adolescent women just as Monroe was doing the same for men. Brando had been virtually silenced in *The Wild One* but the fall-out from *A Streetcar Named Desire* confirmed him as "the Valentino of the bop generation." Bringing up the rear was another angry young man, the aforementioned James Dean, an actor credited with "inventing" the term "teenager" in the U.S. He would die in 1955 in a car crash but despite (or because of?) that tragedy he would come to personify every disaffected young person's need to revolt against the status quo. Was he a rebel without a cause? Perhaps, but sometimes these are the ones who exert the most long-lasting influence. Over half a century on, Dean's image still adorns the walls of impressionable young men and women who distrust anyone over 30, or who are looking for another path to self-fulfillment than the one outlined by their parents.

Brigitte Bardot was another iconic figure of this time, the Legion of Decency having failed to block her breakthrough movie *And God Created Woman* in 1956. That movie's poster carried a nudge-wink tagline, "But the devil invented Brigitte Bardot," thereby signaling the movie's intention to launch a new sex bomb onto the world. In Lake Placid, New York, church authorities offered an exhibitor $350 if he cancelled a scheduled showing of the film. He refused, and the cinema in question was closed down for six months as a result.[108]

If Marilyn Monroe was merely a "tease," as some alleged, Bardot was the real deal: "Just the kind of girl to take home to mother ... if you want to give her a heart attack."[109] The joke went that Bardot had met Jean Harlow one day and Harlow said to her, "Our names sound similar." To which Bardot replied, "But the 't' is silent in yours."

"The former convent schoolgirl," John Cooney wrote, "disturbed Vatican sensibility with her comment 'It is better to be unfaithful than to be faithful without wanting to be.'"[110] But what could they do? She was French, and different laws seemed to apply to the continent than the U.S. or Britain. Billy Wilder quipped, "What they call dirty in our movies they call lusty in foreign ones."

Marjorie Rosen described Bardot as "the best thing to come out of France since *foie gras*. 'That blonde baby pout — the successor of Williams' taunting *Baby Doll* and predecessor of Nabokov's *Lolita* — commingled with a knowing

3. Decades of Revolt

sexuality. Her style ... tapped the fantasy tradition of the succulent child-woman."[111]

Of 27 films condemned by the Legion of Decency, seven starred Bardot. In a famous scene from *Love Is My Profession* (1959) she lifts her skirt up above her waist to repay lawyer Jean Gabin after he's defended her successfully on a robbery charge. What she's wearing underneath doesn't leave much to the imagination, but as Baxter Philips revealed, "The scissors saved the Anglo-Saxon world from seeing the scene."[112]

By this time, independent distributors were opening doors previously locked firmly against the cinema chains. Lurid B-movies and cheap "nudie flicks" crept in under the net for those who got their kicks in back streets after dark.[113] Sexploitation followed liberalism, as the censors feared. By 1964 over 700 cinemas were openly exhibiting such films.[114]

The profits were enormous. One of the first of such delights was Russ Meyer's skinflick *The Immoral Mr. Teas*. It was shot in just four days in 1959 for $24,000 but went on to gross over $1 million in the next four years.[115] The story of a messenger boy who has hallucinations of nudity every time his job brings him into contact with a beautiful woman, it was based on the rather far-fetched premise that the eponymous gentleman was able to see inside women's clothing as a result of an anesthetic he received for a tooth extraction. It was banned in Britain but played for years in Hollywood, escaping the many prosecutions brought against it on the premise that nudity *per se* wasn't obscene.[116]

Meyer went on to direct such delights as *Eve and the Handyman* (1961) and *Wild Gals of the Naked West* (1962) before

When Brigitte Bardot's films made their way from France to Hollywood the censors' scissors went into overdrive to prevent the sex siren from corrupting the morals of the youth.

extending his range with *Lorna* (1963), which added rape and murder to the sexual content for good measure. "I realized the nudies had had it," he pined — prematurely, it must be said.[117] Thereafter his films grew more brutal, as may be gleaned from their titles: *Motor Psycho* (1965), *Faster, Pussycat, Kill, Kill* (1966) and *Vixen* (1969). The last of these was prosecuted 23 times for obscenity in the U.S. and finally trimmed down by the British censor from 71 minutes to 47.

In 1970 Meyer made *Beyond the Valley of the Dolls*, an unashamedly trite confection about an all-female rock group sleeping their way to the top — or at least the middle. It was so bad it was good and became something of a camp classic, mixing violence and bed-hopping in a manner that blurred the distinction between mainstream sex and underground porn. Twentieth Century–Fox, a studio that had been in dire financial straits before its release, laughed its way to the bank. So did Meyer, who continued his odyssey into risible depravity with *The Seven Minutes* (the alleged time it's imagined it takes a woman to reach orgasm) in 1971.

But this is to run ahead of our theme. Back in 1959 Father Thomas Little, an assistant to Cardinal Spellman, actually went so far as to castigate *Some Like It Hot*. Today this is regarded as one of the most innocuous films of its era. It often turns up in lists of people's all-time-favorite films but Little, pointing to the transvestism at its core, lambasted it for having "clear implications of homosexuality and lesbianism."[118]

If this weren't so serious it would be funny. What Wilder was after here was farce, not innuendo. He actually employed a coach to help Jack Lemmon walk like a woman but Lemmon, after a few preliminary lessons, sent her home. He didn't want to walk like a woman, he told him, he wanted to walk like a man trying to walk like a woman. This was an insightful interpretation of the essence of the role — not surprising from such an astute performer as this man.

Pillow Talk went on release that year as well. This mindless fluff acquired something of a reputation for ushering in a spate of "sophisticated" sex comedies. Star Doris Day was a girl-next-door type who personified blandness. (Oscar Levant famously said he knew her before she was a virgin.) Her co-star Rock Hudson looked cotton candy too, at least to a generation unaware of his homosexuality.

The film had a naughty subtext, Hudson playing a serial seducer who says of his prospects with Day, "I think five or six dates ought to do it." He didn't get a chance to do "it" though, the film content to be primarily verbal. The most popular scene used a split-screen device which featured both of them in their baths (in two separate dwellings, of course) speaking on the phone. Michael Gordon, the director, wanted Hudson to put his hand through the screen in what would have been a daring visual joke for the time, but the Hays Office pooh-poohed the idea.

John Simon alleged that Day's only talent "is that of being absolutely sanitary: her personality untouched by human emotions, her brow unclouded by human thought, her form unsmudged by the slightest form of femininity."[119] For Dwight MacDonald she was "as wholesome as a bowl of cornflakes and at least as sexy."[120]

If Day, as James Skinner posited, only surrendered her maidenhood "after wedding bells had pealed," her continental counterparts, like Bardot, Sophia Loren and the lubricious Gina Lollobrigida, carried "looser morals in their baggage."[121]

Molly Haskell didn't think there was too much difference between Presley, Monroe and Day. For her, the trio pedaled an image rather than the real thing: "They were all about sex, but without sex. The fabulous fifties were a box of Cracker Jacks without a prize; or with the prize distorted into a forty-inch bust, a forty-year-old virgin." In the forties, she held, sex was drowned in sentimentality, "but now it was deflected into a joke ... with breast fetishism combining with Lolita lechery."[122]

Otto Preminger gave the guardians of virtue more grief with his 1959 feature *Anatomy of a Murder*. Again the script was the main culprit rather than the action. It featured many explicit sexual terms like "penetration" in its tale of the alleged rape of a young girl, played by Lee Remick.

The film has dialogue that often resembles a legal transcript but at no point does it leer, or become coy or suggestive. Nobody ever thought they'd see James Stewart brandishing a pair of panties to a crowd and getting away with it but he does here. Preminger offers an almost forensic appraisal of a crime, or suspected crime. We hear words like "sperm" and "contraception" but we don't squirm in our seats because of their context.

The Chicago Censorship Board refused to grant the distributor of the film a permit for its exhibition in that city because of the use of the words "rape" and "contraceptive" but Preminger brought the case to the U.S. District Court, which ruled that "the film cannot be placed in the category of the obscene or immoral, because the dominant effect does not tend to excite sexual passion or undermine public morals."[123]

The censors originally clamped down on the film but two appellate courts reversed their decision, ruling that the candid script was "not likely to so much arouse the salacity of the normal viewer as to outweigh the film's artistic presentation."[124] A different kind of censorship to the usual acted as a tag here when Stewart's father took out an ad in his local newspaper advising his neighbors not to go and see it. Stewart admitted he "got an awful lot of letters after [the film]. 'You let us down,' they said. 'I'm not going to your pictures any more. I take my children to a Jimmy Stewart picture and you're up there in court talking dirty and holding up women's panties.'"[125] He took it all in his stride, though, and said he'd have done it all again with pride.

And then came *Suddenly Last Summer*. With a quality director (Joseph L. Mankiewicz), a quality scriptwriter (Tennessee Williams) and a quality cast (Elizabeth Taylor, Montgomery Clift, Katharine Hepburn), it still managed to be a mess — no mean achievement. Clift is a neurosurgeon trying to get Taylor to remember the circumstances behind her cousin's death as the film rambles through a series of dizzy *longueurs*. British film censor John Trevelyan was amazed that it was granted a Code Seal, considering it "included almost all known sexual perversions."[126]

The Legion didn't know what to make of it all any more than the general public did. They had a feeling it was dangerous, but too obscure and eerie to know exactly why. They eventually gave it a separate classification. They knew it wasn't commercial so felt it wouldn't do much business, despite the stellar cast and reputable names of the director and screenwriter. The authors of *The Rough Guide to Cult Movies* made an astute point when they wrote that the film is scary in the way that horror films aren't because the sense of evil springs from the central characters rather than anything extrinsic to them.[127]

Williams himself was underwhelmed by the film. He wrote in his memoirs about the phone call producer Sam Spiegel made to him about it: "Sam asked what I wanted for the movie rights. I said, 'How about fifty grand plus 20 percent of the profits?' Sam said, 'It's a deal,' and it was. The profits were as good as the movie was bad."[128]

Room at the Top, another 1959 release, became one of Britain's most successful exports, making the journey to Hollywood with style, unlike so many of its predecessors which didn't have stateside "legs" despite national success. The story of a man who sacrifices emotion for career goals, it has Laurence Harvey as "local-boy-makes-good" Joe Lampton. A class parable as well as a sexual one, it forces Harvey to throw up the older woman he loves (Simone Signoret) for the boss' daughter (Heather Sears) because she signifies social success. When Signoret more or less commits suicide through heartbreak, Harvey could be left like the Anthony Quinn of *La Strada,* bemoaning the fact that, to use a Shakespearean term, he "threw a jewel away worth all his tribe." Instead he slots himself into his new situation with only brief pangs of guilt. He has achieved his life's dream, pulling himself up from his blue collar background, but at the cost of spiritually killing two people: Signoret and himself.

Room at the Top broke new ground for British films — indeed films anywhere — because it dealt with a man who sold his soul and survived. Yes, he was miserable at the end, but he was still functioning. He had the plum job and the society wife, if not inner peace. The woman he loved had died, but not before he threw her over. He caused her death — indirectly — so he had that coming to him.

But the ethical compass of the film is compromised. This sinner isn't punished as much as his celluloid predecessors. He has the decency to feel deflated at the film's end, but not enough to throw up the creature comforts his compromises have vouchsafed him. His life is left dangling but it won't be until six years later, with *Life at the Top,* that we will see the slow degeneration into the abyss that was always inevitable. Only the delay was surprising. (And, one supposes, the replacement of his wife by a more high profile actress, Jean Simmons. Which is a different kind of compromise.)

In one scene in the movie, after Harvey and Sears have sex, Sears exclaims "Oh Joe, wasn't it super!" This was long before girls were "allowed" to enjoy sex, especially pre-marital sex. Harvey is more subdued, in a kind of reversal of the expectable male-female roles. His grumpiness doesn't so much result from moral guilt over the act itself as the fact that he knows he's been intimate with her more for the prospect of career favors than natural affection. He's punished, as mentioned, at the end after Signoret dies in a car crash, but ten years earlier one imagines he would have been in the car with her, another burnt offering to the gods of Puritanism.

The film proved that Britain could be just as decadent as France with its "nouvelle vague" *auteurs*— a dubious distinction. *Room at the Top* was banned in some American states but also received widespread praise, most particularly from Reverend Malcolm Boyd, an Episcopalian chaplain at Colorado University who rightly realized it told a moral tale exceedingly well. He made the interesting observation, "Churches frequently stood by and witnessed the spectacle of kudos being bestowed upon artistic and religious trash in the form of very bad movies that are dubbed religious merely because they deal with Biblical subjects or sentimentally pseudo-religious themes."[129] If only every priest were as perceptive as this, the whole history of censorship in films might have been a tad more civilized.

Martin Scorsese outlined the absurdity of the situation:

> When I was a child I remember the church displayed lists of films in categories A, B and C. C meant it was condemned by the Legion of Decency. If you walked into a theater showing that film and had a heart attack, you're in hell. When I was about 18 or 19 I saw *The Seventh Seal,* which was a wonderful religious experience for me. But when I wanted to see it again it was playing with *Smiles of a Summer Night*—a condemned film. So I immediately went to confession and said to my parish priest, a sweet man who's now dead, that because I was studying film at New York University, I had to see *Smiles of a Summer Night.* I explained that I hadn't really understood the sexual aspects. He replied that I could see the film for my work, but that they had to keep these things from the masses.[130]

Signoret won the Best Actress Oscar for *Room at the Top* that year. Audrey Hepburn was second favorite for *The Nun's Story*. The fact that an aging lush beat a pretty postulant was probably enough to make Will Hays spin madly in his grave. The cinema had changed a lot since 1944 when Oscar nominee Leo McCarey, directing *Going My Way,* beat Billy Wilder, the director of *Double Indemnity*. On that occasion Wilder is alleged to have been so devastated he actually tripped McCarey when he was on the way down the aisle to collect his award.[131]

Room at the Top wasn't unduly explicit in sexual terms, but its moral—or rather amoral—perspective seemed to presage a new era in blunt realism. The days of billowing curtains, soft dissolves of firelight scenes and swirling waves crashing on rocks to the backdrop of a pulsating music score were indeed numbered. No longer would married couples sleep in separate beds. No longer did they have to be faithful to one another for fear of terrible fates. No longer were viewers locked outside the doors of raunchy boudoirs "for the good of their souls." People were about to do on screen what they did out in the big bad world, and woe betide the consequences.

Messages wouldn't be thrown at people willy-nilly any more, but conveyed by means of the films themselves—or not so, as the case might be. This wasn't indicative of a purer age—or a purer art—on the come. No, it was just filmmakers saying to their former censors: "This is how things are. You may not like them, and I may not like them either, but I'm going to show them, and if you get something out of them beyond themselves, hey, that's a bonus."

"As the sixties opened," Molly Haskell pronounced, "the Production Code was relaxing, inch by inch. With successive revelations on the screen the decade progressed like a stripper, though awkwardly—like a novice in a hurry to get off the stage."[132]

The times, they were a-changin'. In deliberately refusing to marry the fathers of their children, Haskell continued, Mia Farrow and Vanessa Redgrave were "applauded, or ignored, for doing what Ingrid Bergman had been ostracized for only ten years before."[133]

The single mother had arrived with a vengeance.

4

The Liberal Ethos

In more ways than one, 1961 was the start of a new era in more ways than one. First off, it was the year John F. Kennedy was elected president of the U.S., promising a brave new world of transparency and idealism. Many people saw him as the "Hollywood" president, an image he was happy to endorse by his very public friendship with the likes of Frank Sinatra (if not Marilyn Monroe) before political expediency caused him to renounce both. (Common rumor has it that Sinatra lobbied the Mafia to secure his election, which made Kennedy's subsequent ostracization of him all the more reprehensible.)

The February edition of *Life* magazine commented on the "frank" and "dirty" films Hollywood was putting out "that wouldn't have been permitted even a year ago." It finished by stating:

> Two of John O'Hara's most libido-centered novels, *Butterfield 8* and *From the Terrace*, are now being shot, and director Billy Wilder's new film *The Apartment* is the story of a young man who rises swiftly in his firm by lending his apartment to his bosses for their dalliances after the working day. Even *Lolita* will go into production this spring. Stanley Kubrick will direct filming of Vladimir Nabokov's wildly controversial novel about an older man and a 12-year-old girl touring the country's motels together — surely the epitome of that ancient movie blurb, "The Picture They Said Couldn't Be Made."

Wilder himself added, "The times are almost ripe for a movie about a young man who has a passionate love affair with his mother. At the end he learns that she's not his mother and commits suicide."

This was also the year Jules Dassin's *Never on Sunday* was released. This had happy hooker Melina Mercouri prancing around Athens proclaiming the joys of prostitution to the leering males who followed her like lapdogs. It was made on a shoestring and Dassin (a blacklisted director) also starred in it to save money. "A whore can't be happy," he tells her at one point, but she proves him wrong with her untamable *joie de vivre*. The film exudes an aura of casual paganism and while it's no masterpiece it's carried along on a tide of frenetic *bonhomie*. The censors were outraged by its celebration of a *louche* lifestyle but it did huge business around the world, which was one more in the eye for the moral right.

Elvis Presley came out of the army in 1960 and in the next eight years made 31 movies, some of them in less than three weeks, without breaking sweat. About 27 of these were rubbish, the other four just about watchable. He only walked away from them when they stopped making money, any Method ambitions he once harbored cauterized out of him by his manager Colonel Tom Parker, who promised to make him rich and did so, forgetting to add that he would have to make a deal with Mephistopheles in the process.

By contrast, Fellini's *La Dolce Vita* went on release in America in 1960, having been banned by most Catholic countries in Europe. The Pope condemned it but many factions of the Legion of Decency felt it was an inspired study of a profound theme, so here again there was a split of loyalties from two factions that had previously been tooth-in-jowl.

This was a major surprise from the Legion of Decency as the opening scene, featuring a statue of Christ being carried across Rome by helicopter, left no one in any doubt about the kind of film they were about to see. It was a post–Catholic take on life as it was lived by the bored rich, with an existential undertow personified by the character of Marcello Mastroianni, the only person in the cast who seems to have the gift of self-knowledge or self-doubt.

This is a film about the spiritual bankruptcy of café society. Many members of the Legion felt it glorified decadence; others were hip to the fact that it was more like a satire of it for it's a very vacuous form of hedonism Fellini puts on display here. People with holes in their souls party as if there's no tomorrow, but then tomorrow comes, and in the aftertaste of gay abandon we watch them try to pick up the pieces of their fractured lives. Neil Sinyard expressed it like this: "[Fellini] rarely just luxuriates in the societies he depicts, but thinks dramatically about how they operate. Far from being a scandalous artist, he might be something of a traditional moralist."[1]

In a radically divergent view, Pauline Kael argued that Fellini's "orgies of modern Rome" can be equated with Cecil B. DeMille's "pagan infernos" of ancient Rome.[2] "Like a naughty Christian child," she continued, "Fellini thinks it's a ball to be a pagan, but a naughty ball ... which can't really be enjoyed." This made him "the new DeMille — a purveyor of the glamour of wickedness."[3] She noticed that Fellini frequently talked in interviews of society's need for miracles and mythologies, but in her view "as a Catholic, and a notably emotional one, [he] has small knowledge of, or interest in, any forms of control outside the church. As an artist he draws upon the imagination of a Catholic schoolboy and presents us with a juvenile version of the Grand Inquisitor's argument.[4]

The anal retentive, or myopic, saw it as an underlining of debauchery rather than an undermining of it and worried about its corrupting effect on impressionable minds. In time it would become a classic but when first shown it was regarded as a work by a dirty-minded little Italian man playing havoc with raw passion in a series of orgiastic vignettes. It was also accused, mystifyingly, of serving a Communist interest. (This was a charge also laid at the door of many films in the past which weren't even remotely political: *White Heat* in 1949, *The Asphalt Jungle* in 1950, *High Noon* in 1952 and so on.)

The film chronicles the descent of a gossip columnist into the bowels of Rome's sensuality. The city almost becomes another character in the film as he samples its lubricious riches, becoming more tainted each passing day until by the film's end he's become sucked up into the morass he once only wrote about.

A suicide, a striptease, an encounter with the chattering classes — these are just some of the picaresque adventures of our beleaguered hack. Fellini places him in a milieu that's disconcertingly intense and also singularly bereft of idealism. As is the case in *8½*, Mastroianni acts like a *tabula rasa* upon which this *carpe diem* society writes its instructions.

Fellini shot a whopping 56 hours of film altogether, afterwards whittling it down to just less than three, which is probably why it's so full of riches. What's even more amazing is that its episodic nature doesn't jar, the parts all resembling pieces of a jigsaw that eventually fuse into an overall vision of the madcap sweetness of the title.

It came out just as Pope John XXIII was getting ready to convene the Second Vatican Council. *Il Quotidiano,* the newspaper of Catholic Action, at first enthused about it but then had second thoughts, possibly as a result of Vatican influence. Neither were church leaders much impressed by the spectacle of Anita Ekberg as Sylvia prancing in a fountain in clerical garb, which she then proceeds to shed.

It was eventually slated for blasphemy and obscenity in a blatant about-turn. Catholics were ordered to shun it and any priest who spoke favorably of it was warned he would either be demoted or moved to another parish. Fellini himself was accused of being an atheist who mocked everything that smacked of Catholicism. Even his mother turned against him, asking him why he made a film like that. Years later, he claimed she was still known as the mother of the man who made the notorious *La Dolce Vita*.

Federico Fellini's *La Dolce Vita* brought Italian exoticism — some would say decadence also — to the screen in 1960.

In his book *Cinema, Religion and the Romantic Legacy,* Paul Coates writes about the manner in which Fellini goes from an air motif (the Jesus statue being carted across Rome) to a water one where Sylvia dances in the fountain. "Rome may contain the Holy See," he argues, "but its descent into unholiness is prefigured by the statue's homelessness."[5]

It seems somehow right, he states, that the film concludes at the seashore where innocence meets experience in a head-on collision. The city mentality, Coates suggests, has made the protagonists unable to recognize the significance of the statue, thereby completing the downward trajectory "from Jesus in the sky to the earth-goddess in the fountain, to the sea-creature in the depths. As it's ratcheted downwards, the idea of the sacred becomes less and less readable with each notch."[6]

There are many possible reasons why the Legion of Decency gave it a wide berth. The most obvious one is probably because Fellini was a genius and his film a beguiling masterpiece. Even if the Legion did condemn it, one got the impression not too many of its adherents would have abided by its decision.

Never before had a pen-pusher's immersion in a vortex of excess resonated with such sultry magic. The film even gave a new word to the world's vocabulary. A man named Paparazzo is Mastroianni's sidekick and the term entered the language as shorthand for those celebrity-hungry snappers who dog the movers and shakers of the media world.

Also in that year, Burt Lancaster appeared in *Elmer Gantry,* directed by Richard Brooks. He clearly relished the role of a fiery evangelist finally undone by a sexual encounter. Many of the major studios were slow to back a film "whose essence was a broadside against religion" but United Artists finally took it up.[7] Lancaster plays Gantry as a silver-tongued devil with half his mind on the Bible and the other half on women's bosoms.

Expelled from theological college after seducing the dean's daughter behind the altar, he inveigles his way back into the revivalist movement by charming his way into the affections of one Sister Sharon (Jean Simmons) who's also edgy and unpredictable. His past comes back to haunt him in the guise of Shirley Jones, who sets him up for a sexual sting.

It was based on a 1927 Sinclair Lewis novel about a Baptist minister. Lewis had created him as a rather one-dimensional character so Lancaster and Brooks wrote a script that fleshed him out. This was racy to say the least. In the seduction scene, Gantry says to Sister Sharon, "I'd like to tear those holy wings off you and make a real woman out of you. I'd show you what Heaven's like. No golden stairways or harp music or silvery clouds, just ecstasy comin' and goin.'"

For Brooks, Gantry wanted "what everyone is supposed to want — money, sex, religion. He's the all-American boy."[8] "We got him interested in dames and drinking," Lancaster boasted, "as well as hollering hellfire and brimstone. We weren't trying to uglify him. We were merely trying to make him into a recognizable, full-blooded human being with common weaknesses and vanities."[9]

The energy Lancaster brought to the role was uncanny. He claimed it was the easiest part he ever played "because I was playing myself."[10] This was easier to believe than the *non sequitur* that followed: "Actually I partly based him on John Huston."[11] We know Gantry is a fraud but we still can't stop ourselves being won over by him.

"Thousands shouted his praises," the poster said of Gantry, "but women damned his soul." Or did he damn his own soul? Audiences didn't seem to ask such questions. They took him as they found him. He was like a raw nerve, a man with so much adrenalin he looked as if he could harness the whole nation's electrical supply.

Religious groups were outraged by the story of a man who sold religion like a snake oil salesman but the Legion of Decency, to the surprise of everyone, took it in its stride. Was this because the focus was on another religious faction? "As a portrait of Protestant vice and venality," Lancaster's biographer Kate Buford wrote in *Burt Lancaster: An American Life,* "the film seemed a justification of the Catholic Church's vigilance, through the Code, as guardians of American morality. Worldly, carnal, passionate and dangerous, Gantry personified the American religious alter ego." (Or should that be "altar" ego?) She concluded that the film told us, "There, but for the Catholic church, went the nation."[12]

There were many letters of complaint about the film. One went: "Make a sequel about a Roman Catholic priest who is a louse. I'll even write it from my own experience. We'll call him Father O'Reilly or Father Mozzarelli or Father Foulzanski. We'll get Bing Crosby for the role of the priest. We can even get him to sing a song or two. 140 million non-Catholics will see it."[13] A businessman from Indianapolis suggested Brooks make a film dealing with "the connection between the Roman Catholic church and Senator McCarthy."[14]

Brooks saw his film as a portrait of the "vulgar, slickly charming, huckster soul of America in love with success because it is the mark of the elect. Flaunt yourself, your body, sell your God-fearing soul. Lure attention to yourself because that is all you have in this big lonely land with no past. In that transaction is the glamorous, corrupt heart of the circus, vaudeville, the movies, commerce, the politics of democracy, religion."[15]

The Legion's main objection to it was the final line where a reporter played by Arthur Kennedy says to Gantry, "See you around, brother." Gantry replies, "See you in Hell." Lancaster was furious when the line had to be excised as he felt it encapsulated the evangelist's frustration at everything he'd been through. The Legion also insisted on a pre-credits disclaimer: "The conduct of some revivalists makes a mockery of the traditional beliefs and practices of organized Christianity."[16]

Like all such disclaimers — one remembers particularly the epilogue to *Duel in the Sun*—this had the effect of distancing audiences from what they were about to see, which diluted the passion Gantry had in spades. It was like a contradiction in terms, showing something and almost in the same breath telling you not to accept it. But for Lancaster it was half a loaf. He also knew such *sang froid* went with the territory. All he could hope was that audiences would trust the tale, not the teller. They did. He received an Oscar for his all-stops-out performance.

Stanley Kubrick's *Spartacus*, also 1960, was a powerful story of a slave leader (Kirk Douglas) rebelling against the mighty Roman Empire before the birth of Christ. The Legion of Decency made Kubrick cut much of the violence but he was allowed to keep some in due to what we might call the "Cecil B De Mille clause." In other words, because he was operating on a Biblical tapestry, different rules applied. Other Legion of Decency members were indignant about the fact that Dalton Trumbo — one of the "Hollywood Ten" screenwriters blacklisted by the McCarthy witch-hunt for Communist allegiances — had contributed to the script.

Trumbo had been working under a pseudonym, Robert Rich, since the ban was imposed on him, but for this film (and, incidentally, Otto Preminger's *Exodus*) he was allowed to use his real name. Not surprisingly, when his identity was uncovered, the Legion started to read Marxist manifestos into the story. One consulter complained that all the slaves in the film were well-bred and utterly wonderful people, while all the Roman characters were ruthless, greedy and sick.

A scene deleted from the film for over thirty years involved Laurence Olivier (as Crassus) revealing a pronounced homosexual interest in Tony Curtis (as Antoninus) during a bathing encounter. Olivier asks Curtis if he likes oysters or snails, which is his coded overture to what his sexual preferences were. Olivier says he likes both and the scene ends there. It's heavily laden with innuendo and Kubrick wasn't surprised when he had to take it out. (I once asked Curtis if Olivier, who was rumored to be bisexual, had come on to him for real on the set of the movie. "No," he replied jocosely. "As far as I was concerned he just liked oysters, not snails!")

Maybe the changing times were most evinced by the fact that the film that won Best Picture of 1960, plus Best Story, Best Screenplay and Best Director, was one which centered on illicit sex. *The Apartment,* as mentioned, was couched in a seedy format, Jack Lemmon lending his dwelling out to his corporate bosses for trysts. One of these involves the woman he loves (Shirley MacLaine), who attempts suicide when Lemmon's immediate employer (Fred MacMurray) refuses to leave his wife for her.

Lemmon and MacLaine were also nominated for Oscars. Billy Wilder was supreme behind the camera too but what was most interesting was that a film which had the apartment of the title doubling as a bordello could win so many awards. No matter how brilliantly it was directed, in a previous era this would have been strictly off-limits, even allowing for the fact that it's really a love story at base.

It qualified for an A3 rating, probably because Lemmon finally flies the flag for love over careerism, but the foregoing scenes probably lingered longer in filmgoers' memories. Lemmon decides to trade in the key of the executive washroom to his two-timing boss in exchange for MacLaine's delayed affections but for most of the movie he turns a blind eye to all forms of marital duplicity.

Liz Taylor played a hooker in *Butterfield 8* in 1960 as well and won an Oscar for her troubles. Alexander Walker wrote, "The Hollywood Prostitute is the favorite playgirl of film censors. She bears little resemblance to the prostitute found in other cities of the world. She is the creation of movie morality. Traditionally she is depicted with a heart of gold. And this is not her only organ which has been adapted for the screen's peculiar morality.... She must never be shown as actually willing and able to sell her body for money: the transaction should be sentimental rather than commercial and yet must not be made enjoyable."[17]

Taylor fits the bill here because she's looking for love. "The censors might have been anxious at her persistence in seeking this quality in motel rooms instead of in marriage."[18] She dies remorsefully in a car crash. Maybe it was her penitence that won her over to the people dispensing the Oscars that year.

MacLaine deserved one much more for her amiably wry turn in *The Apartment* but she didn't die, or show too much remorse over her fling with the married MacMurray. One of Taylor's lines in *Butterfield 8* was "Mamma, I was the slut of all time." She felt the script was pornographic and confined to friends, "It stinks."[19]

The film was unutterably bland. *The Apartment*, on the contrary, had much more bite but was more subtle on the sex front. MacLaine may have suffered on this score, having frequently played "tarts with hearts" before. She once confessed, "I've played so many hookers they don't pay me in the regular way any more. They leave it on the dresser."[20]

Off-screen events perhaps contributed to the Academy's eventual decision, Taylor having a throat problem that almost killed her after the film wrapped. An emergency tracheotomy saved her life. Taylor appeared at the Oscar ceremonies proudly displaying her tracheotomy scar and waltzed home with the award. MacLaine hadn't even bothered to attend as everyone in the industry seemed to suspect that Taylor would get the sympathy vote.

Sex was becoming more cuddly than dangerous in films at this point. It wasn't so much the elephant in the room any more as the unspoken theme of treacly vehicles like *Pillow Talk*. Marilyn Monroe was even winding down, her performance in *The Seven Year Itch* and suchlike making sex seem homely, almost like Mom's apple pie. Murray Schumach groaned, "What was violent controversy in the days of Clara Bow became innocent merriment with Monroe."[21]

Not everyone viewed the situation like this. Geoffrey Shurlock visited Monroe on the set of the provocatively titled *Let's Make Love* expecting the worst. "So you're Shurlock," she cooed upon seeing him, informing him that it was the first time she'd ever met a censor.[22] The breed hardly fazed her. She liked to say, "The trouble with censors is that they worry if a girl has cleavage. They ought to worry if she doesn't have any!"[23]

He was unhappy with a scene where she was rolling round a bed with Yves Montand because he said it suggested she was preparing for what he called "the sex act." His problem was that her position in the scene was horizontal. Monroe informed him that one could have sex in the vertical position as well. He had no answer for that.

So once again sex was the enemy, especially sex as Monroe presented it, which was like an activity quite removed from any ethical considerations, but still not sleazy. Such a mix couldn't work for the likes of Shurlock, or indeed his British counterparts.

It's interesting that a scene in *The Entertainer* was passed by the censor in Britain in the same year because the male character in the scene, played by Laurence Olivier, "had obviously been making love mechanically, and without any pleasure."[24]

The most talked-about film of that year, though, was Alfred Hitchcock's *Psycho*. Today its handling of schizophrenia looks decidedly ropey but few could challenge Hitchcock's ability to create almost unbearable tension. He knew he was on to a good thing with his explosive plotline, so much so that he issued a directive to cinemas that nobody was to be allowed in after the film started.

Some worthies claimed to have predicted the surprise ending but one suspects their prescience came with 20/20 hindsight because the split personality of Norman Bates (Anthony Perkins) was pioneering territory for 1960. Hitchcock also cleverly diverted our attention from Bates by pretending to give us a tale of infidelity and larceny, as personified by the character of Marion Crane (Janet Leigh).

At the beginning of the film, Crane is having a lunchtime romp with a married man (John Gavin). She subsequently steals money to help him pay for his divorce so she's both adulterous and a thief to boot. When she meets the meek and mild motel-keeper Bates, who's so obviously under the thumb of his screeching mother, there are no prizes for guessing where the audience's sympathies are going to lie.

But now the film shifts gear. Crane has a change of heart, ironically as a result of her conversation with Bates. She decides to give back the money she's stolen. At roughly the same point we see Bates peeping at her as she undresses for a shower, and becoming sexually aroused. Not long afterwards Bates, dressed up as his mother, stabs her to death in the film's most celebrated scene.

A nation, allegedly, was terrified of taking showers for years afterwards — just as a future generation would fear going for a swim after Steven Spielberg's *Jaws*. From the Legion of Decency's point of view, the $64 question was whether there was actual nudity involved. (Most other viewers were probably too scared to notice.)

A double stood in for Leigh during the scene and though she was indeed nude, Hitchcock used so many editorial jump-cuts it was impossible for those guardians of purity to see any naked flesh. One would have had to view the film in slow-motion for that to have occurred.

We never see Bates' knife touch his victim's flesh. Hitchcock also shot the film in black and white to avoid a splurge of blood, which would have infuriated both Hays and the Legion of Decency. Hitchcock liked to joke that blood always looked more realistic in black and white. He also exclaimed, "Blood is jolly!"[25]

Janet Leigh simulating her shower scene scream in *Psycho* (1960) before Anthony Perkins emphasizes the importance of first checking things out with Mother.

"I do not like to see blood in life or on the screen," Hitchcock insisted. "I made *Psycho* in black and white because I knew I didn't want to show all of that red blood in the white bathroom."[26] Taken to task over the violence, he said he thought film violence only had an influence on sick minds, not healthy ones.

After the film was released, a man was arrested in Los Angeles for murdering three women. He said he was inspired to murder the third woman after seeing the film. Hitchcock justifiably inquired what film had he seen before murdering the second woman, or the first.

When the censors first saw the shower scene, they were divided about whether it actually contained nudity or not, except for a final aerial shot of Leigh, or rather her stand-in, sprawled over the bathtub after Perkins (who also used a double) has finished with her. Hitchcock knew this would have to go but he drove a hard bargain for the rest of the scene in a manner Mae West would have been proud of.

Of the five censors who saw the first cut — no pun intended — three claimed they saw nudity while the other two didn't. On the second viewing all five of them changed their mind: the three who had seen the nudity didn't see it now, where the two who didn't now did. Hitchcock must have been chuckling at his ingenuity to provoke such consternation. We're almost into voyeurism here if the exposure was this flimsy.

Danny Peary thought Hitchcock may have been making a mischievous analogy between Bates' knife in the shower and the "mad censor who wanted to cut out all the nudity in his picture."[28]

In the end the Legion didn't condemn *Psycho* but they gave it a B certificate, which signified that it was "morally objectionable in part for all," a very Jesuitical phrase. The bottom line was that it was out there in the public domain, Hitchcock being wilier than Norman Bates at avoiding "detection" for his "murder" of Ms. Crane.

Leigh afterwards revealed that Hitch planned things all along to manipulate the censors, putting things in the film that were so bizarre, he could come back to them and say he would agree to their demands if they agreed to his. In most of his movies he deliberately inserted questionable shots in first drafts, knowing full well they would be unacceptable, but with each disallowed one he gained leverage in his bargaining for the ones he'd really wanted all along.

The removal of the final aerial shot was his olive branch. He sacrificed it, poignant and all as it was, to keep the masterly editing of the slashing itself, counterpointed by the music score where each piercing note corresponds to an equally piercing incision in the hapless Marion Crane's body. After the film was released, he got a letter from a woman saying that since her daughter had seen the movie, she pointedly refused to have a shower, so what should she do. "Have her dry-cleaned," Hitchcock replied with his usual deadpan humor. The Irish censor Liam O'Hora banned it, claiming it was "horrific in the most sadistic manner."[29] Perhaps it was, but it was also fascinatingly innovative.

Thomas Doherty believed that *Psycho* is where the Code fell apart. "The notorious montage of murder in the bathroom of the Bates motel," he wrote in *Pre-Code Hollywood*, "is the scene of the crime, the place where Joseph Breen's moral universe went swirling down the drain." After this, it was "walking dead."[30] The contentious films that followed (*Lolita, Kiss Me, Stupid, Dr. Strangelove, The Pawnbroker,* etc.) merely drove the nails into its coffin. The rating system that replaced it meant that Hollywood was no longer saying "Viewer, be assured" to audiences, but rather "Viewer, beware."[31]

In 1961 moviegoers finally discovered women had navels because that was the year Christine Kauffman showed hers to Kirk Douglas in *Town Without Pity*. In the same year, the Legion had a problem with *Splendor in the Grass* on the grounds that "the denial of pre-marital relations may lead to serious mental problems."[32] No doubt Warren Beatty and Natalie Wood were left scratching their heads, imagining that they were merely appearing in a lyrically made love story. The fact that it was directed by Elia Kazan no doubt brought it to the attention of the killjoys sooner than a similar film from a man with a less checkered past.

Perhaps the most surprising phenomenon of 1961 was a western, Robert Aldrich's *The Last Sunset*, which featured an incest sub-theme, something that would have been unheard of a few years previously. But then Dalton Trumbo, the screenwriter, was always a man who liked to sail close to the wind. There was a suggestion of incest in the relationship between Natalie Wood and her father in *Rebel Without a Cause* six years previously but here the bond between Kirk Douglas and Carol Lynley was much more pointed, and in the last genre one would have expected it.

Alan Bates was mistaken for Jesus in *Whistle Down the Wind* in 1962 but the film raised nary a whimper with censors, unlike *The Miracle* a decade before. Then, as now, sex proved to be the most consistent moneyspinner. Warner Brothers paid $200,000 for the rights to Helen Gurley Brown's book *Sex and the Single Girl* but only used the title, employing a string of writers to think up a plausible story to be built around it.[33]

4. The Liberal Ethos

Lolita also came out in 1962. Director Stanley Kubrick again ran into trouble with the Legion of Decency with his adaptation of the highly-charged Vladimir Nabokov novel, which in some people's minds tried to rationalize (or even romanticize) pedophilia. (Similar charges were leveled against the 1997 remake with Jeremy Irons and Dominique Swain. As one might have expected, the latter was exponentially more graphic.)

Written in 1954, the book had done the rounds of publishers without much luck. Simon & Schuster rejected it after Mrs. Schuster informed her husband in no uncertain terms, "I won't have my name on that dirty book!"[34] The following year a frustrated Nabokov submitted it to a Parisian publishing firm called the Olympia Press, which had a history of hardcore porn on its lists. This pained Nabokov deeply but he saw nowhere else to turn. He was an old-fashioned man who was light-years away from any sexual aberration in his own life, having been married to the same woman for nearly forty years. The most exciting thing he got up to was "classifying butterflies."[35] In 1958 an American publisher, G.P. Putnam, brought it out in the U.S. but the *New York Times* dismissed it as "repulsive."[36]

Many studios shied away from *Lolita,* including Columbia, United Artists and Warner Brothers, fearing the film wouldn't get a Seal and be condemned by the Legion. Kubrick sensed the danger and capitulated on many fronts. But he stoutly refused to remove the central thread of pedophilia which was the film's *raison d'être.*

Tuesday Weld was the first choice for the precocious temptress. "I didn't have to play it," she huffed, "I *was* Lolita."[37] But Kubrick was looking for a younger star and eventually settled on the unknown Sue Lyon, who looked much older than her 14 years even if she didn't exude as much obvious oomph as the gorgeous Ms. Weld.

Shurlock told Kubrick that *Lolita* was unfilmable as per Nabokov's text, featuring as it did a sexual tryst between a married man and a girl young enough to be his daughter. Kubrick thought that if they were married in a state that allowed 14-year-old girls to go to the altar it might work. Shurlock agreed, though this possibility wasn't developed.

James Mason was chosen to play the tortured Humbert Humbert and the cameras rolled as the purity squad sharpened their scissors. One of the first lines to go was Lyon's description of her sweater as being made of "virgin" wool, which drew the response from Mason, "The only thing about you that is, kiddo." A subsequent one about her needing to have "a cavity filled" was allowed only when it was emphasized that she needed her teeth capped."[38]

The film opened to open hostility from the public, some viewers seeing Lyon as a real-life love-slave to Kubrick. (One misguided soul believed she had actually been sold to him by her parents.) There were so many cuts in the final version that the *New York Times* critic answered the movie's own tagline "How Did They Ever Make a Movie of *Lolita?*" with a blunt "They didn't."[39] Kubrick afterwards described the Production Code as "the loose suspenders that hold up the baggy pants of the circus clown. It allows the pants to slip dangerously, but never to fall."[40]

It was eventually released with an "Adults Only" rating from the Legion of Decency. The fact that it was passed by this organization at all, with any kind of caveat, was of course a huge leap. (A decade before, it would surely have been banned.) The laxity came not so much from liberal thinking as the knowledge that it would have seen the light of day anyway, with or without its blessing. The Legion's involvement with that "anti–Christ" Kubrick was nothing more than damage limitation. They knew they couldn't totally extinguish the fire so they merely tried to douse it. Put another way, it was better to have him inside the ecclesiastical tent peeing out than outside peeing in.

Kubrick wasn't happy with the finished product, complaining, "It wasn't possible to portray Humbert Humbert's obsession on the screen with all the eroticism suggested in Nabokov's novel."[41] He saw off an obvious onslaught from the censors by raising the age of his main character from 12 (which she'd been in the book) to 14. This decision, in one critic's view, made Humbert "less a child molester than a doomed romantic."[42]

According to *Variety*, moralists could rest easy because *Lolita* was like "a bee from which the stinger has been removed."[43] *Time* magazine wrote, "Wind up the Lolita doll and it goes to Hollywood and commits nymphanticide."[44] This was both a trivialization of the plot and a dire misreading of its intent. Lyon wasn't allowed to see the film herself, being three years short of the "Over 18s" classification to secure entry.

Britain introduced a homosexual theme into many films at this time, the most prominent being *Victim* (1961) with Dirk Bogarde. He was brave to take the role considering he was gay in real life as well, though this wasn't picked up on by the media. (It would have been in today's more intrusive era.) He told Barry Norman in *The Times* that *Victim* was the first film to treat homosexuality seriously. It was also the first film in which a man said "I love you" to another man. Sadly for Bogarde himself, this phenomenon also coincided with him losing his heart-throb status among the young women who'd flocked to his films heretofore. But it was a price he was willing to pay.

Up until now, being gay was the love that dared not speak its name. In *Rebel Without a Cause* (1955) Sal Mineo displayed a pronounced affection for James Dean — and a picture of Alan Ladd (rather than Betty Grable) in his locker. Such thinly-disguised homosexuality netted Mineo the inevitable fate of an early death.

Gay filmmaker Marion Riggs alleged, "The charge of being too graphic offered the perfect pretext for silencing a disenfranchised minority's attempt to end its subjugation and challenge the cultural terms of the majority's social control."[45] So the "straight" moguls continued to reign.

Whenever the censors encountered what they referred to as "a pansy flavor" in a script, they reached for a scalpel. That's why Paul Newman's "weakness" in *Cat on a Hot Tin Roof* (1958) had to be transmuted into impotence. As for Mineo and Dean in the aforementioned *Rebel Without a Cause*, the Hays Office forced director Nicholas Ray to "tone down the script's erotic element," Geoffrey Shurlock penning a memo to Jack Warner reminding him that there was to be "no inference of a questionable or homosexual relationship" between the pair.[46] The general fate of movie homosexuals at this time was to be relegated to "mincing, effeminate sissies in comedies" or as "murder and suicide victims in dramas."[47]

Screenwriter Gore Vidal wanted to introduce a homosexual element into the relationship between Charlton Heston and Stephen Boyd in *Ben-Hur* (1959) but director William Wyler knocked the idea on the head, feeling it was unnecessary and also that it would drive Heston wild if he was told about it. Vidal felt the film was screaming out for it. He thought it was evident in Boyd's every expression even if Heston was in denial about this.

Christopher Fry, another screenwriter on the film, delivered a script that made no reference to homosexuality. This was the one that made its way onto the screen. Vidal felt Heston somehow strong-armed Wyler into favoring this script over his own one. After Heston published his memoirs, I met him and asked him for his view on the matter. "They're putting homosexuality into things nowadays for reasons that are beyond me," he said. "It seems modish. But it wouldn't have worked in *Ben-Hur*. If that view makes me sound old-fashioned, so be it. It was a great story of a broken bond and you don't need any subtext to bolster it up."

The following year, a more overt exchange between Laurence Olivier and Tony Curtis manifested itself in *Spartacus*, as already mentioned, the scene in question having to be excised from the final cut, much to Stanley Kubrick's annoyance. The bottom line was that neither film was intrinsically "about" this theme so the scenes were expendable. Also, the price that could have been exacted at the box office if the censors were defied would have been too high considering both films' lavish budgets.

But by 1960 there were two films about Oscar Wilde in general release, *Oscar Wilde* and *The Trials of Oscar Wilde*, so it wasn't only Dirk Bogarde who was "coming out." Michael Hordern found Bogarde heavy going as an actor and put some of that difficulty down to his life in the gay closet: "I've read that Bogarde's cruel streak can be attributed to his fight for acceptance as an actor, as a homosexual man, and as a writer," he droned, "and all the time I thought it was just because he's quite an unpleasant fellow!"[48]

In *A Taste of Honey* (1961), Rita Tushingham is helped through her pregnancy by a homosexual friend but this is just a subtheme of the film so it didn't get the attention it deserved. Roman Polanski's *Knife in the Water* was passed without cuts in Ireland in 1962 despite having strong homosexual overtones. The reason? "It was argued that homosexuality was quite unknown to the Irish and what they didn't understand couldn't harm them."[49] (Had the censor not heard of Oscar Wilde?)

The Children's Hour (1961) had a good Broadway run in the years 1934 and 1935 but when it was filmed by William Wyler in 1936 the lesbianism theme couldn't get past the censors, causing Wyler to comment, "Miss Hellman's play has not yet been filmed."[50] In the sixties version, the word "lesbian" is never used, though the plot kicks off when a pampered child makes up a story about having seen two female teachers embracing. The advance publicity for *The Children's Hour* prepared one for the creepy treatment of its lesbian theme: "Did nature play an ugly trick and endow them with emotions contrary to those of normal young women?" But maybe this is the only way it would have been permitted.

A similar bowdlerization appeared the same year in *A Walk on the Wild Side*. Here Capucine runs a brothel. Or does she? It hardly looks like one or the PCA wouldn't have passed the film. Its identification is so tentative, Alexander Walker observed, that Laurence Harvey, as Capucine's ex-beau, "imagines she is housed in some kind of YWCA hostel, in spite of the girls who drift around in lacy nighties in mid-afternoon."[51] Clearly, in instances like this the cosmetic superstructure applied to lewd *mises-en-scenes* bordered on the comical.

Audrey Hepburn was a teacher accused of lesbianism in *The Children's Hour*. She fared somewhat better as a happy hooker in *Breakfast at Tiffany's* (1961). This was a watered-down version of Truman Capote's novel. He wanted his friend Marilyn Monroe to play the flighty heroine but when Hepburn landed the gig, the die was cast: It was going to be cleaned up beyond recognition. Capote "adored" Hepburn but knew she was miscast. He exclaimed, "She's no hillbilly!"[52] Orson Welles described her as "the patron saint of the anorexics."[53]

"Titism has taken over the country," Billy Wilder offered in consolation. "Audrey single-handedly may make bazooms a thing of the past. The director won't have to invent shots where the girl leans forward for a glass of Scotch and soda.[54]

Sanctuary was released in 1961 as well. Based on William Faulkner's novel of the same name, it had already been filmed as *The Story of Temple Drake* (1933), a film which gave the censors many problems as Miriam Hopkins cavorted about as a flapper playgirl. A problematic rape scene was allowed to stay in by having the lights go out as a scream is heard.

There were two versions of the 1961 version released by 20th Century–Fox. The U.S. one had a rather tame love scene between Lee Remick and Yves Montand. In the foreign one Ms. Remick wore less clothing, which gave Montand more flexibility in courting her. Continental temperaments had always been more lusty. The censors seemed to accept this if not to overtly cater for it. Whatever, blind eyes were turned more often than not.

The Italian sex comedy *Boccaccio 70* (1962) proved to be another irritant for the censors. A collaborative effort co-directed by such luminaries as Luchino Visconti, Federico Fellini and Vittoria de Sica, it was never going to be the film for which any of these men would be remembered. Nonetheless, its significance in a shifting of the moral compass of the time was immense. The Fellini segment, "The Temptation of Dr. Antonio," features Anita Ekberg. No longer dancing around a fountain as she was in *La Dolce Vita*, Ekberg now adorns a huge billboard encouraging the public to drink more milk. The problem is that the milk is coming from her breasts. Later in the movie the billboard comes to life and a huge Ekberg becomes a dream fantasy of the eponymous doctor, who's been campaigning for its removal on moral grounds.

The second segment, directed by Visconti, centers on a woman (Romy Schneider) who decides to charge her husband for sex after she discovers he's been frequenting a brothel. This leads us into De Sica's final one which has Sophia Loren as a carnival sex object who falls for a church sexton.

All in all it was a heady brew, partly generated to settle old scores with censors than to create high art. Doing good business without a PCA seal, it was condemned by the Legion without any adverse effects at the box office.

Catholics were now making up their own minds about what they wanted to see so the ecclesiastical system of checks and balances was effectively on its last legs from both commercial and ethical perspectives.

Amazingly, the Legion passed Tony Richardson's *Tom Jones* (1963) despite its bawdiness, one scene having Albert Finney being seduced by a woman who could actually have been his mother. Was the world becoming more tolerant? There was no pattern in censorial decisions any more, it seemed, and apparently few enough filmgoers worried about the eunuchs in the movie harem.

In 1963, Shropshire art teacher Mary Whitehouse became alarmed when she found some of her pupils "apparently faking sexual intercourse."[55] When she asked them what they were doing, they replied that they were copying Christine Keeler and Mandy Rice-Davies, the women embroiled in a vice scandal involving government minister John Profumo. The following year, on May 5, Whitehouse booked a hall in Birmingham and called a public meeting. Over 200 people attended from all over Britain and launched the "Clean Up TV" campaign, which then morphed into the National Viewers and Listeners Association.

Whitehouse, whose name somehow seemed apt, went on to become the conscience of sexual liberals with declarations like "If they didn't show it on the screen, most people would never know about oral sex."[56] She even demanded a post-watershed slot for the children's TV show *Doctor Who* on the grounds that it offered "tea-time brutality for tots."[57]

The U.S., like Britain, seemed to be comprised of a radically divergent set of citizens, some clamoring for more latitude in what could and should be shown both on the "big" screen and the "boob tube" at home and others desperately clinging to the solemn (and sometimes straitjacketed) values of yesteryear.

The stars themselves were often confused too. Many of them didn't reprise their directors' liberalism, or agree with an "Open Sesame" policy for viewers. Sometimes the stars even had different opinions of the characters they played to those displayed by audiences. Marlon Brando, for instance, always professed a thorough distaste for Stanley Kowalski in *A Streetcar Named Desire* (1951), perhaps due to the fact that many people afterwards identified him with Kowalski, expecting him to behave piggishly in public. Brando liked to oblige in this regard, though often with the motive of shocking rather than any other reason.

Actually what he objected to most in Kowalski wasn't his thuggish behavior but his arrogance. In his autobiography he explained that he himself was the antithesis of Kowalski: "I was sensitive and he was coarse, a man with unerring animal instincts."[58] Brando always feared the synonymization of himself with Kowalski that went on in press circles, leading to the unwanted sobriquet of "Slob" that followed this supremely cultured man wherever he went. But then Hollywood has always thrived on stereotypes. Its image of this man was copperfastened by Brando's rebellious behavior offscreen. He could never quite live down Kowalski no matter how many refined parts he essayed in the years afterwards.

When Paul Newman played *Hud,* he expected audiences to regard him as a love rat. Let's not forget that this character's typical sexual overture was "What time does your husband come home?"—a novel chat-up line for a Hollywood hero. But such was Newman's charisma that women drooled over the guy with, as the billboards proclaimed, "the barbed wire soul." Newman objected to this. He didn't try to portray Hud with any attractiveness. Perhaps that's why his sexual charisma oozed off the screen—because it wasn't forced.

As if to add insult to injury, even the censors seemed to be losing their convictions, and sounding off in skittish vein about films they were expected to be shocked by. John Trevelyan, the British censor who was something of a freethinker, famously remarked of his trade, "We're paid to have dirty minds."[59] Going against this very edict, he refused to act as a moral watchdog without qualification. The British Board of Film Censors, he believed, couldn't assume responsibility for the guardianship of morality. It couldn't refuse for exhibition to adults, films that showed behavior which contravened the accepted moral code. Neither could he refuse to pass films that criticized the establishment and/or expressed minority opinions.

Another ethical bugbear was the irregular marital status of some stars. After Sophia Loren became involved with Carlo Ponti, who was already married, the Italian Men's Catholic Action Organization demanded that all Catholics boycott her films. (She exhorted them to pray for her soul instead.) One magazine suggested that if she'd been living in the Middle Ages she'd have been burned at the stake.

Loren met Ponti when she was fifteen and started living with him four years later. He was twenty-two years older than her and already married. He divorced his wife in Mexico but this wasn't recognized in Italy so the Vatican deemed him to be bigamous when he went down the aisle with her. (Her mother's advice to her was "Wait around for him and you'll wind up as an old maid lighting candles.")

For church folk, sex always seemed to be the major (if not the only) sin stars could commit, but it was becoming out of step with the flighty purveyors of free love. And then *Playboy* arrived. And the pill...

Scottish psychiatrist G.M. Carstairs said on BBC2 in 1962 that in the eyes of Christ, the cardinal virtue was charity, not chastity. "It was his intemperate disciple Paul," he argued, "who introduced the concept of celibacy as an essential part of Christian teaching. Centuries later it was the reformed libertine St. Augustine who placed such exaggerated emphasis upon the sinfulness of sex. It has always been those whose own sexual impulses have been precariously repressed who have raised the loudest cries of alarm over people's immorality."[60] A rare oasis of sanity.

The Hays Code was finally undone by a brace of New Wave directors who modeled themselves on the *nouvelle vague* movement prevalent in Europe. A fresh wind was blowing through celluloid and these movie brats — the Coppolas, the Altmans and the Arthur Penns — picked up the slack, turning their backs on the studio system that had created the superstars of yore in favor of movies that would stand in their own right with or without an iconic personality to parlay their virtues.

In 1964, however, nude scenes were still cut from films like *The Sandpiper* and *The Carpetbaggers*. The following year, the same fate befell *The Cincinnati Kid*. Though the cuts were agreed to, they were performed with anger from the directors and a certain amount of sympathy from filmgoers, even Catholic ones.

The wall of censorship was being attacked from all comers but it hadn't yet crumbled. Nonetheless, the number (and degree) of excisions that were being made suggested the frustration was at boiling point. Sooner or later the excrement was going to hit the ventilator and when it did a deluge of formerly forbidden footage was going to seep through. Even Geoffrey Shurlock seemed to twig this, though he didn't admit it, perhaps even to himself.

The world and his wife hit Billy Wilder's *Kiss Me, Stupid* over the head in 1964. This was a naughty, but hardly debauched, farce about a musical aspirant (Ray Walston) pretending to willing to let his wife sleep with a famous singer (Dean Martin) in order to secure a recording contract for himself. Considering the number of *double entendres* flying about the place, it was hardly surprising it would run into trouble with Father Thomas Little, the executive secretary of the Legion, who was dispatched to veto it.

Kim Novak appeared as the hooker whom Walston tries to substitute for his wife. Father Little had problems with her *decolletage*, as well as most other things about the film. One line he insisted Wilder remove was when Felicia

4. The Liberal Ethos 133

Farr (playing Mrs. Walston) says, "Who ever heard of a groom playing the organ at his own wedding?" Wilder couldn't (or pretended not to) get the innuendo but Father Little was adamant. He felt the film condoned wife-swapping and also that the script was laced with thinly-disguised sophomorish filth. Wilder argued that it was merely intended to be a comedy.

Kiss Me, Stupid, the film in which the censors finally caught up with Billy Wilder in 1962. Pictured here are Kim Novak, Ray Walston and Dean Martin (Marilyn Monroe and Peter Sellers had originally been slated to appear).

The fact that he set it in a town called Climax, however, let us know in no uncertain terms what *kind* of comedy it was intended to be.

Shurlock, amazingly enough, gave it a Seal, though not without hissing, "If dogs want to return to their vomit, I'm not going to stop them."[61] One wonders if he would have found it less offensive if Marilyn Monroe had been in the lead. She was originally slated for the part but died in the interim.

As far as the Legion was concerned, Shurlock's decision to grant a Seal to the film appeared to be "yet another instance of his capitulation to the rising tide of permissiveness."[62] And there were other factors bothering Legion members. They were particularly perturbed by a scene where Martin importuned Novak to go into a garden with him with the suggestive line: "She can show me her parsley." An indignant Wilder suggested changing parsley to broccoli to satisfy them but they wanted the scene re-shot. Wilder couldn't organize this as Novak was filming in Britain.

Kiss Me, Stupid was subsequently given a Condemned rating, which meant that this hilarious film never got the audiences it deserved. It was as if the Legion was getting its revenge on Wilder for the way *The Apartment* somehow flew under its radar.

Apart from these two movies, Wilder had also dirtied his bib with *Some Like It Hot* and the infinitely more inflammatory *Irma La Douce* (1963), a protracted bore starring Shirley MacLaine as a prostitute (again!) and Jack Lemmon as a *gendarme* ostensibly trying to protect her but really more interested in keeping her for himself. In a sense, both of them were reprising their roles from *The Apartment*, but in a much saucier context. With each new outing, Wilder seemed to be sailing closer to the wind. With *Kiss Me, Stupid*, his past finally caught up with him.

The film Novak was filming in Britain was *The Amorous Adventures of Moll Flanders*, a raunchy romp that convinced her critics that her already tarnished soul was incontrovertibly beyond salvation. The U.S. censor asked for no less than fifty cuts, mainly due to Ms. Novak's mammarial assets. In this sense, she was like the new Jane Russell.

Looked at today, it's a lot funnier than it was given credit for, even if Novak was no Marilyn Monroe. If Monroe lived, she could have been hilarious in this role. Coincidentally, she overdosed during the making of another Dean Martin movie, the uncompleted (and, for her, aptly-titled) *Something's Got to Give*. She was sacked from this production for repeated lateness and absenteeism.

Similarly, if Peter Sellers hadn't had one of his many heart attacks during the first few weeks of shooting *Kiss Me, Stupid*, he would have been in the finished cut — he was Wilder's first choice over Walston — and it would have been a different film. Which is no disrespect to Walston, but as far as this kind of screwball comedy is concerned, Sellers was head and shoulders over everyone else. Wilder knew that too.

Because audiences weren't laughing, they were more inclined to detect smut. So was the establishment. The film's condemnation by the Legion of Decency was the first of its kind since Elia Kazan's *Baby Doll* in 1954, a dubious distinction that seems to be the thing most people remember about it today, which is a pity.

As the sixties went on, the power of the Legion of Decency steadily eroded, both due to changing social attitudes to sex and religion and also the rise of a barrage of independent filmmakers who found ways of distributing their works without the formerly coveted Seals. Martin Quigley also died that year, his passing seeming to symbolize the end of an era. Peter Biskind summed it up: "The changes in sexual mores, along with the softening of the blacklist, the virtual dismantling of the Production Code and above all the fast-growing disenchantment with the Vietnam war, created climates increasingly conducive to the production of films so critical of American institutions they would have been unimaginable in the fifties."[63]

Vociferous campaigns against controversial movies met with only limited success as the winds of liberalism blew through the new decade. Rules formerly set in stone were relaxed and a new rating was introduced. An X rating traditionally meant only Over-18s could attend a particular film. Now an R rating also came into play, allowing those under that age to see X-rated movies provided they were accompanied by an adult.

The Hays directives drowned in the swirling tides of permissiveness. Young people had disposable income, and views their forbears would hardly have vouchsafed them. Authority was dying and sex a matter of preference rather than ethical directives. In 1964 Gore Vidal, who had suggested homosexuality in the screenplay he contributed to *Ben-Hur,* as we saw, used the word itself in the screen adaptation of his own play *The Best Man*. A year later John Schlesinger introduced bisexuality in *Darling,* the film in which Julie Christie tells Dirk Bogarde, "Your idea of fidelity is having just one girl in bed with you."

But some diehards refused to go away. By the end of that year, Breen had made such a blitz on the movie industry that of the 270 films the Legion vetted, only 42 were passed as suitable family viewing. This was the lowest tally in thirty years, signaling the fact that directors were either fed up of being snipped or Breen's tolerance threshold was on the wane. Maybe both.

Geoffrey Shurlock cast a wider net. He passed the James Bond adventure *Goldfinger* in 1965 despite its apparent endorsement of frolics in the boudoir on the part of its central sleuth. In an early scene, Sean Connery is in bed with one of his conquests when he's summoned to the phone by his boss. He says, "I can't talk now because something big has just come up." The fact that Shurlock was willing to allow crude innuendos like this, which seem to belong more to *Carry On* films than espionage yarns, suggests that he was more threatened by intellectual sex scenes than juvenile snuff.

By this point of his career, Shurlock seemed to be losing his marbles, possibly as a result of seeing too many sexually suggestive features. "It's only a little fucking," he said to fellow censor Jack Vizzard after watching the Bond movie, "What's all the shouting about? My God, what do women think they are, that to give them a little of what-comes-naturally brings the sky down on everybody's heads, like something out of Chicken Little? The deification of the female waterworks is too much."[64] He had become so lax that he allowed one of Bond's playmates, played by Honor Blackman, was allowed to be called Pussy Galore.

In 1965, Pope John XXIII banished liturgical cobwebs by offering the laity more power, more responsibility and more respect. If the church was indeed the people, this ceded ground away from church leaders in deciding what was "good" for the public.

"The Bishops," in one writer's view, "were not foolish old men. By the middle of the sixties they clearly recognized that the Legion had a negative image among Catholics and the movie-going public."[65] Soon afterwards it changed its name to the National Catholic Office for Motion Pictures (NCOMP). This seemed to be little more than a tokenistic sop to modernity that only copperfastened its waning influence. It was, in essence, a busted flush.

In Sidney Lumet's *The Pawnbroker* (1964), Rod Steiger emphasized this, playing an irascible Jew haunted by memories of a Nazi concentration camp where his wife was tortured. In a pivotal scene, a black hooker strips to get Steiger to pay more for the product she's hocking. This causes him to remember his naked wife being sexually assaulted by the Nazis.

Father Little viewed the scene with some concern. He realized the nudity, which sends the reclusive Steiger into a tailspin of angst during a flashback sequence, wasn't inserted for gratuitous reasons. Nonetheless, if it was passed by the Legion, he feared that the baring of breasts in movies would become "just as common as blowing your nose."[66] He felt rowing back on Legion policy would "open the floodgates to a host of unscrupulous operators out to make a quick buck."⁶⁷

Marjorie Heins remarked in her book *Sex, Sin and Blasphemy* that the Catholic Church had a history of trying to control nudity in all branches of the arts, including "painting and sculpture throughout the Middle Ages and well into the Renaissance. Under Church decrees, nudity was permitted for classical mythological themes but not for religious ones."⁶⁸

The Pawnbroker was refused a Seal but this decision was appealed to the Motion Picture Association of America, which overruled the Legion. Shurlock was instrumental in the appeal. It was a landmark decision. According to Jack Vizzard, a former Jesuit novice who worked under both Breen and Shurlock, Shurlock had lost belief in the whole credo of censorship by this time. Apparently he one day said, "We'll never have moral pictures unless producers think in terms of morals themselves. We're tired of playing nursemaid to the industry. It's keeping pictures perpetually adolescent."⁶⁹

Shurlock assured conservatives that the decision wouldn't cause chaos but many people on the inside track felt it would, for good or ill. Hard cases usually made bad laws, at least if one was prudish. The NCOMP gave the movie a "Condemned" rating, which showed how out of touch it was. Rod Steiger received an Oscar nomination; he was surprised to be beaten by Lee Marvin, cast against type in the comedy western *Cat Ballou*.

In June 1965 the bishops issued a statement saying that in and of itself, nudity wasn't immoral, and had "long been recognized as a legitimate subject in painting and sculpture." Nudity in the cinema, however, was in their view "never an artistic necessity."⁷⁰ This seems to contradict Heins' point.

The progressive Episcopal bishop James Pike praised *The Pawnbroker* as "one of the truly significant films of our time."⁷¹ Dr. Pike, remember, had put his head on the liturgical block when he championed Elia Kazan's *Baby Doll* after Cardinal Spellman had condemned it from the pulpit.

Lumet's movie, unlike Kazan's, cleaned up at the box office. Most people seemed to agree that its condemnation was "a major miscalculation by the Legion and the church. It gave critics of the church's failure to speak out against the Holocaust additional evidence of Catholic insensitivity, if not overt anti–Semitism. It also reinforced the view of critics of film censorship who cast that organization as narrow-minded."⁷² The editors of the magazine *Film Heritage* underlined that view when they opined, "If all a movie patron can see in *The Pawnbroker* is nudity, then all the censorship in the cosmos won't save him as a human being."⁷³

There was another maelstrom in 1966 when Michelangelo Antonioni's *Blow-Up* hit the screen. It was refused a Seal and was roundly castigated by church authorities but MGM released it through a subsidiary company, Premier Films, and it ended up making $7 million in its first six months. For rebellious directors, clearly this was the way to go from now on.[74] Neither were MGM unduly concerned about a Condemned rating from the NCOMP. The movie was a smash wherever it played, and not only for the elite.[75]

Just as Rossellini had tilted at a religious windmill in 1951 and Fellini at another one a decade later, now a third European was cocking a snook at convention. The common wisdom was that the film industry was being run by Jews. Maybe it was truer to say it was being dictated to by Europeans, at least as far as precedent-creating was concerned.

Antonioni's willfully *avant garde* movie was condemned by the Catholic Office because of highly-charged scenes involving Sarah Miles and David Hemmings. "The more familiar shot of Vanessa Redgrave nude to the waist," Alexander Walker noted bemusedly, "did not cause any similar concern, since she was holding her arms crossed over her breasts in that peculiar way girls seem to adopt in movies, but hardly anywhere else in real life."[76]

The censors didn't quite know what to make of Antonioni, a man who once droned, "Hollywood is like being nowhere and talking to nobody about nothing."[77] Some would accuse his films of espousing that haziness, drenched as they are in suggestion. One is reminded of Karl Kraus's "A satire which the censor is able to understand deserves to be banned."[78]

In the most talked-about scene from *Blow-Up*, Hemmings romps with the naked Jane Birkin and Gillian Hills, both of whom display pubic hair in the entanglement. Was this "art" (because it was directed by Antonioni) or smut? The debates raged. Gloria Leonard gave this view: "The difference between pornography and erotica is lighting."[79] Whether one agreed with her or not, *Blow-Up* was the first film distributed widely in the U.S. to feature full frontal female nudity.

Mike Nichols directed *Who's Afraid of Virginia Woolf?* in the same year, adapting Edward Albee's acclaimed play with great power as he gave a new term to the screen: "love-hate relationship." The highly inflammatory material would never have crept through the net in a previous era. Here it was garlanded with honors and rapturous praise. The film revived the career of Richard Burton and won Elizabeth Taylor an Oscar.

Shurlock rejected it but his decision was rescinded by the Production Code Review Board. Albee dug his heels in when Warner Brothers, who'd stumped up $500,000 for the rights, asked him to water down the script. They employed scriptwriter Ernest Lehman for the job. Lehman's last commission had been *The Sound of Music* (dubbed *The Sound of Mucus* by its male lead Christopher Plummer) so alarm bells went off in Albee's head. He had to listen to Lehman change lines like "Hump the waitress" to "Hop the waitress." Nichols was empathetic to his frustration and reminded Lehman of a Gary Cooper movie of yore where the line "He's so poor he hasn't got a pot to ... put flowers in" fooled nobody in the audience, and in fact patronized them.[80]

The Hollywood Reporter believed *Virginia Woolf* was "the straw that broke the PCA's back." Albee's original play represented "a powerful literary pedigree, and there was no way the material could be softened without turning it into an embarrassing travesty."[81]

It's a shame that we remember *Virginia Woolf* today more for the ruckus it caused with the censors than the incredible performances of its gilt-edged cast, and for its coarse language rather than the poignance behind that language as four people threw their hearts across the screen as they crawled dubiously towards pained self-knowledge.

The years 1965 and 1966 broke the PCA's back mainly because of the three classic reversals of its decisions with regard to *The Pawnbroker*, *Who's Afraid of Virginia Woolf?* and *Alfie*. Such films became sociological benchmarks in people's appraisal of the justifiability of screening nudity, verbal profanity and abortion respectively.

Alfie had Michael Caine in the title role. He played him like James Bond without the finesse, bedding women for fun and bragging about it afterwards. He was a low-rent 007, chalking up as many notches on his bedpost as opportunity allowed and then vamoosing. His speeches to camera were risible, at least to male chauvinists. He didn't give a toss about consequences.

When one of his "birds" became pregnant and had to have an abortion in a seminal scene, Shurlock was apoplectic with rage. Both he and the NCOMP condemned the film. In times past, such a ruling would have killed it at the box office but this was the "enlightened" sixties and nobody was really listening. It was eventually passed with a rating of A-IV, which stood for "morally unobjectionable for adults, with reservations," a phrase that seemed to cover itself on all fronts but in reality meant very little. We were dealing with semantics here.

Alfie divided the censors down the middle. Jack Vizzard felt the abortion scene, which ended with Alfie "peering down in stark horror at the pitiful remains of the embryo, his child, that had just been taken from his friend's wife. The shock led him to a scene in which, for the first time in his life perhaps, he exhibited feelings toward another human entity. It was a powerful therapeutic encounter and showed the fact of abortion in all its shabby reality."[82]

Vizzard thought "the very offensiveness of the sequence was its antidote," an interesting insight and a huge leap in lateral thinking from the old days.[83]. In former times such a scene, or theme, would surely have resulted in the refusal of a Seal or a Condemned rating. Here it became just another event in the cocky Cockney's irresponsible lifestyle.

Mai Zetterling directed (or rather mis-directed) the sex farce *Night Games* in 1966. Featuring scenes of homosexuality and masturbation, it was barred even from the San Francisco Film Festival, which was saying something considering this city was regarded as the gay capital of the U.S. Shirley Temple walked out of its test screening after the masturbation scene, which features a young boy relieving himself after being sexually excited by his mother. The manager of the cinema showing the film, spotting Ms. Temple walking out, played "On the Good Ship Lollipop" during the intermission. Asked for his reason, he's alleged to have replied, "She popularized my picture. Why shouldn't I give some advertising to her song?"[84]

That year also, *This Picture Is Censored* was released by Barry Mahon Productions. It featured an hour of material excised from other films, showing scenes of nudity, seduction, assault, torture and even dismemberment. Not surprisingly it was banned but upon appeal the ruling was reversed by a court that decided that while it contained "a most generous display of the female epidermis, both fore and aft, the whole thing is about as titillating as a ton of coal."[85]

Monsignor Little announced his resignation from the Legion in September 1966 to devote himself to more clerical duties. He had had his fill of salacious movie material, he explained, and professed a wish "to die in the Stations of the Cross not looking at Gina Lollobrigida."[86]

Jack Valenti became president of the Motion Picture Association in that year too. He immediately set about disposing of the Hays Code which, he said, was "an anachronistic piece of censorship that we should never have put into place."[87] Valenti came into the movie industry because the Production Code was on life support and there was little or no liaison between censorship boards in different states, which meant that "films with inflammatory subjects would sometimes end up playing in a checkerboard pattern across the country."[88]

Distributors were also challenging such censorship boards in courts, and almost always winning. The passing of the nudity scene in *The Pawnbroker* created an untenable loophole in the Code, suggesting that one standard existed for good films and another for ordinary ones. Films like *Who's Afraid of Virginia Woolf?* were allowed to take advantage of that loophole, causing Jack Warner to exclaim at a screening of it, "My God, we've got a $7.5 million dirty movie on our hands!"[89]

Valenti replaced the Code with a ratings system that varied for every film: in effect the same one we have today. Was the abandonment of the old system a Good Thing? Michael Medved argued that directors like Hitchcock, Hawks, Wilder, Capra, etc., "all somehow managed to create their masterpieces under its auspices."[90] (But maybe this is beside the point.)

There were four broad categories: G for General, M for Mature, R for Restricted (under-16s to be accompanied by an adult) and X for over-16s only. The U.K. had G for General, GP for Parental Guidance, R for Under-18s to be accompanied by an adult and X meaning No Under-18s.

Valenti realized the new system was flawed. What system wasn't? "You cannot get perfection in this world, my friend," he reasoned. Jack Vizzard saw it as "an exercise in an American brand of the old black magic in that it seeks to find a niche for everything that comes along and then presumes that by naming it, it's brought under the control of the conjurors."[91]

Medved makes the point that the following year, 1967, the average weekly audience going to films in the U.S. dropped from 38 million to less than 18 million, a decrease of more than 50 percent. Were people bored by the new liberalism or was this just a coincidence? The toothpaste was out of the tube but not that many people wished to buy it.

Michael Douglas poked fun at the new ratings system when he said, "I get it. GP means the hero gets the girl. 16 means the villain gets the girl. And 18 means everyone gets the girl!"[92]

It was easy for Douglas to be frivolous as he hadn't suffered under the old system where "the glimpse of a stocking was looked on as something shocking." Or having to kiss athletically. James Stewart remarked, "Everybody makes a joke of censorship now, but in the old days when you were in bed — it didn't matter whether it was with your mother or your wife or your sister or a prostitute — you had to keep one foot on the floor."[93] This is the way Albert Finney saw it: "In love scenes on beds you had to keep one foot on the floor at all times, which made it rather like playing snooker or pool."[94]

In 1967 we also had Dustin Hoffman romancing both a mother and her daughter in *The Graduate,* the film that made him a star. The PCA refused to approve Michael Winner's *I'll Never Forget Whatsisname* in 1967 because it contained an oral sex scene. Likewise for Finney's *Charlie Bubbles* the following year. In both cases, revolt followed. The films were released through subsidiary companies, thereby sidestepping the Administration and hastening its end.[95]

A film version of James Joyce's masterpiece *Ulysses* was also released in 1967. It was treated rather lightly by the censors. Was this because its sexual content was primarily verbal rather than visual, in the expectable genuflection towards Joyce's linguistic dexterity? Alexander Walker commented: "The book was made the passport for the film. And a nod of approval from the Catholics made it easy to do without a Code Seal."[96]

Ulysses was the first (semi?) mainstream film to pass the word "fuck," and also feature a man nude from behind. Vincent Canby took pains in *The New York Times* to explain that females and "normal" males are not sexually stimulated by rear-view male nudity.[97] Did that mean "normal" females might be?

Directed by Joseph Strick, it certainly pushed the boat out with its boudoir (and bathroom) candor but the Legion felt it would appeal more to students of Joyce than the lascivious trenchcoat brigade. This is probably true, though the final stream-of-consciousness soliloquy of Molly Bloom was surely something that would have been banned outright a few short years earlier. Yes, yes, yes.

Joyce believed he had a Jesuitical strain injected backwards in him. Religion formed him but it also caused his rebelliousness against the Church. He became anti–Catholic but not non–Catholic. As was the case with his native Ireland, which he couldn't escape even in exile, religion made an indelible mark on him. (So did movies, by the way: He was Ireland's first cinema manager.)

Ironically, *Ulysses* was banned in Ireland by the censor Dermot Breen (no relation to Joseph). The decision was upheld by the Films Appeal Board. Seven years later it was re-submitted and again rejected. It was finally unbanned in 2000, a whopping 31 years since its first submission, receiving an Over 15 certificate. Joyce would have been amused.[98]

The British Board of Film Censors refused to give it a certificate unless substantial cuts were made. Strick dug his heels in at this, referring to the censor as "your friendly neighborhood film mortician."[99] (He should actually have been overjoyed that so much was left in.) He decided to take the film

4. The Liberal Ethos 143

to the Greater London Council who, as the licensing body for London, could sidestep the Board's decision. The GLC passed it without a single cut. Why? "It was later revealed that the sound production in the projection room was so faulty that none of the censors had heard a word of the dialogue!"[100]

Arthur Penn fell foul of the Legion of Decency with his groundbreaking movie *Bonnie and Clyde* (1967). J. Hoberman wrote in *The Village Voice* that,

Warren Beatty and Faye Dunaway about to make a large withdrawal at a bank, without having a bank account, in *Bonnie and Clyde* (1967).

for Penn, crime was defined as "a game ruined by a grown-up society's tedious insistence that acts have consequences."[101] In other words, not the kind of thing that Hays & Co. could have countenanced without a lot of sleepless nights.

The audience is very much on the side of the outlaws, Warren Beatty and Faye Dunaway. They're infinitely more free-spirited than those who pursue them. Michael J. Pollard, the snitch, shifts loyalties and thus, for the viewer, becomes one of "them." The violent deaths of Beatty and Dunaway confirm their status as victims. The killing of the two leads took longer to film than any other scene in the movie, mainly because Penn, like Alfred Hitchcock in the shower scene in *Psycho*, used different camera angles to film the same set-ups or, alternately, filmed from the same angle but at a different speed. Beatty and Dunaway were rigged with blood packets that exploded upon impact, Penn even attaching a piece of prosthetic scalp to Beatty's head that a crew member pulled off with an invisible nylon thread. He tied one of Dunaway's legs to the gearshift of the car so she would be wrenched every which way as the bullets sprayed her before gravity took over and she fell like a marionette behind the steering wheel.

"There's a moment in death," Penn took pains to explain, "when the body no longer functions, when it becomes an object and has a certain kind of detached ugly beauty. It was that aspect I was trying to get."[102] These were techniques that would be fine-tuned in the years ahead by directors Sam Peckinpah and, in our own time, Quentin Tarantino. Maybe George Stevens (a director who influenced Peckinpah) pioneered it all with the shooting of Elisha Cook Jr. in *Shane* (1953): He had ropes pulling Cook backwards after he was gunned down in the mud by the reptilian, black-gloved Jack Palance. Stevens reasoned that heretofore people died in cowboy films, if not all films, by falling forward, when it stood to reason that the force of a bullet could be expected to do the opposite. Stevens went for raw, grisly horror, whereas Penn was looking for something "spastic and balletic."[103]

Jane Mills argues that the graphic nature of *Bonnie and Clyde's* violence here, and in the films of Peckinpah and Tarantino that were to follow, "certainly contains more realism than the anodyne world of *The Lone Ranger* in the 1930s, where characters killed and maimed without drawing blood — and, equally miraculously, their clothing remained undisturbed."[104]

Hoberman felt that the film's unrelenting violence, especially in the final reel, "foregrounded carnage as choreographed spectacle."[105] Jimmy Breslin, still smarting from the real-life violence of 1963 when John F. Kennedy was gunned down in cold blood in Dallas, viewed it differently: "Pretty people kill, and the killing they do is pretty too. If you want to see a real killer then you should have been around to see Lee Harvey Oswald."[106]

The real Bonnie and Clyde, by all reports, were a thoroughly ruthless pair. Penn romanticized them, making them insecure and emotionally vulnerable (not to mention laughable in some of their attempts to rob banks). This caused the film to be (unlike, say, *Scarface* or most other crime flicks of yore) an indictment of a society that brutalized them even as they brutalized it. Their slo-mo deaths, in a stylized final sequence that would become something of a fad in later years (*The Wild Bunch* and *Butch Cassidy and the Sundance Kid* being perhaps the most notable examples), strengthened this impression. One of the reasons the film threatened censors was because their deaths became almost like the deaths of martyrs. Only a few movies had attempted this kind of thing before — *They Live By Night* (1949) being one.

Ian Grey thought the final scene graphically portrayed what forty years of gangster epics stringently denied: Death is "without glamour or any reassurances."[107] In *Newsweek*, critic Joe Morgenstern initially dissed the film as "a squalid shoot-em-up for the moron trade" but as its reputation grew he retracted this view and gave it guarded praise. The cinema-going public in general was both amused and shocked by it in turns.[108]

The irony was choice. In the old days, heroes used to protect society from its enemies; now it was society itself that was the enemy. Jerzy Toeplitz drew a conclusion about the movie in his book *Hollywood and After*: "Its philosophy was extremely simple: The world is vile and badly run and the likable heroes are quite right to set themselves against it. The fact that they also kill is of secondary importance."[109]

Stanley Kubrick felt that audiences' interest in violence reflected the fact that on the subconscious level we're very little different from our primitive ancestors. Peckinpah, who directed *Straw Dogs* around the same time, echoed this viewpoint. "I regard all men as violent," he confessed, "including myself. We're just a few steps up from apes in the evolutionary scale."[110]

Beatty's innocent "We rob banks!" is a schoolyard boast — particularly when he exhibits the fact that he doesn't do it very well. Neither is he a Lothario in the bedroom. Making him impotent changed the whole texture of what "macho" meant.

Before *Bonnie and Clyde* even went into release, the Legion of Decency, in a panic that the morals of the nation were at stake, designated a priest called Father Patrick Sullivan to oversee it. As he did so, he expressed severe misgivings about the fact that Dunaway wore no bra in the opening scene. After Beatty showed him a rough cut, he repeatedly exclaimed he could see Dunaway's breast through her dress. According to Beatty, "He kept running the film back and forth saying, 'Oh no, that's her breast.' And we'd say, 'No, Father, it's just her dress. It's silk.' And he'd say, 'No, no, I see her breast! Wait, I think I see a nipple!' We'd say, 'No, no, that's just a button.'"[111] And so the madness continued.

The film came with the audacious tagline, "They're young, they're in love … and they kill people." For many viewers this was a desecration of the sacredness of life, a romanticism of thuggery with a casual disregard of whatever trails of destruction the bandits left in their wake. It seemed to matter little that, if you looked deeper, this wasn't so much a celebration of a pair of "natural born killers" as a poetic, lyrical study of two young people who simply fell prey to a craving for adventure. The fact that they suffered the ultimate penalty for their wild philandering (in slow motion as well) made the film not so much an ode to violence as a cautionary fable that portrayed bloodletting as it had never been portrayed before, in all its gore.

A huge talking point across the U.S., if not the world, it was eventually nominated for ten Oscars. Just as the ceremonies were about to start, Martin Luther King was assassinated. Now there was real obscenity, real crime, real violence. Another martyr lay on the chopping block. Could Father Sullivan censor this too?

Penn had a certain amount of leverage with the film considering the fact that when he made it, both the Legion of Decency and the PCA were on the ropes.[112] But nobody could deny its honorable intentions. He was making the point that violence was part and parcel of American life and he was merely reflecting that. He said in his defense: "Kennedy was shot. We're in Vietnam, shooting people and getting shot. We haven't been out of a war for any period of time in my lifetime. Gangsters were flourishing during my youth. I was in the war at 18, then came Korea, now comes Vietnam. We have a violent society. It's not Greece, it's not Athens, it's not the Renaissance. It's American society, so why not make a film about it?"[113]

I Am Curious (Yellow), a Swedish film that became notorious for different reasons, also came out in 1967. This had almost as many sexual positions as the Kama Sutra, showing oral and genital activity in a manner unprecedented up until this. It has since become a byword for liberation. That's fine insofar as it goes, but what really rankles about this is the facile political subtext. Intercut with the boudoir frolics are a number of street scenes where soundbites are proffered on issues like class and racial equality. Does it feel it needs these to give the bump-and-grind routines legitimacy? This is where the real exploitation comes in. Footage of Martin Luther King and the Russian poet Yevgeny Yevtushenko try to ratchet up its street cred but only end up making it look even more ridiculous. Apologizing for the sex is the thing that really makes it dirty.

Another 1967 vehicle, *Reflections in a Golden Eye*, saw Marlon Brando give perhaps the most courageous performance of his career as the preening, homosexual Major Penderton. The sixties is often castigated as Brando's nadir decade. Almost everything he did in the fifties seemed to be Oscar-nominated, and he had his famous "renaissance" in the early seventies, but in this decade his lack of concern over his films seemed to show in every other frame.

Such wasn't the case here. John Huston's moody adaptation of Carson McCullers' novel throbs with tension and portent as Brando becomes humiliated by his wife (Elizabeth Taylor) and fantasizes about a young soldier (who's more interested in Taylor than Brando) before the shocking *denouement*.

Audiences didn't go for it and it was condemned by the NCOMP because of the nature of the material. But it remains a classic study of repression and retribution, expertly handled by the ensemble cast. Brian Keith and Julie Harris are exemplary as well but it's really Brando's film. He succeeds in making us empathetic towards a tortured army man driven to a reckless act as he finally confronts an unbearable revelation.

The Killing of Sister George (1968) featured the first lesbian love scene in a mainstream movie but had little to distinguish it apart from this. If anything, it reinforced stereotypes of lesbians as being "butch" so it really set the sexual clock back instead of forward. It was initially thought to champion gay rights but Dawn Sova wrote, "Its portrayal of lesbians as sick, depraved or unhappy realized the lesbian community's worst fears."[114] (In one scene, Susannah York subjects herself to the humiliation of drinking Beryl Reid's dirty bath water to prove her love for her.)

Roman Polanski's *Rosemary's Baby* (1968) became a trendsetter for diabolism, "a kind of blueprint for the occult renaissance of the late 1960s."[115] A chilling adaptation of Ira Levin's novel, dealing with an emotionally fragile woman (Mia Farrow) recruited by a coven of witches to bear the devil's child, it was predictably condemned by the Legion for its mockery of religious practice. But as Stephen Tropiano pointed out, part of the reason for the outrage was Polanski's talent: "The technical excellence of the film serves to intensify its defamatory nature."[116] It became the seventh-highest grossing film of the year, raking in over $12 million. As Tropiano wrote, "In the, end, evil triumphed over good at the box office, while the Catholic Church's 35-year reign of terror had at last come to an end."[117]

Midnight Cowboy pushed the envelope in a number of other directions in 1969. John Schlesinger secured bravura performances from both Dustin Hoffman as the tubercular Ratso and Jon Voight as his unlikely buddy in a film that was really about loneliness. (Both actors were Oscar-nominated but lost, incredibly, to John Wayne's bog standard turn as an aging cowpoke in *True Grit*.) It was given an X rating on account of its uncompromising depiction of New York's gay and drug-ridden underbelly but by now viewers were able to recognize a masterpiece when they saw one and such scenes were regarded as necessary to the rich texture of Schlesinger's vision of depravity. A 50-year battle for self-expression seemed finally to have been won.

It was the first X-rated film to win a Best Picture Oscar. This sounded like a contradiction in terms to those weaned on the false altar of restrictiveness. To them it was like saying, "Beware of this—but applaud it all the same." John Lyden believed that the film received critical acclaim from religious groups, who "shifted gears to accommodate the new era," because of its "gritty realism and its moral message of the possibility of self-sacrifice and friendship even among those whom society has rejected."[118]

Time has been kind to it. Even its dated scenes, like the one at the drug party, have a kind of quaint appeal. But where it wins out most is in its lack of self-consciousness. There's no hidden homosexual agenda in the relationship between Voight and Hoffman, the hustler and the hobo, and no hamfisted attempt by Schlesinger to wring tears from their fractured liaison. Basically, they end up rooming together because they're both misfits. Whatever tenderness they share on that score is very delicately handled. Schlesinger doesn't beg for an emotional investment from the viewer and therefore gets it on the double.

Julie Salamon relievedly wrote in, of all places, *The Wall Street Journal*: "There are no speeches about homelessness or homosexuality or child abuse or friendship, as there surely would be if it were made today." In so many modern movies, she cannily notes, characters always seem to be commenting on their emotions instead of just having them. *Midnight Cowboy* didn't fall into that trap.[119] As the Robert De Niro of *The Deer Hunter* might have said, "This is this." There were no frills.

Though *Midnight Cowboy* wasn't a homosexual film, it could have been seen as a "closeted" form of one. The suggestion of it made the theme stronger. (Likewise, as we saw, in John Huston's *Reflections In a Golden Eye*.) Rod Steiger

4. The Liberal Ethos 149

was convincing in a gay role in *The Sergeant* (1968), though he chewed the scenery a bit more than Brando — something Steiger tended to do in a lot of his later work.

The Fox (1967), based on a D.H. Lawrence novella, which had come out the previous year, featured scenes of both lesbianism and masturbation. John Trevelyan said he wouldn't ban homosexual scenes *per se*. For him it was all about attitude and tone. Things were slightly different here because it was a woman (Anne Heywood) who was pleasuring herself. Another taboo had been broken.

Under Trevelyan's stewardship, sensitive material became a matter of "negotiation or horse trading" in contrast to decisions that had "previously been imposed by unilateral *diktat.*"[120]

Trevelyan was instrumental in raising the age limit for an X-cert film from 16 to 18. This prevented many movies from being banned, a fate that could have befallen the likes of *A Clockwork Orange* and *Last Tango in Paris* (which I'll look at in the next chapter). He did his best to censor violence in films which he felt might lead to violence off-screen, being mindful of the context in which it was portrayed. In his autobiography he confessed that he wasn't always successful in his ambition, but "we did what we could, and we reduced as far as possible scenes in which a helpless person was brutally beaten up, a degrading spectacle that could only be enjoyed by someone who was mentally sick."[121] He also quipped that he viewed so many sex education films he had to have been "the most sexually educated man in Britain!"[122]

Humor was one of his most admirable qualities. Another was his ability to empathize with filmmakers, something the people from the Hays era couldn't (or wouldn't) do. He prided himself on the fact that many high-quality directors like Schlesinger and Joseph Losey invited him on to the sets of the films they were making so he could get the "feel" of what they were about.[123]

So here was another crucial change, the erstwhile hermetically-sealed world of the censor was opened up by Trevelyan in a manner that was gleefully welcomed by those at the coalface of the industry. In one's wildest dreams, could one imagine Otto Preminger inviting Geoffrey Shurlock onto a film set? Or Will Hays or Jason Joy?

Audiences were also becoming more independent. In 1970 a priest told Trevelyan that a film he had condemned from the altar was playing in no less than forty cinemas in Chicago, a sure sign that the clergy had lost their teeth as far as the public was concerned.[124]

The sixties closed with the humorous, New-Age farce *Bob & Carol & Ted & Alice*. This 1969 film poked fun at orgies, extramarital sex, group sex and quasi-intellectual notions of "open" relationships. The fact that the wife-swapping on display (not to mention the navel-gazing) doesn't quite work out isn't so much a nod towards fidelity as an underlining of the emotional bankruptcy of everyone involved.

The so-called sexual revolution had become dissipated into a campy send-up of its own excesses. Flower power was shown for what it was — or rather wasn't — and we were on the brink of one long post-coital hangover. In such a trivialized psycho-sexual milieu, the intergalactic striptease of Jane Fonda in Roger Vadim's psychedelic *Barbarella* (1968) was somehow apt.

The sex in this futuristic slice of pop-trash is effected not by taking one's clothes off and going to bed with one's lover, but rather by the woosome twosome swallowing pills and placing their upturned hands against one another "until their exaltations are in perfect compliment."[125] Pauline Kael went to it expecting it to be "good, trashy, corrupt entertainment." She concluded rather disarmingly that it wasn't good trash, "but it's corrupt all right, and that's something."[126]

Marjorie Rosen gave this cautionary coda to the decade: "If the sexual cornucopia released in the sixties has truly contributed to our alienation and impotence, if our emotions live in vacuums and our libidos can only be resuscitated through violence, pornography or freaky sex, what's left?"[127] She was speaking in the context not only of *Barbarella* but also of four 1967 films where oral sex was implied: *Hurry Sundown*, *Charlie Bubbles*, *Bonnie and Clyde* and *I'll Never Forget Whatsisname*.

From now on, all the stops were out. It was like pre–Code Hollywood all over again — with attitude. The censors were running scared and film directors were dizzy with their new sense of power. No Fatty Arbuckle or William Desmond Taylor could threaten the "indie" revolution now. The most seismic decade in the history of film had seen to that.

The decade was notable for something else too: the almost total invisibility of *film noir*. Mick LaSalle gave a probable explanation for this: "You can't have *noir* without evil women, and during a time of sexual freedom and exuberance, movies that portray sexual women as inherently evil look ridiculous. *Noir* films, like vamp films, depend on the implicit link between sex and death. It was only when that link returned in the eighties with AIDS — that *film noir* enjoyed a ten-year resurgence of popularity."[128]

5

Nothing Succeeds Like Excess

Peter Bogdanovich's beautifully muted elegy to a dying era, *The Last Picture Show* (1971), ushered in the new decade. This monochrome masterpiece featured veteran Ben Johnson in a supporting role (he won a Best Supporting Actor Oscar). Bogdanovich also drew wonderful performances from Jeff Bridges, Timothy Bottoms, Ellen Burstyn and Cloris Leachman (who won an Oscar for Best Supporting Actress). It was a coming-of-age drama that was also a paean to an age of simplicity; what a pity it all became mired in moralistic squabbles about a swimming pool scene where Cybill Shepherd appeared nude for a few seconds, leading to intricate discussions about what exactly constituted the exposure of "human genitalia." Such squabbles, and their resultant nuances, seemed much more obscene than anything Bogdanovich showed on screen. They led one to believe that there were little old men with magnifying glasses in viewing booths who knew nothing about art but a lot about promiscuity. One was reminded of the mathematician Howard Hughes had employed in 1941 to measure Jane Russell's ample breasts off against those of other starlets to decipher just how far he could go with the Hays Office to get a seal.

The censors were also concerned with *A Clockwork Orange* as Danish *avant garde* director Jens Jorgen Thorsen released his modish adaptation of Henry Miller's *Quiet Days in Clichy*. It was an aimless descent into cheap thrills featuring a struggling writer and his equally dissolute friend wandering around Paris looking for food and sex, though not necessarily in that order. They consort with prostitutes and other women in trysts that are more vulgar than arousing. In between, Thorsen gives us many quasi-documentary-style scenes (some without dialogue) where little or nothing happens.

The film depicts women as discardable sex objects and it was justifiably prosecuted in the U.S. for its offbeat philandering. A Californian judge, however, overruled this decision, believing the film to have artistic merit. In coming to this conclusion, perhaps he was influenced by Miller's literary reputation. Whatever his reasons, the film led to some reviewers coining a new term to describe it: "sexploitation." Whatever genre it fell into, it had few saving graces, its smug, self-congratulatory mood trying to pass itself off as bohemian liberalism. The British Board of Film Censors banned it completely but it was passed by the Great London council three years later.

A year later, another maverick director, Stanley Kubrick, adapted Anthony Burgess' satirical futuristic novel about a bunch of juvenile delinquents terrorizing society. The fact that he used classical music as a backdrop to the bloodletting was a new and, to many, a sinister departure from previous violent movies. But then there was never going to be anything predictable about *A Clockwork Orange*.

Stanley Kubrick brought a new form of psychedelic violence to the screen in his controversial adaptation of Anthony Burgess' novel *A Clockwork Orange* in 1971.

Was he entitled to use classical music as a counterpoint to his violence? In the view of Walter Evans, he was. Evans believed that Beethoven's art was "profoundly violent and profoundly sexual."[1] Vivian Sobchak went further, stating, "Art and violence spring from the same source; they are both expressions of the individual, egotistic, vital and non-institutionalized man."[2] Critic Michael Eric Stein even suggested that "with violence comes passion, and with that passion comes our ability to choose what we love, what we dare, who we want to be — our humanity."[3] Justin Smith felt that the stylization of the violence ran the danger of sanitizing it and "inuring us to its reality."[4]

Kubrick defended it by

5. Nothing Succeeds Like Excess

arguing that rough, graphic violence was less harmful than the kind of "fun" violence one saw in the James Bond films and Tom and Jerry cartoons. He surmised that "any kind of violence in films serves a useful purpose by allowing people a means of vicariously freeing themselves from the pent-up aggressive emotions which are best expressed in dreams, or the dreamlike state of watching a film."[5]

He accepted the X rating the MPAA put on the original cut, but Smith contends that after nine months of the film's release Kubrick removed the gang rape scene from it to secure it an R rating. Kubrick thereby benefited from the "high level publicity and word of mouth generated by the initial release [of the film] for its 1972 reissue."[6] It won the New York Film Critics Award for Best Picture in 1970, which weakened the case against its moral condemnation by those outraged by its excesses.

For many viewers, the charge of "intellectual pornography" surrounding it was, more than anything else, a testament to its disturbing power.[7] Molly Haskell imagined Kubrick to be both a misanthrope and a misogynist. The violence that Alex (Malcolm McDowell) perpetrates against women is cold and intellectual, in her view, and the women themselves merely "pasteboard props in the pop-art scheme of the film, pinballs to be toppled in Kubrick's nasty bowling ballet." She would have preferred if he hated them more: "As it is, they're merely ugly peripheral figures in a color magazine spread, executed by a man whose strongest emotion is a slight aversion to the human race."[8]

This is fine writing, to be sure, but is Ms. Haskell not in danger of confusing Kubrick with Alex? If we're to continue this logic, he would be a pedophile like Humbert Humbert as well, or a martyr like Spartacus.

A curious postscript followed the release of the film. Kubrick withdrew it from circulation when he learned that some British youths were carrying out violent acts like those of McDowell in the movie, and even dressing like him while doing so. He refused McDowell permission to have the film screened at a retrospective of the star's films in aid of the victims of Chernobyl as a result of this.[9]

Sam Peckinpah pushed the boundaries of both sex and violence out further with *Straw Dogs* (1971), wherein a timid professor (Dustin Hoffman) has to endure his wife (Susan George) being anally raped in a remote British village and his house besieged by testosterone-charged local yokels in a shocking finale. The American censor cut the sex scene significantly while the British one saw the violence as more offensive.

Summer of '42, also in the same year, had a scene featuring a teenage boy buying a condom in anticipation of a night of passion with the significantly older Jacqueline Bisset, a war widow promising him a gentle rite of passage into adulthood. (Alan Bates had attempted to buy a condom in the British working class drama *A Kind of Loving* way back in 1962 but became too embarrassed to order one from the female shop assistant.)

Two actresses playing ladies of easy virtue vied for Oscars in 1971, Jane Fonda winning for her hooker turn in *Klute* and thereby denying Julie Christie, who played a brothel madam in Robert Altman's atmospheric western *McCabe & Mrs. Miller*. Another Oscar contender that year was Glenda Jackson, who cavorted with both the bisexual Murray Head and Peter Finch in John Schlesinger's *Sunday, Bloody Sunday*. Jackson also peeled off her clothes in *The Music Lovers*, Ken Russell's overblown biopic of Tchaikovsky. It set tongues wagging once again about the eccentric director's penchant for appearing to turn all of his movies into extensions of his own personality.

There was a bigger hoo-ha over Russell's *The Devils*. This contained scenes of priests and nuns practicing witchcraft in 17th century France, plus exorcisms and scenes of unmitigated brutality. Russell angered the censors when he went on to state that he was a devout Catholic. *The Devils* broke so many taboos that it made some viewers long for a return to the days when the Code had directors quivering in fear. Russell was never going to make a restrained film but in this tale of a group of nuns in Loudon during the reign of Louis XIII, his catalogue of sexual perversity made the Marquis de Sade look like a Trappist monk. Oliver Reed and Vanessa Redgrave played the leads. Reed is Grandier, a sensual priest who sleeps with women and then grants them absolution the following morning. He's eventually burned at the stake after being accused of sorcery. Redgrave, a hunchbacked nun, is rejected in love by Reed. For revenge she accuses him of raping her. Thereafter she feigns demonic possession. It's a very decadent concatenation of diseased Catholic iconography.

When John Trevelyan insisted on a number of cuts, Russell wrote him in order to try and preserve as much of his work as he could. "What I set out to do," he said, in a missive that raised some eyebrows, "was to make a deeply felt religious statement, and I believe that despite the fact that I have butchered the film at your bidding far and away beyond anything I dreamed of, what remains still just about retains my intentions."[10]

Trevelyan allowed one of the most violent scenes as the film to escape his scissors. It was the one where the priest is willing to suffer torture rather than renounce his faith. (Trevelyan wrote in his autobiography, "Milder violence would have failed to make a valid point."[11]) He had many discussions with Russell over what might trouble the censors in the film. Russell chronicles how detailed such discussions were: "Of all the dozens of hours I spent arguing the pros and cons of this and that with John, only one moment still sticks in my mind. He said, 'I'm afraid we can't have Vanessa saying 'cunt.' It's taken me ten years of fighting just to get 'fuck' accepted: I'm afraid the British public isn't ready yet for 'cunt.'"[12]

Russell shot a scene which Trevelyan wisely told him to leave out of the final cut. It featured the possessed nuns "raping" a life-size figure of the crucified Christ as a priest looked on, masturbating. Russell used a musical backdrop of Stravinsky's "Rite of Spring" which he played "flat out."[13] He also beat on a set of drums to "whip up fervor" among his cast.[14]

Russell fairly reveled in the bacchanalian camerabatics. In his autobiography, Reed tells us that one day he unashamedly carried on to the set a "huge figure of Christ naked on the cross, and well endowed."[15] Russell always insisted *The Devils* wasn't so much about sex as politics: "To me it was about brainwashing, about the state taking over."[16]

Judith Crist spoke for herself and her colleagues at *New York* when she droned, "We can't recall in our relatively broad experience (400 movies a year for perhaps too many years) a fouler film."[17] Penelope Gilliatt went one worse: "The epileptic rhythms of the editing are revved up with a score that might be programme music for the onset of psychosis."[18] It's hard to know if Russell would have been flattered or insulted. Alexander Walker dismissed it all as "the masturbatory fantasies of a Catholic boyhood."[19]

But it was Russell's apogee, even with its flaws. He was referred to as a "fish and chips Fellini."[20] He worked on a histrionic tableau as he recounted a tale he believed was historically true and therefore he felt validated in filming it. Reed agreed, as is attested to by his rhetorical question at a press conference: "Why is it permissible to describe historical events in books and plays, though they must not be shown on the screen?"[21]

'No medieval painting of hell," one writer bristled, "exceeded Russell's images of sexual degradation."[22] Outside the cinemas, Mary Whitehouse and her cronies sang songs and said prayers to try and exorcise the celluloid demons. No less than 17 local councils in Britain banned the film. Russell's biographer Joseph Lanza surmised that this might have been a contributory factor in Trevelyan's leaving his post soon afterwards.[23]

We don't know for sure. He said he'd had his fill of *What the Censor*

Saw—the title of his autobiography. "I've got nothing against sex," he explained. "It's a marvelous human activity. It was watching others do it all the time that got me down."[24]

Before he left office he declared, "I would like to think that the role of film censor is beginning to disappear."[25] Two years after his retirement, he joined the campaign for the Abolition of Film Censorship for Adults. His successor Stephen Murphy described the job of censor as "impossible." Trevelyan commented, "In retrospect I think he was right."[26]

The world Murphy entered was light years away from the one Trevelyan faced in his early career. What, for instance, was he to make of *Carnal Knowledge* (1971), a film that ends with an impotent Jack Nicholson trying to masturbate with the aid of a prostitute? It was scenes like this that caused the movie to be banned in Georgia. Nicholson was so convincing in the part that he soon became "a prominent name on the Women's Lib hit list."[27]

The film, also starring Art Garfunkel, caused feminists to have a collective seizure. No matter how hard Nicholson tried to explain that he was merely replicating what the script required of him, the women's libbers refused to listen, ranking him public enemy number one along with other reprobates such as *Playboy* owner Hugh Hefner. Jack probably didn't do himself any favors with quotes such as "I've balled all the women, I've done all the drugs, and I've drunk every drink." So despite protesting that "I'm not trying to get into the pants of every woman I'm interested in," his role in the film pretty much cemented in the minds of the public an image of him as an "out-of-control shagging machine."[28]

Molly Haskell felt *Carnal Knowledge* typified a chauvinist view of sex as "an adolescent competition that, with many Americans, persists well into middle age." The film purported to indict the male members of the cast, in her view, but in effect defended them "not least through the satisfaction they take in degrading the women."[29]

It was acclaimed by the critics as one of the greatest films of 1971, yet in March 1972 a criminal jury in Albany, Georgia, declared that it was obscene and convicted theater operator Billy Jenkins of distributing obscene material. He was found guilty, fined and sentenced to a year's probation. An appeal to the Supreme Court of Georgia went nowhere. Then Jenkins appealed to the U.S. Supreme Court, which reversed the original verdicts.

In the seventies in general, most of the edicts of the Hays Code on matters sexual went by the board. The thin blue line that used to exist between underground and mainstream cinema became increasingly more tenuous. The

NCOMP withdrew its support of the ratings system in 1971, depressed over the number of contentious films that had avoided X certificates and the general relaxation of censorship dictates. Ireland tended to lag behind Britain and the U.S. in terms of liberalization but in 1972 the repressive censor Christopher Macken was replaced by the more tolerant Dermot Breen. "The dark ages of censorship," wrote Ciaran Carty, "which saw either the suppression or mutilation of virtually every movie of any artistic significance," seemed to be over for good.[30]

The most outrageous film of the year was *Last Tango in Paris* with Marlon Brando as Paul, a U.S. expatriate trying to come to terms with his wife's recent suicide. He meets pretty young French girl Jeanne (Maria Schneider), who's about to be married. This is *A Streetcar Named Desire* two decades on. Norman Mailer believed that Brando cashed the check Stanley Kowalski wrote for us many years ago by his sexual gymnastics. Mailer described the sound of him tearing Schneider's knickers as the most thrilling to be heard in world culture since the four opening notes of Beethoven's Fifth Symphony. As for Schneider herself, she was every eighteen-year-old in a mini-skirt and a maxi-

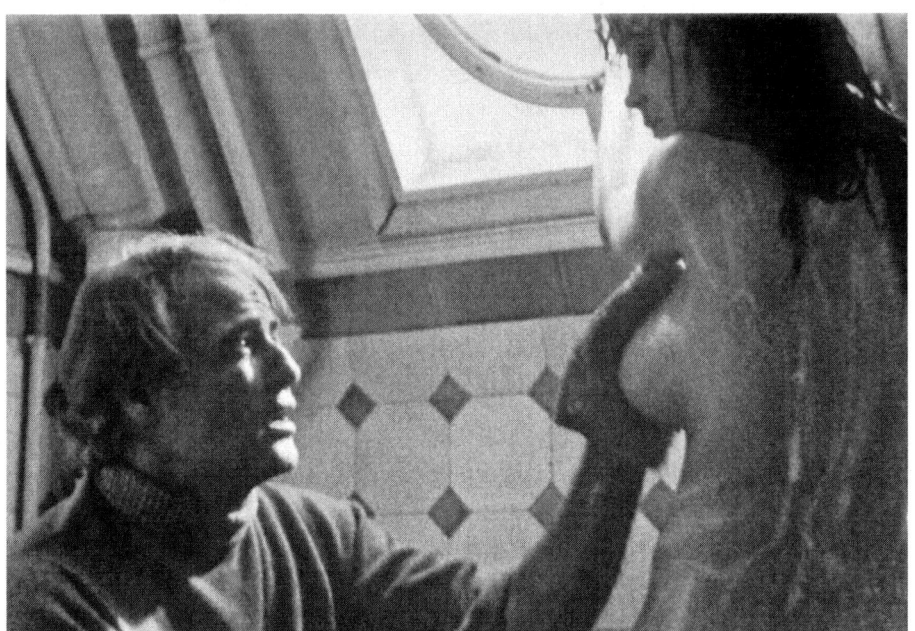

Marlon Brando cashing the erotic check he wrote in *Streetcar* twenty years previously as he squares up to Maria Schneider with lust and *ennui* in *Last Tango in Paris* in 1972.

coat who ever promenaded down Fifth Avenue with the inner arrogance that proclaimed her "cunt" was her chariot.

Mailer rightly pointed out that Brando looked too distinguished to be the proprietor of a cheap flophouse and that the film didn't carry through on its improvisational overtones because we could all see the ending coming a mile off. Unlike Vivien Leigh in *Streetcar*, Schneider had the freedom to tell Brando that she loved the animal in him, but this was really only a mask for his inner turmoil — something Kowalski would never have understood.

The central roles were originally to have been played by Jean-Louis Tringinant and Dominique Sanda but this fell through because Sanda was pregnant. In some ways the film would have been more authentic (though obviously less of a sensation) if such casting materialized.

Paul and Jeanne begin a brutal sexual relationship which is conducted in the stark apartment where they accidentally meet. At Paul's insistence, no names or personal details are exchanged. Anonymity is the keynote. The apartment is to be their escape hatch from the world, the place where they have physical intimacy but little else.

The film was most noted for a scene in which Brando uses butter to "lubricate" Ms. Schneider before he penetrates her anally. He also asks her to renounce values like church, family and home before doing so. The director of the film, Bernardo Bertolucci, actually wanted Brando to perform real sex on screen but Brando drew the line at this, thinking it would have made "our sex organs the focus of the story."[31]

One writer called this "the most famous sex scene in the history of the cinema."[32] Schneider afterwards said she felt raped "both by Marlon and Bertolucci."[33] (This was a bit rich considering the reason she was chosen for the part was because she stripped off all her clothes so readily at the audition.) The dialogue throughout is crass. "What will you do if I die?" Jeanne asks Paul at one point. "Fuck a dead rat," he replies.

Brando changed the script dramatically, inserting many biographical details of his dysfunctional past, exposing not only his body in the film but his mind as well. He was called upon to descend to the very depths of his being before attaining a kind of perverse epiphany at the end.

When Paul finally utters the forbidden words "I love you," we know his goose is cooked. He will die, but before that he deposits a piece of chewing gum under a rail — a final trivial gesture in a trivial, tortured life. His tryst with Jeanne has been absurd but necessary, inconsequential but fulfilling. She's a microcosm of a larger *anomie*, the symbol of his own spiritual vapidity.

Their relationship was never about longevity so he can't complain. It ran its course and now he's getting out. Maybe he's the lucky one.

The film was regarded as revolutionary when released. Today it looks contrived and over-stylized, a cute parable that telegraphs its intentions too baldly. Brando is best in the scenes he doesn't share with Schneider. His bestiality with her is like Puritanism turned inside out. A genuine Continental like Tringinant or Marcello Mastroianni would have played it less stridently (and it probably would have disappeared without trace as a result — which might have been no bad thing).

The *cognoscenti* saw it all as poignantly progressive. The reality was that it was jaded, re-treaded sixties liberalism. Paul doesn't want to know anything about Jeanne. Hey, there's nothing to know. As played by Schneider, she's too empty-headed for us to accept that she could intrigue a man like Paul, whose mind is a cauldron. How could this pair spend their lives together? What would they talk about?

The relationship is much more credible when it's undergoing its "unreal" phase, i.e., the time when Paul wants no names exchanged. When he decides he wants to become confessional and expose his psyche as well as his genitals, already things are becoming artificial. Many of the scenes are so mannered you find yourself almost screaming for some lowbrow naturalism.

Neither is it acceptable that she would want to kill him. He may be a pest but he isn't violent or dangerous. Is it herself she's afraid of when she shoots him? If so, Bertolucci hasn't directed her enough or she hasn't the depth to convey this. At the end of the day it's Brando's movie, more autobiographical than his actual autobiography perhaps, and to that extent we should treasure it.

The comeback that Brando kickstarted with *The Godfather* a year earlier was galvanized by this, but Brando produced better work elsewhere, as in *Quiemada*, a film that died due to lack of interest on the part of its distributors. *Quiemada* remains Brando's proudest performance but few people know about it. *Last Tango* was high-profile because of the manner in which it broke down boundaries but its pretensions towards existential significance are just that: pretensions.

It tackles too many themes to properly engage. The intensity of Brando's bereavement over his dead wife sits uneasily with the cavalier contrivance of his adolescent escapades with Schneider. Jean-Pierre Leaud (Schneider's fiancé) might have been capable of such juvenilia but not this man. His scatology is too self-serving, too self-consciously sensationalistic. At times it verges on the farcical, which makes it all the more amazing that Brando took it all so seriously. He felt that in our daily life almost everything was squalid. Things which were too true gave us a sense of annoyance and the film captured that, as well as the desperate melancholy and self-hatred of middle age.

In Italy, obscenity charges were filed against Brando, Schneider and Bertolucci. All were eventually acquitted but Bertolucci lost his right to vote for five years and was also given a four month suspended prison sentence. "A bit extreme," one writer hissed, "for the nation that gave the world fascism."[34]

The film was banned in Italy until 1987, which pained Bertolucci deeply as he saw it essentially as a romantic work. He believed the basic question it asked was whether it was possible for a man and woman to have a relationship outside traditional social patterns. That's why it takes place inside the anonymous room. The moment the characters depart that hermetically-sealed environment, he contended, their innocence turned to anguish and guilt.

Audiences were divided about its artistic merit. Many found it unwatchable but Pauline Kael hailed it as a masterpiece, predicting that the date of its premiere, October 14, 1972, would in time become a date in artistic history comparable to the night in 1913 when Stravinsky's "Rite of Spring" was first performed, and ushered in modern music. Brando felt Kael's OTT review "revealed more about her than about the movie."[35]

If it wasn't for the presence of a screen legend like Brando, *Last Tango* might have been consigned to the forbidden vaults of hard porn cinemas, but his commitment to the role was huge. It took so much out of him he said he'd never go that deeply into his psyche again — it pushed the film into a different league. (The downside was that he could never ask for butter in restaurants afterwards without getting funny looks from the waiters.)

Richard Roud believes its lasting power is that it's "explicit without being pornographic"[36] The Church, if not the state, was always more threatened by something like this because it was anarchic but it couldn't be dismissed as being (s)exploitative. One priest, though, was able to see the funny side of the whole farrago when he suggested that it should have been condemned because it proved, if nothing else, that Brando could "mumble in French quite as well as in English."[37]

Molly Haskell thought *Last Tango* enabled women to "surrender to their sexual fantasies and still emerge with their souls intact." She saw Schneider as "too knowing for her fate, too sexually advanced for an oedipal fixation," but the film, for her, wasn't so much pornographic as a psychic exploration of two tortured souls: "That we turn invariably from their bodies to look at

5. Nothing Succeeds Like Excess

their faces is at once the glory and defeat of the erotic, which is at its most intense just as it's turning into its opposite, the spiritual and romantic."[38]

Deep Throat, also released that year, featured a young lady whose clitoris was located in her throat so she could only achieve orgasm through oral sex. Her doctor tries to cure her problem by performing this service for her. (One wonders how many men in the audience wished they'd become doctors as they watched this scene.) The film, made on a shoestring, it cleaned up at the box office. It was banned in many American states, which gave rise to a number of court cases. Linda Lovelace became famous for all the wrong reasons as a result of it and later went on the record as saying she was corralled into making the movie. She then found Jesus, before her untimely death.

The acting throughout was painfully amateurish but few viewers noticed this, or wanted to. Just this once, the "dirty raincoat" brigade disappeared into the throngs of "respectable" citizens who turned up to watch a woman with a peculiar biology being serviced by any lascivious man in sight.

Many states predictably judged it to be obscene, which meant it was unceremoniously pulled out of cinemas. In others there were hung juries and mistrials. In California, a Citizen's Decency Association even took out an ad in a newspaper to condemn it, but by now it was a runaway train and even casual voyeurs wanted to find out what all the fuss was about. The harder the watchdogs tried to douse the fire, the higher the flames rose. The legal battle to censor the film, Stephen Tropiano insisted, "only fueled the public's interest in it. The phrase *Deep Throat* became part of the American lexicon, while Linda Lovelace became a household name."[39]

It was written and directed by Gerard Damiano, who had a budget of $25,000 and a shooting schedule of just six days. How much oral sex can you film in that time? (Answer: a lot.) It went on to gross over $25 million. The male fantasy that women actually enjoy this type of activity was heightened by Lovelace's total commitment to the role. (She really made you believe going down on a man was floating her boat.) Nora Ephron disagreed. She found the film not only anti-woman but anti-sex as well. Ephron subsequently interviewed Lovelace and rowed back on that view as a result of being taken in by her statement that she totally enjoyed the whole experience, but these views are in doubt today because we know from Lovelace's 1981 book *Ordeal* that she was exploited.

In 1972, though, she was still high on free love, and when a New York judge ordered the film to be put out of circulation she protested, saying it made her mad that sex films were called obscene when movies full of slaughter were rated GP. This taught kids that killing was accepted by society. She felt that if instead they were taught that sex was good, there wouldn't be so many neurotics in the world. The irony is that sex caused a lot of Lovelace's own neuroses.

The fact that her character's clitoris was located in her throat made her, for one writer, "an ultimate fantasy which neatly does away with the female genitalia. Her vagina is desensitized, unimportant; the only juices of her that flow are saliva. Fellatio can now satisfy both her partner and, by some generous masculine imagination of re-location, her too."[40]

It's all based on a physiological abnormality, of course — one that conveniently allies itself with a classic example of male wish fulfillment. To date, the feminist corollary to *Deep Throat*, i.e., a film where a man's primary sexual equipment resides in his tongue, thus enabling him to receive as much pleasure from cunnilingus as Lovelace did from fellatio, has yet to be made.

The other bombshell of 1972 was *The Exorcist*, based on a book by William Blatty, which dealt with the demonic possession of a twelve-year-old girl played by Linda Blair. The evangelist Billy Graham was so enraged by it, he reputedly asserted there was an evil "buried within the celluloid of the film itself."[41] *The Exorcist* performed the ingenious feat of using religion as a stick to beat religion with, in a kind of post-medieval freakshow. "By deleting the theological context," Les and Barbara Keyser wrote, "the film fixed its focus even more intently on ceremony: incantation replaced faith and chant replaced charity."[42]

The film, these authors argued, "begins the most Jansenistic chapter in the Hollywood catechism, a disgusting procession of demonic interventions in human life, where at best God, through the clumsy agency of very ignorant and incompetent priests, painstakingly crawls his way back to a stand-off with a devil who makes his task look easy and fun."[43]

Pauline Kael called it "the biggest recruiting poster the Catholic Church has had since the sunnier days of *Going My Way* and *The Bells of St. Mary's*.[44] Her point was that it got people thinking and talking about religion again. Jon Landau, writing for *Rolling Stone* described it as a "religious porn film, the gaudiest piece of big budget schlock this side of Cecil B. DeMille."[45] John May had a more corrosive reaction: "It strains credibility so severely that one need not be particularly attuned to religious sensibility to be so offended."[46]

Getting more specific, Nikolas Schreck expressed his derision for the kind of devil that possesses Regan, the central character: "Regan's demonic presentations of the devil on screen strike me as absurd, the kind of spookhouse effect trotted out by evangelists to scare their congregations.... It seems like the devil could come up with something more threatening to the social order than pissing on Mom's rug, playing with herself, throwing up, or saying 'Fuck.'"[47] Schreck agrees with Jeffrey Russell that Blatty was naive in giving us a devil who was "stupid enough to choose to possess a little girl rather than a national government."[48]

The Archbishop of Canterbury, Dr. Ramsey, put his finger on the nub of the issue when he said, "If there's an immense craze on the subject, it's a sign of spiritual immaturity."[49] The film, surprisingly, escaped with an R rating when one might have expected a harsher judgment. According to Julian Petley, this was an example of the rating system going easier on movies produced by big studios.[50]

The Exorcist gave rise to many similar films in the years following, cinematic horror shifting into a "higher, more viscerally demanding gear" in the early 1970s, "directly proportional to the nudity flooding art-house cinemas courtesy of continental soft porn."[51] Nobody was to know this in 1972, though, and the shock waves produced by the film went worldwide. A Los Angeles cinema manager estimated that each screening of it resulted in an average of "four customers fainting, six vomiting and many fleeing in panic."[52] In Germany a boy was alleged to have shot himself in the head after seeing it. A man who claimed to have been himself possessed underwent an all-night exorcism in his church before killing his wife with his bare hands.[53]

There were calls for the movie to be banned and riots outside many cinemas from outraged members of the public. Some cinema managers were arrested but it all really ended in a puff of smoke. For better or worse, the devil was here to stay and if he wanted to get sexy with Ms. Blair, the public, generally, were interested in riding shotgun.

Perhaps inevitably, it spawned a sequel, *Exorcist II: The Heretic* (1977). Perhaps equally inevitably, the latter bombed, This was mainly due to the fact that John Boorman, the director, tried to make a complex psychological thriller when all audiences wanted was more and more shocks. This, combined with a thoroughly wretched performance by Richard Burton as the token priest, conspired to make the whole package into an unmitigated farce.

Boorman had a lot of trouble with Burton on the set as the actor was trying (unsuccessfully) to get off alcohol at the time. Boorman spat out these words about the aging legend: "He's like all those drunks — impossible when he's drunk and only half there when he's sober. Wooden as a board with his body and relies on doing all his acting with his voice."[54]

The big mistake they made with *The Heretic* was employing an intellectual to deal with a franchise that was, by definition, crassly commercial. It didn't have much to do with art and still less with religion. It was gimcrack melodrama couched in spiritual iconography. Nobody ever felt *The Exorcist* was consciousness-raising. No, the only thing this baroque film raised was Linda Blair's bed. It went from Christ to anti–Christ with deft precision, carrying us all along on a tide of scatology that wouldn't have been out of place in the Salem witch-hunt.

By the mid-seventies everything seemed to be fair game in the cinema. If the sex in *Last Tango* was explicit, it did at least have some kind of existential underpinning, even if this was at times pretentious. Films that followed it didn't always have that kind of reach, or ambition. Neither did the censors seem to pay too much attention to the new world order. Sex was now a "given" between couples rather than a concession.

Time was that permissiveness had to be the *theme* of a sexual movie. Now it was just sort of "there." Not like an elephant in the room so much as a mouse. In Clint Eastwood's *Magnum Force* (1973) we had a young Japanese girl coming up to him and asking, "How does a girl get to go to bed with you?" Eastwood gives the dry response, "Try knocking on the door." Exchanges like this were almost ho-hum in a raft of movies made around this time. Where were Mae West's innuendoes now? Gathering dust in the vaults of a hundred censors' vaults.

Emmanuelle arrived on the world's screens in 1974 and spawned a bevy of sequels, each more abominable than the one before, though Sylvia Kristel was undoubtedly an erotic lady. Her undulations seemed to awaken the libidos of viewers not only in France, the film's country of origin, but the world over, for reasons that still remain unfathomable, because this hymn to kinkiness has little to distinguish it from any other soft-porn vehicle of the time, or any other time. Georges Pompidou banned it in France but after he died his successor Giscard d'Estaing, a man of eminently less taste, permitted it to be screened. The rest is history — or herstory.

From the devil to sex and back again: In 1976 we got another demonic offering from Richard Donner about a five-year-old anti–Christ who has to be consigned to movie hell by his foster father. What threw many people about *The Omen* was the cast. Once you got highly respected mainstream performers like Gregory Peck and Lee Remick on board, the film automatically acquired a kind of ballast, if not *gravitas*. They acted as the kind of establishment platform from which it could depart with such gleeful irresponsibility.

5. Nothing Succeeds Like Excess 165

Donner was, in effect, writing himself a blank check to be decadent because he had the imprimatur of Hollywood's A-Team to do so.

The U.S. Catholic Conference described *The Omen* as "one of the most distasteful films ever put out by a major studio." Donner countered with "The church must admit that the devil can be alive and well on planet Earth, and, if so, isn't it important to gather our religious strength to ward off this evil?"[55]

The remaining years of the seventies were characterized by decisions as erratic as they had been in the past four decades. Woody Allen's anti-blacklist film *The Front* (1976) made MPAA history because, even though he said "fuck" in one scene, it emerged with just a GP rating.[56]

Martin Scorsese's *Taxi Driver* (1976) brought blood-spattering to a new level as Robert De Niro's avenging angel tried to rid New York of its seediness, but it was sexually coy. Cybill Shepherd is predictably shocked when De Niro's Travis Bickle brings her (inexplicably) to a pornography theater on their first (and last) date. In a later scene the sound of teenage hooker Jodie Foster pulling down Bickle's fly was cut by the British censors. This despite the fact that De Niro casually blows away anyone threatening his mission as avenging angel on the mean streets of the Big Apple.

Looking for Mr. Goodbar (1977) seemed to celebrate promiscuity in its presentation of a woman who cruises bars for no-holds-barred sexual liaisons. David Shipman thought the fact that the leading lady (Diane Keaton) is killed at the end made it "as moralistic as any Code movie: the wages of sin are death."[57]

In 1979 we got more sacrilege with Monty Python's *The Life of Brian*. Here we had a reluctant messiah whose life roughly parallels that of Christ, with the (minor) difference that this Christ specializes in making funny speeches which his listeners repeatedly misinterpret in that Pythonesque kind of way. The satirical spoof was banned in Scotland for its sacrilegious content. The director Terry Jones told the world it didn't mock religion but only mocked *organized* religion. Hmm. Outside some cinemas where scenes were cut, pro–Python picketers carried banners with the message "Resurrect Brian. Crucify the censors."[58]

The writers of the book *God Goes to Hollywood* allowed that behind the "vulgarity and delightful silliness" of the film lay two messages. The first was that we all have to be our own saviors and the second is that we need to laugh: "Failure to do so has resulted in far too many religious wars already."[59]

Roy Kinnard and Tim Davis admitted that, though the jokes often went too far, "there's cogent truth in some of the movie's observations about society's frequent corruption of religion."⁶⁰ The *Monthly Film Bulletin* concluded that the film "might be taken seriously as an attempt to demystify Christ and religious fanaticism but it unsuccessfully sends up the kind of reverent, choir-laden, star-studded gospel dramatizations habitually perpetrated by the cinema industry on behalf of God and Mammon."⁶¹

It's interesting to note that, apart from *The Exorcist*, *The Life of Brian* was the only film to be banned on grounds other than obscenity up to this time. A Pythonesque twist of fate accompanied its release in Runnymede, England, for blasphemy ... and then it was revealed that Runnymede didn't have any cinemas in their jurisdiction. How Terry Jones must have guffawed at that.

For Pauline Kael, it was all too much. By the end of the seventies, she felt, we were living in a world where movies somehow seemed to "thrive on moral chaos."⁶² Was there any way out of this? Or would the next decade prove to be even more venal?

Cruising (1980) was a rather dull film that infuriated the gay community because of what it felt was a skewed depiction of its seedy underbelly. A thriller directed by William Friedkin, famous for having brought *The Exorcist* to the screen seven years before, it was based on a series of murders of gay men that took place in New York in the late 1970s. Al Pacino played an undercover cop who infiltrates the gay scene to find the murderer. Here he comes into contact with many of the unsavory elements of the "cruising" scene: bondage, S&M, and the crass, casual sex of unfeeling transients.

To research the film, both Pacino and Friedkin visited the sex clubs that had leather-clad *habitués* heavily into funkiness. When Pacino was accused of trawling in the sewer of gay life, he defended himself with a heated "That's the point of the movie! At first I didn't know these fringes existed. I took the role because my character is fascinating, a man who's ambiguous both morally and sexually, who's both an observer and a *provocateur*."⁶³

In reply to the charge that the film could provoke even more violence against gays, Friedkin replied, "If I believed that, I'd stop shooting today. The character in the film who's the killer is not gay. He's a sick person who takes his sickness out on gays. Also, it isn't clear that there's only one killer in the film." In fact, nothing at all was clear as daily rewrites went on, partly as a reaction to the gay protests. The film ends ambiguously with the audience wondering if Pacino himself is the actual killer.⁶⁴

There were bomb threats on the set, with bottles and rocks being hurled at the cameras and trucks, and even the actors. Gay activists proclaimed,

"This film will kill people"—a prediction that turned out to be true because in November of that year a minister's son parked his car outside a bar where much of the filming had taken place and began indiscriminately shooting an Israeli submachine gun. He killed two gay men and wounded many others.

Friedkin tried to make the point that the film was about the way in which suppressed sexuality, be it homosexual or heterosexual, could foster violence, but not too many people were listening. Gay activists continued their crusade but it lacked direction. At one point Pacino was labeled a homophobe. Some time later he was being spoken of as a closet gay. Likewise for Friedkin. Would-be moralists called the movie filth without bothering to investigate on what side of the sexual border its loyalties lay. Maybe it didn't matter. It was going to get up people's noses one way or the other.

Many protesters came to the premiere. Hundreds of cinemas were picketed but the film itself failed to captivate audiences. It was like a white elephant. Most of the excitement surrounding it preceded its screening, which was anticlimactic. When the film died, so did the protests.

Before *Cruising* begins, we get a disclaimer: "This is not intended as an indictment of the homosexual world. It concerns one small section which is not representative of the whole." Imagine if every film where the killer was an accountant, or a plumber, or nurse, had to grovel to the Thought Police like this. Pretty soon every plotline would have baggage. And an agenda, real or imagined. The industry couldn't survive.

Another film from the same year which got a lot of people talking because it featured a respected star in a compromised role was Brian De Palma's *Dressed to Kill*. This shattered the squeaky-clean image of Angie Dickinson by having her play a sexually repressed wife who has a dalliance with a man she meets at a museum, thereafter getting murdered by a cross-dressing psychopath played by Michael Caine.

Re-titled *Undressed to Kill* by some wags who were offended by the sexual material on view (as well as the gorefest), it was widely viewed as a misogynistic enterprise that also misrepresented people with personality disorders. And unfairly blackened cross-dressers. (The latter aspect of the movie obviously called up parallels to Hitchcock's *Psycho*.) Feminists picketed it but only succeeded in drawing more attention to it as a result. De Palma, never a man to be intimidated by abuse (he's suffered his fair share of it, as well as the ubiquitous taunts of being a Hitchcock clone), was grateful for all the free publicity.

Dickinson's early scene in the shower is also reminiscent of *Psycho*, as indeed is her brutal stabbing by the sexually conflicted psychotic. Caine's character also bears more than one resemblance to Anthony Perkins' Norman Bates, having perverted desires warring with guilt inside his intensely Catholic soul.

People are generally punished for their sins in Hitchcock's films and De Palma has been quite happy to carry on this strain in his repeated *hommages* to the great director. Skewed Catholic iconography also ran through De Palma's breakthrough feature *Carrie,* where menstruation (the beginning of one's sexual life, as it were) became the prelude to the film's more sensationalistic elements. Sissy Spacek's mother here was also a religious nut.

After imagining herself being violated anally by her dream lover (an experience she enjoys), Dickinson has a mechanical sexual session with her husband, after which she makes her way to Caine, with whom she flirts. It proves to be a bad decision—and one of her last ones. She then meets a man in a museum and he masturbates her afterwards in a taxi while the driver watches. This is exhibitionism amplified to a new level, and definitely not the Angie Dickinson we thought we knew.

De Palma was annoyed about the MPAA's attitude to the violence in the film. Even though he only implied most of it, he still got censored. He saw his work thrown in with *The Texas Chainsaw Massacre* as though he were eviscerating people. The film finally got an R rating because he agreed to make concessions. He took out the sight of some pubic hair in the shower scene and a close-up of the razor cutting Dickinson's throat in the elevator. In the end, it came down to crazy game-playing: The trading of pubic hair against expletives wasn't exactly what he had in mind when he first had his vision of the movie.

Films like *Dressed to Kill* were shocking in their way, but also shockless. The abnormal had become normal by now and people were reaching saturation point. The church and the NCOMP felt manacled by time.

This is how one writer viewed the overall fall-out from that organization's flagship publication: "The conservatives within the church felt betrayed by its liberalism; the more liberal church members dismissed it as irrelevant. Father Sullivan informed his few remaining readers that it would no longer publish reviews after September 1980. What had started with such a fury in 1934 died in 1980 with hardly a whimper of protest."[65]

Caligula, another 1980 scorcher, was an unmitigated exercise in excess for its own sweet sake. Seeing as it was both produced and partly directed by Bob Guccione, the publisher of *Penthouse* magazine, this wasn't unduly surprising. What *was* surprising was how he managed to coerce such stars as Peter O'Toole, Helen Mirren and Malcolm McDowell into being a part of it. When they saw the finished cut they disassociated themselves from it but it was too late by then.

It remains a particularly nasty evocation of the eponymous tyrant and the empire over which he presided. Even Gore Vidal asked to have his name removed from the final screenplay because of its gratuitous carnality, which was surely saying something considering this man's taste for, well, gore. There are many ways to portray decadence without appearing decadent oneself but this wasn't one of them.

Guccione accepted the fact that he was dealing with torrid material but argued that comparing an X-rated film to *Caligula* was a bit like comparing the shoot-out at the O.K. Corral to the Second World War. After it opened in New York on February 1, 1980, the cinema manager was arrested. Over 3,000 Catholic clergymen signed a complaint against it in New York, Chicago and Los Angeles, but by autumn of that year it had been shown in over 100 cities. Eventually it became one of the largest grossing independently produced X-rated films ever made in the U.S.[66]

Bob Guccione's *Caligula* (1980) contained orgiastic excesses that would have shocked even Cecil B. DeMille. Helen Mirren, shown here, played the part of Caesonia.

In 1981 a remake of *The Postman Always Rings Twice* featured an erotic scene between Jack Nicholson and Jessica Lange on a kitchen table that burned up the screen and seemed to be screaming for cuts from the censor. In the same year, Steven Spielberg, of all people, caused alarm with *Indiana Jones and the Temple of Doom*, which has a scene in which a Hindu priest rips the heart out of a human being who has been offered up as a sacrifice. Considering this was a film which many children were expected to attend, it caused the introduction of a new PG-13 rating. This made concerned parents aware that certain scenes might be unsuitable for children under that age.

In 1985 Jean-Luc Godard caused more liturgical ripples with *Hail Mary*, a film in which the Virgin Mary alternates between playing basketball and serving petrol. Not your average Madonna...

Ken Russell had to slice fifteen minutes off *Crimes of Passion* the same year after CARA (the Code and Ratings Administration) expressed its disapproval of the sex on display. Sex was also the bogey in features like *Betty Blue* and *9½ Weeks*, both made the following year, as it was in three 1987 films: *The Big Easy*, *Fatal Attraction* and *Angel Heart*, the latter also featuring demonic content. In 1988 we had a controversial treatment of rape in *The Accused*, which won an Oscar for Jodie Foster, and also *Naked Gun*, which trivialized *coitus* by having Leslie Nielson and Priscilla Presley trying to get it on inside bodybag-sized condoms.

Fatal Attraction was a kind of horror movie crossed with a thriller about a man involved in what might be euphemistically classed as an "amorous indiscretion." Put bluntly, Michael Douglas cheats on his wife, played by Anne Archer, with the hydraulically-charged Glenn Close. Feminists were outraged that the movie's sympathies nearly all lie with Douglas, a family-loving guy who just "happened" to stray while Close ramps up the shock-shlock quotient. In the original ending she committed suicide but the film went for *grand guignol* rather than poignance as she rises from a bathtub in the final scene like a witch you can't kill. The other ending was re-inserted for a DVD version but it was really too little too late.

Of course the most inflammatory film of the decade, if not the century, was Martin Scorsese's *The Last Temptation of Christ*. "I've always wanted to do a spiritual movie," he explained, "but religion gets in the way."[67] He'd planned making it a decade before he got it off the ground as he searched for a studio "willing to risk the wrath of Christian fundamentalist groups who had used intimidating tactics against studio officials."[68]

He knew he was playing with fire. The book, written by Nikos

Kazantsakis, had caused havoc when it was first published in 1948. The following year, hardly surprisingly, Kazantsakis was excommunicated from the Eastern Orthodox Church and his novel put on the Catholic Church's Index of Forbidden Books. When he died, he was denied a Christian burial.

The film caused a lot of anger among die-hard Catholics because of its suggestion that Jesus fantasized about marriage and Mary Magdalene, and also because he had doubts about his divinity. Scorsese knew it was blasphemous in the extreme but felt it was also necessary for people to challenge their faith by thinking, as it were, outside the box.

Michael Bliss praised him for the bravery of his vision: "The Christ in films such as *The Greatest Story Ever Told* and *Ben-Hur* passes through each film with a halo of adoration swirling around his head. Such films speak only to people already convinced of Jesus' divinity so they accomplish nothing in the way of widening his appeal. It's precisely his uncertainty, the foundation of his agonies and temptations, that paradoxically makes the crucifixion story so glorious."[69] Scorsese underlined this when he explained, "I wanted to use Kazantsakis' concepts to tear away at all those old Hollywood films — even though I love them — and create a Jesus you could maybe talk to, question, get to know."[70]

Apprehension greeted the film's eventual release. In New York, 100 police officers were drafted in amid fears of violence while 1,000 protestors swarmed outside a theater.[71]

Richard Corliss raved about it in *Time*: "Scorsese's first achievement in *Last Temptation* is to strip the Biblical epic of its encrusted sanctimony and showbiz. By jolting the viewer to reconsider Hollywood's calcified stereotypes of the New Testament he wants to restore the immediacy of that time, the stern wonder of that land, the thrilling threat of meeting the Messiah on the mean streets of Jerusalem."[72] Corliss wasn't convinced it was a Christian movie, "but it sure is Catholic. Iconographically it springs from the luxuriant Catholicism of the Mediterranean peasant, for whom the church is a pervasive shepherd, cop, forgiving mother and town scold, and Christ is a living, bleeding presence, as familiar as a best friend or a guilty conscience."[73]

Scorsese put it this way: "I don't really see a conflict between the church and the movies, the sacred and the profane. Obviously there are major differences, but I can also see great similarities between a church and a movie house. Both are places for people to come together and share a common experience. And I believe there's a spirituality in films even if it's not one which can supplant faith. It's as if movies answer an ancient quest for the common unconscious."[74]

Christopher Deacy thought Scorsese took issue with "the Alexandrian portrait of Jesus that Scorsese was taught at his Roman school in his youth, whereby the figure of Jesus effectively glowed in the dark and carried his celestial choir around with him everywhere."[75]

The emphasis on Jesus' humanity was necessary. If Christ was totally God then "temptation is meaningless, resistance is easy and struggle is absent," which makes the film lose its *raison d'etre*.[76] Christ triumphs "not simply because as God he can do no less but because as man he faces down his demons."[77] He's a salvific figure not despite his struggles but because of them.[78]

Peter Fraser expressed Scorsese's ambition with profundity: "Scorsese inadvertently challenged the authority of a weakened church in America and embarrassed popular evangelicalism by attempting a form of popular evangelism according to evangelicalism's own subjectivist and materialistic tendencies. [He also] demythologized the holy aura that surrounded the old Hollywood epic."[79] Scorsese defended the film by insisting it was made as "a prayer, an act of worship."[80]

It was, if anything, even more daring than the book on which it was based, giving us a Christ who was insecure about his mission, prone to hallucinatory delusions, tortured by identity crises and driven demented by passionate feelings towards Christianity's especial *femme fatale*, Mary Magdalene.

Was the world ready for such a film? Yes and no. Stephen Tropiano attempted to see it in perspective considering the hype surrounding it: "The world did not come to an end. The earth continued to spin. California did not sink into the ocean. As the number of demonstrators started to dwindle outside the theaters, so did the audiences inside."[81]

Sheamus Smith, the Irish film censor, found himself buried in a blizzard of missives from irate citizens even before it reached Ireland. Many of these contained "prayer pamphlets, rosaries, holy medals and various publications on the lives of the saints." Groups of people also sang hymns outside his office.[82] One woman asked him if he could help a "special friend" of hers. He thought she might be looking for a favor but when he asked who the friend was, she answered "Jesus." She thought the screening of the film would bring a curse to Ireland. Smith even got a warning from the Archbishop of Dublin, Desmond Connell.[83]

He passed it uncut and gave it an Over 18 certificate. Cinemas showing it were obliged to display a notice in the foyer pointing out that it was based on Kazantsakis' book rather than the Gospels. Smith felt the biggest problem with it wasn't the blasphemy but rather its lengthy running time. His colleague

Jerome Hegarty agreed. His reaction after seeing it was "Jaysus, I thought they'd never get him up on that bloody cross!"[84]

In Salt Lake City, thieves stole the print of the film that was to be shown and the screen was slashed. Los Angeles vandals ripped up seats and spray-painted threats against the distributors of the movie. Scorsese got hate mail and death threats, though the treatment he got was mild in comparison to that accorded to another blasphemer. Shortly after *Last Temptation* was released, Salman Rushdie published *The Satanic Verses* and the Ayatollah Khomeini issued a *fatwa* against him, calling on Muslims to assassinate him because his book insulted the prophet Muhammad. Donald Thomas alluded to this point after *Last Temptation* was shown on television in 1995: "Thereafter, the adage of debunking Judaism is fascist, debunking Islam is racist, but debunking Christianity is free speech acquired a certain plausibility."[85]

Sydney Pollack's reaction was more upbeat. "Christianity survived for 2,000 years," he chirped. "It will survive Martin Scorsese's movie."[86] Clint Eastwood gave a very Clint Eastwood reaction: "Freedom of speech is the American Way."[87]

Paul Coates argues in *Cinema, Religion and the Romantic Legacy* that the controversy surrounding *Last Temptation* mirrors the anger that greeted Godard's *Hail Mary* a few years before: "Both films place their Biblical protagonists uncomfortably in the context of the body and its desires. Insofar as the text mocks the spirit, it does so as the ventriloquist's dummy of these desires."[88] Coates thinks that many of the people who accuse these films of being blasphemous haven't even seen them, "for to do so would seem to endorse sacrilege."[89]

Peter Fraser agrees. Though both of these films were regarded as blasphemous for "drawing portraits of Christ, that appeared too human," what they were actually attempting was the opposite—"attempting to lift the human to an understanding and embrace of the divine. The films move towards a convergence of heaven and earth, as did the older epics."[90]

Michael Medved thought the film had little more than "shocking gore, arid stretches of appalling boredom, laughable dialogue and unbearably bad acting."[91] This was harsh but he suspects other people he knew felt the same way. One colleague definitely did, but yet wrote a glowing review of the film. When Medved asked him why, he replied, "Look, I know the picture's a dog, and probably Scorsese knows it too. But with all the Christian crazies shooting at him from every direction I'm not going to knock him in public."[92]

What we're witnessing here is a view of a man rather than his work. Or rather the man's liberal ideology. This is just as reprehensible as the blanket approval of the soft-centered clerical films of yore which Medved mentions.

But many critics did come out against *Last Temptation*. Medved believes this negative response made Scorsese even more anti-clerical than he had been heretofore. So much so that when he remade *Cape Fear* a few years later he portrayed the villain (Robert De Niro) as a religious freak, in marked contrast to the character that was his template in the original 1962 film. Emphasis on the religious dimension of the villain in *Cape Fear*, Medved suggests, "might well be Scorsese's revenge on the born-again believers who had so passionately protested against his previous picture."[93] He feels there's a lot of rubbish turning up on our screens these days and a part of him pines for the era of the much-maligned Production Code, which today is "generally reviled as a misguided attempt at repression."[94]

Medved cites the attempt of Cardinal Roger Mahony of the Archdiocese of Los Angeles to reinstate the Code in 1992. Addressing a public forum at the Hollywood Roosevelt Hotel on February 1 of that year, Mahony proclaimed to the congregation before him: "Perhaps the time is ripe for the entertainment industry to consider the advisability of having such a code. I would encourage the media to look upon calls for reform not as a censorship issue but rather as an issue of human rights and dignity."[95]

Not surprisingly, his remarks caused bewilderment among the wider community. The American Civil Liberties Union ran an ad in *Daily Variety* with the headline "What? Back to separate beds?"[96] Medved was a lone voice in seeing the cardinal's point. He realized the re-introduction of the Code would be impossible in today's world, as indeed would any self-policing scheme, but he's still glad we have media watchdog organizations like the Christian Film and Television Commission, the American Family Association, Focus on the Family, etc.

Peter Greenaway's *The Cook, the Thief, His Wife and Her Lover* fell foul of CARA in 1989 on account of its scatology, nudity and cannibalism. It got an X rating, which it exploited in cavalier fashion with the billboard tag-line: "X for Xtraordinary." As so often happens in matters of these kinds of strictures, it ended up making much more money than it would have done if it hadn't become embroiled in controversy.

Or is this to adopt too simplistic a view? Jack Valenti, the president of the MPAA, cogently commented, "If you make a movie that a lot of people want to see, no rating will hurt you. And if you make a movie that few people want to see, no rating will help you."[97]

5. Nothing Succeeds Like Excess

"The correlation of nudity and sex with frankness and cinematic realism," Jody Pennington wrote, had been associated with European films and independent American ones in the 1950s and 1960s, but by the end of the 1980s had become "a Hollywood convention" in PG-13 or R-rated films.[98]

Director Philip Kaufman's *Henry and June* (1990) dealt with the steamy affair between two literary giants, Anaïs Nin and Henry Miller, and also Nin's fascination with Miller's wife June. CARA slapped an X on it, largely on account of its lesbian material but also, intriguingly, because one scene had a Japanese postcard showing a woman with an octopus. Kaufman complained, "I can't imagine who that's going to offend unless there's a 17-year-old octopus in the audience."[99]

He had to cut the film to pacify CARA but in September of that year the X rating was scrapped altogether in favor of one called NC-17. This meant that nobody under 17 years could be admitted to a given film. It sounded like a fair compromise but the film still caused a flood of protest, and many cinema owners who bemoaned the demise of the "X" refused to screen it.

By now, viewers might have been entitled to feel they'd reached scandal fatigue. What they didn't reckon on was a blonde bombshell, the veteran of a string of forgettable movies, being snatched from oblivion by a Dutch director to play a new kind of villainess in a big-budget slasher movie.

Basic Instinct (1992) was the film which made Sharon Stone a sex sensation overnight, largely on the strength of "that" scene in the police station where she uncrossed her legs during her interrogation and revealed, well, practically everything. She afterwards accused her director Paul Verhoeven of showing more than he said he would. "You could see all the way up to Nebraska," she joked.[100] But she could hardly quibble. After a lengthy film apprenticeship she was suddenly rich, famous and in huge demand.

"If you have a vagina and an attitude in this town," she snorted dismissively of Hollywood, "that's a lethal combination."[101] Stone-bashers countered by claiming she herself always exhibited more of the former than the latter in her films. Katharine Hepburn complained, "It's a new low for actresses when you have to wonder what's between her ears instead of her legs."[102] Other viewers aligned her exposition to a gynecological procedure.

Stone played a lesbian murderess. She was castigated for both misogyny and homophobia as a result. Michael Douglas, her co-star, remarked commonsensibly that somebody has to be the villain in a crime movie, and it couldn't always be the Italians. Stone was bemused by the fact that people seemed more shocked by the fact that her character was a lesbian than the fact that she was a serial killer.[103]

A group called Queer Nation met up with the director and asked for script revisions. They also demanded that the film feature the murders of women as well as men "to avoid labeling lesbians as hating men."[104] It was picketed upon its release, and regarded not only as homophobic and misogynistic but also "lesbophobic." Once again Douglas, who had outraged feminists with *Fatal Attraction* not too long before (Glenn Close being regarded as the human personification of AIDS), was in the wars. Verhoeven made many cuts to rather to ensure his $50 million film would recoup its profits.

Natural Born Killers (1994) turned the heat up even higher. This is a film which makes *Bonnie and Clyde* look like *Mary Poppins*. Even the title seemed to be an endorsement of its violence, as if there is indeed such a phenomenon as a "natural born" killer which would exculpate him/her in some way for their misdeeds.

Director Oliver Stone wallowed in such violence, which was galvanized by jumpy editing and a disconcerting soundtrack. He didn't appear to even adduce a reason for the two main characters' wanton slaughter until co-star Juliette Lewis told him one day on the set that he would have to show that something happened to her character, callousness and cruelty coming from pain rather than irresponsibility. After this conversation, Stone added a

Sharon Stone in *Basic Instinct* (1992) demonstrating some, er, basic instincts with Michael Douglas.

5. Nothing Succeeds Like Excess 177

Woody Harrelson and Juliette Lewis show the world a trendy way to blow people away in Oliver Stone's *Natural Born Killers* (1994).

flashback scene in which she was abused by her father, played by Rodney Dangerfield (a discernibly unlikely role for the stand-up comic).

Lewis chooses her victims at random, going "Eenie, meenie, miney, mo" as if tossing up between two flavors of ice cream she might purchase. Audiences were divided between revulsion at what they saw and a curious kind of hero worship. Stone incited the kind of adrenalin stars like James Cagney had called up in the 1930s as his woosome twosome went on the rampage in a blood-curdling orgy of sick kicks.

Many viewers seemed able to put their normal humane instincts on the back burner for the film's duration, which increased the danger for those who remained immune to its dubious charms. In the end, when the media catch up with them, their fate becomes a circus.

The film was castigated for excessive displays of sex and violence but Stone suggests much more of this than he shows, which may account for some of its subversive appeal. Much of it looks like a video, the kind of thing Marilyn Manson or Eminem might market in our own time. It has all the hallmarks of an MTV ad, Stone's now-familiar *Blitzkrieg* style of direction giving his killers a kind of dispensation by having them cast as victims of a culture where soundbites are spewed at them by the nano-second from various cacophonous outlets. In such a context, it's "society" (yawn) that's the real murderer because it murders people's souls. This would perhaps have been acceptable if Woody Harrelson spent more time acting instead of posturing, and if Stone leavened his OTT camera-wielding somewhat.

He was lauded by the critics because his frenetic bag of directorial tricks hadn't, as yet, become a mannerism. Lewis was impressive as the traumatized child but it's really an *auteur* movie and when the *auteur* in question persists in drawing attention to his own psychedelic shenanigans, we feel we're being emotionally blackmailed. If this doesn't negate our sympathies, it certainly dilutes them.

The film is an unapologetic homage to *A Clockwork Orange* but Kubrick made his film at a time when it was revolutionary to play with such anarchic notions. By 1994 (the "Stone" age?) they were pallid rehashes of a departed vision. Neither did the presence of Robert Downey Jr., another overrated actor out of his depth, help Stone's cause, the satire here being too blatant. Downey is the token redneck TV host, "Everyman" if you like, who unleashes the expectable amount of outrage on the hapless pair. Bonnie and Clyde would never have allowed things get this sloganistic.

Owen Gleiberman agreed that the film resembled *A Clockwork Orange* in the way it depicted violence, "both real and imagined, as a kind of drug, a ruthlessly addictive force that hooked an entire society."[105]

In Britain, James Ferman did something unusual for a censor: He asked for a scene that had been deleted by the MPAA to be re-inserted. It was the one where Harrelson kills a woman after having sex with Lewis. He felt the conjunction of the two activities would make the murder more repugnant instead of having it disappear "among the general mayhem of the film."[106]

Stone told Irish journalist and anti-censorship campaigner Ciaran Carty that he didn't see it as an exercise in sordid bloodletting but rather "an indictment of the media's opportunist role in fomenting the modern culture of violence."[107]

Garrison Keillor rowed in with "Censorship can't eliminate evil, it can only kill freedom."[108] Carty liked this appraisal. He didn't think *Natural Born Killers* was subversive of public morality but that censorship itself was.[109] He took issue with the Irish film censor Sheamus Smith, who banned it. Smith only banned seven films in his 17-year tenure as censor (1986–2003), in contrast to his predecessor, Dermot Breen, who banned 46 films in only six years. Smith saw his role not as a "restrictive force" but rather a "responsible purveyor of consumer advice and guidance on film and video material."[110] But he felt he had to take a tough line on this film as "Ireland was living with a gun culture; IRA murders and atrocities were daily occurrences." He feared copycat killings as he'd heard these took place in France and the U.S.[111]

David Cronenburg went one further in 1996 with his weirded-out movie *Crash* where the sex impetus this time is provided by car accidents, the ensuing wrecks and physical pain acting as commodious aphrodisiacs for the characters. It was passed in Britain without cuts but the Westminster City Council banned its showing in London for fear that "sexually inexperienced people may look to the main characters as role models."[112] One writer outlined the ludicrousness of this view by demonstrating the hypothetical reaction of such "sexually inexperienced" people: "Honey, let's crash the car tonight and have sex in the back seat like they did in that movie!"[113]

The following year a *Lolita* remake boasted scintillating performances from a tortured Jeremy Irons as Humbert and Dominique Swain giving an Oscar-worthy performance in the title role. This was light years closer to Nabokov's character than Sue Lyon could ever have dreamed of in the 1962 original. Lyon had looked like a snooty teenager but Swain was a sultry seductress all too well aware of how she was pushing Irons' buttons even as she grew from girl to woman.

Four months before the film was completed, a real-life disaster struck as JonBenet Ramsey, a beautiful little girl from Colorado, was found dead in her home. It was a story that captivated and shocked the world almost as much as the O.J. Simpson murder had. JonBenet was a pageant beauty, groomed by her parents for glory and now they were suspects for her murder. Was she sexualized too early? Did her case expose a disease in the American culture that turned little girls into sex symbols when they were hardly out of the cradle? These were the water cooler conversations that intrigued the nation ... and perhaps killed the new *Lolita* at the box office.

The U.S. shunned the movie and it didn't do much better in Europe. Arthouse cinemas appreciated its undeniable quality but the subject matter was far too close to the bone. Some years later, Ben Affleck's brilliantly convoluted directorial debut *Gone, Baby, Gone* (2007) would suffer a similar fate, its projected release coinciding with the death of Madeleine McCann, another child whose terrible real-life fate made shocking headlines and put the film into cold storage. Today, both of these movies can of course be seen on DVD, but sometimes art must bow to the raw pain of people involved in traumas too deep for words — or images.

A new phenomenon of the depiction of sex and violence in the cinema is its over-the-top-ness, which sometimes descends into farce. We see this in everything from the Wes Craven *Scream* films to the work of people like David Lynch and Brian De Palma. David Denby wrote of De Palma's *Dressed to Kill*: "He releases terror in laughter. Even at his most outrageous, Hitchcock could not have been as entertaining as this."[114]

So now we seem to have reached a new frontier in liberalism: the dumbing down of all feeling to worship at the altar of *schadenfreude*. The price we've paid for the voice of the *auteur* has been very high indeed. Maybe there's yet time for that particular check to bounce.

6

After the Deluge

The battle against censorship has long been won, which means that direly bad films with strong sexual and/or heretical content have come through the system as prolifically as artistic ones. This, needless to say, is the price for winning any battle, and the foundation upon which a liberal society is built. But that doesn't mean we have to like it. Freedom of speech should mean people actually have something worthwhile to say.

Neither should we presume that pressures against such liberalism will ever be completely eroded. This is also a good thing—within reason.

In recent times we've had organizations that resemble the Legion of Decency, e.g. the Christian Film and Television Commission, which issues a fortnightly magazine called *Movieguide*. As rigid in its way as the Legion of Decency was eight decades before, *Movieguide* saw fit to diss the innocuous comedy *Mrs. Doubtfire* (1993) because it disregarded Verse 22 of the Book of Deuteronomy which states unequivocally: "A woman must not wear men's clothing nor a man wear women's clothing for the Lord your God detests anyone who does this." (Off the top of my head I can think of perhaps fifty movies which would fail to satisfy *Movieguide* on this score, many of which have won Oscars.)

Films should really be about transparency. William Holden once remarked of his role in *Sunset Boulevard* (1950), "I had to sit on Gloria Swanson's bed in that movie with one foot firmly on the floor, and my overcoat on. Everyone in the audience knew I was living with her as a kept man. Why did we have to be so modest?"[1]

In 1992 Louis Malle earned the wrath of the ratings board when he featured a nude scene between Jeremy Irons and Juliette Binoche in *Damage*. He railed, "Why does America have such a strange taboo about nudity when it allows ice picks to be slashed into the chests of lovers in films like *Basic Instinct?*" There would always be this culture gap between Europe and the U.S.

There have been other curious censorial decisions both in and outside the U.S. What, for instance, is one to make of the PG-13 rating of the 1996 disaster movie *Twister* because of its "intense depiction of bad weather"?[2]

Going My Way (1944) was banned in many Latin American countries because Bing Crosby's priest wears a sweatshirt and baseball cap in one scene. Sweden banned *E.T. The Extra-Terrestrial* (1982) because it was claimed the film showed parents being hostile to their offspring. And then there was the curious decision of Prince Rainier to ban all of his wife Grace Kelly's films in Monaco, where they lived.[3] This man was a publicist's worst nightmare. What price privacy?

Perhaps the poignant nature of censorship in general is encapsulated in an anecdote Frank Walsh relates in his book *Sin and Censorship* regarding the film *Cinema Paradiso*. In this Italian gem set in a small town, the local priest forces the projectionist to excise all romantic scenes from the films he's showing, with the result that one boy in attendance remarks, "I've been going to the movies for twenty years and I've never seen a kiss."[4]

At the end of the film the projectionist dies and the boy, now a film director, goes back to the little town for his funeral. The cinema has long been pulled down but before he died the projectionist spliced together all the excised kissing footage and kept it as a memento for him. As he watches the montage of stars like Cary Grant, Rudolph Valentino and Rosalind Russell engaged in amorous clinches, he's overcome with nostalgia for the old man. And for his own departed youth.

"Working in the national office of the Legion of Decency, in New York," Walsh remarks, "a small group of priests and laywomen performed a task very similar to that of the lone cleric in *Cinema Paradiso*. They, however, assumed the burden of safeguarding the morals not only of a small town but an entire nation. And anyone who tried to splice together all the cuts Hollywood made in the 16,251 feature films classified by the Legion and its successor, the National Catholic Office for Motion Pictures, would face a much more formidable task than the one undertaken by the *Cinema Paradiso* projectionist."[5]

Oscar Wilde put it well when he suggested that there were no moral or immoral works of art, only those well and badly made. Will Hays wouldn't have had much truck with this line of thinking, too busy marketing his wares like soap. Today, of course, sex scenes start where those of yesteryear ended. As Bob Hope joked, "They're doing things in films today that I wouldn't dare to do — even if I could!"

6. After the Deluge

Something else that should be said regarding the explosion of sexual material onto the market since the 1980s is the emergence of video chains, which have transformed virtually every house in the country into a private cinema, and made it more difficult to monitor ratings systems where younger viewers are present. A decade later, DVDs provided another exponential leap in the availability of questionable material to all and sundry.

Jody Pennington comments: "The pornography industry discovered a goldmine in the two formats. Mainstream companies re-released films in uncut or unrated editions that included nudity or sex scenes excised from theatrical releases, a variation of the studios' dual releases for the European and American markets in the 1950s."[6] Such glossy phenomena as "Director's Cuts," "Digital Remastering" and "Bonus Features" have all enabled re-packaging of previously released movies, many of dubious artistic integrity.

Have we gone too far? Will over-exposure to substandard movies eventually result in their non-existence? Gerald Gardner believes this. He argues simply: "Boredom will drive out the smut."[7]

The new millennium began with a film ironically called *Romance* (1999). *Sex* would have been a more appropriate title for here, as would be the case with *9 Songs* some years later, we were given more graphic sex than had ever appeared in a mainstream film before. Indeed, the director, Catherine Breillat, believed her two main stars actually had sex during the filming.[8]

Maybe the ankle bracelet Barbara Stanwyck wore in 1944's *Double Indemnity* was sexier than the robust rompings of actresses like Claudia Cardinale, Charlotte Rampling, Madonna, Isabelle Hubert, Gina Lollobrigida, Diana Dors, Mamie Van Doren, Bo Derek and countless others, as well as the likes of Jessica Alba and Megan Fox in our own time.

Such rompings, frequently with little or nothing to do with the plot of the film in which they feature (which may, indeed, have no plot to speak of *anyway*), have made many people pine nostalgically for the days when directors had to dream up subtle ways to escape the eagle eyes of Mr. Hays and his somewhat draconian clampdowns on lewdness.

The sex symbols that followed Marilyn have let us down. Here's Andrew Sarris on one of them, Raquel Welch: "I don't believe she actually exists. She's been manufactured by the media merely to preserve the sexless plasticity of sex objects for the masses."[9] There's also a problem with the way, even today, censors take a tougher line on sex than violence. Sally Struthers made a good point about the imbalance: "If a man is pictured chopping off a woman's breast, it only gets an R rating, but if, God forbid, he's pictured kissing one, it gets an X. Why is violence more acceptable than tenderness?"[10] These words were spoken many years ago but they're still relevant even if the same exact details don't apply.

Molly Haskell doesn't see too much difference between sex and violence in essence. Violence, for her, is "the indispensable staple of male pornography."[11]

The bare facts of the matter, if that's not the wrong phrase in the context, is that while sex definitely sells, it doesn't sell as well as violence, so there's less to be lost in giving a sexual film an Over 15 or Over 18 cert than a violent one.

There's an argument to be made for the fact that some of the top moneyspinners of all time — *E.T.*, *Home Alone*, the *Star Wars* movies and *Indiana Jones* ones — got "soft" ratings to let younger audiences see them. The MPAA is owned and operated by the major studios. Does it do its best to protect children from violence or is it dependent on it? Restrictive ratings diminish films' profits because the younger age groups can't attend them. Too much blurriness, on the other hand, leads to mixed signals.

It's a vicious circle, and we're all wearing blinkers, bowing to peer pressure and propaganda. In an era which permits the likes of Quentin Tarantino's *Kill Bill* to trivialize violence, this fact becomes even more squalid. Ever since *Halloween* and *Friday the 13th*, children don't know whether to scream or chortle, and the *Scary Movie* series is happy to catch them between the two extremes. This gives rise to more swelling of the coffers for the unscrupulous organ grinders. And all in the name of winnowing out potentially pernicious material.

Surely this would make a good satire for somebody like the Coen Brothers. The material is right there in their own backyard. Traditionally, Hollywood has been honest about confronting the mote in its own eye in film but this theme hasn't, tackled yet. It's high time it was.

Which isn't to say there weren't double standards in the past either. The aforementioned Irish film critic Ciaran Carty attended a showing of *Rosemary's Baby* in University College, Dublin, in October 1971 and was impressed with it, as were the students in the audience. "Why," he asked afterwards, "is it all right for a member of a film society to see it whereas it would be a perversion of public morality for the same person to see it in a Dublin cinema? Is there a moral difference between a person who is a member of a film society and one who is not?"[12]

6. After the Deluge

The former Irish film censor James Montgomery was once asked what he knew about movies and replied alarmingly, "Nothing, but I know about the Ten Commandments."[13] Perhaps this says it all about the mores of the 1930s and 1940s, when he held sway. He saw his job as a missionary one, declaring, "I am between the devil and the Holy See. My task is to prevent the Californication of Ireland."[14] He liked this kind of language, announcing at another time that the main danger to Ireland wasn't Anglicization, as many feared, but its "Los Angelesation."[15]

Carty reminds us that films were ruthlessly censored in the past without a by-your-leave and the public were largely kept in the dark about the reasons for such dissections, as were the movie companies: "Distributors submitting movies claimed they had no idea what the censor or the Appeals board meant by obscenity. Shots passed in one movie might be cut in another. There was no consistency other than to treat every movie with suspicion."[16]

Carty believes that "the essential criteria in reaching a decision on [Over 18] movies should be the intent of the director and overall artistic merit of the movie rather than any possible moral considerations."[17] Not that these should ever be mutually exclusive.

As previously mentioned, Carty devoted much of his journalistic career to highlighting the injustices of the Irish censorship system which either banned or mercilessly hacked to pieces many masterpieces from eminent directors like Ingmar Bergman, Federico Fellini and Michelangelo Antonioni, as well as a host of British and American ones, and indeed some Irish as well. He wrote to many of these directors advising them of the manner in which their works were being butchered without rhyme or reason and received sympathetic letters in reply outlining their disgust at the system and appreciation for his support.

Sometimes he became the target of abusive letters from those who felt he was trawling in mud. He even received threatening phone calls from unknown sources, his wife having to endure heavy breathers on the line when he was out of the house. One letter he received from a Father Tiernan in County Sligo berated him for having "a fixation about the little snippets" removed by the censor. Father Tiernan said he was grateful to the censor for removing "these embarrassing bits of dirt from otherwise good films, just as I thank my victualler when he trims off unwanted bits from my steak before he sells it to me."[18]

Father Tiernan went on to say he felt the people who liked these snippets preserved were largely "pimply youths, middle-aged men with coat collars furtively turned up and hat brims down, a handful of pale bearded students and a scattering of lonely immigrants from warmer climes, all of whom have as much interest in art as a cat has in the law of thermodynamics."[19]

The incensed priest ended his diatribe by asking: "Is anyone naive enough to believe that *I Am Curious (Yellow)* has run so long because of the sociological questionnaire that runs through it? Or that *Hair* is booked months in advance because of the patrons' love of rock music? The old barker in the strip club was at least honest when he announced, 'Yes, sir, it's all for Art's sake, and if Art's in the front row I hope he enjoys it!'"[20]

It's notable that the priest in question didn't refer to any genuinely artistic film in his letter, but his sentiments no doubt were representative of the feelings of many Catholics of the time who tended to equate "foreign" with "salacious" when it came to filmmaking, and to deride those who frequented arthouse cinemas as glorified Peeping Toms with a license for their voyeurism.

The Catholic Church was a very potent force in Ireland when Father Tiernan penned these missives. It's significantly less so today, both in Ireland and the U.S., and this fact has fed into the manner in which priests are depicted on screen, as opposed to yesteryear when they often behaved as though personally anointed by God.

"Priests," Les and Barbara Keyser reminisced in *Hollywood and the Catholic Church*, "were major heroic figures in crime films, shoulder to shoulder with FBI men, revenue agents and other agents of morality. Super Padre was born around the time Superman came crashing down from Krypton, and for years a few Latin mumblings and a breviary could quiet the most savage beast. One imagined that if Bing Crosby, Spencer Tracy and Pat O'Brien traded in their soutanes for battle fatigues they could win the war on racketeering almost single-handedly."[21]

Michael Medved mourns the fact that contemporary films are, generally speaking, rabidly anti-church. In the good old days, he remembers, "if a character appeared on screen wearing a clerical collar it served as a sure sign that the audience was supposed to like him."[22] Today, on the other hand, films present "a view of the clergy that is every bit as one-sided in its cynicism and hostility as the old treatment may have been idealized and saccharine. Whenever someone turns up in a contemporary film with the title 'Reverend' or 'Rabbi' in front of his name you can count on the fact that he will turn out to be corrupt or crazy — or both."[23]

"In the opening decade of the twentieth century," James Skinner stated in his book *The Cross and the Cinema*, "the Roman Catholic Church in the

6. After the Deluge

United States was an Irish immigrant institution above all else."[24] He puts this down to a multiplicity of factors, not least because of the huge Irish population in America that resulted from a common language between the two countries and the massive emigration from Ireland to the U.S. in the aftermath of Ireland's horrendous potato famine in 1847.

The result was that Irish Catholic influences percolated through many early American movies, reaching their apotheosis, perhaps, in the number of priests played by Irish actors like Barry Fitzgerald and Pat O'Brien throughout their careers. The huge numbers of conservative Irish-Americans attending movies obviously had to have an impact on the content of such movies, and this manifested itself most markedly in the censorial restrictions first instituted in the early 1920s. These became infinitely more stringent after 1934 when the Legion of Decency was formed and issued a virtual moratorium on anything smacking of loose morals.

That all changed, changed utterly in the following decades, as we've seen, the church losing ground on a raft of issues upon which its views were once held sacrosanct. In 1995, the Pontifical Council for Social Communication listed 45 films that possessed special artistic and/or religious merit. Among that list were two films that had, half a century before, been branded morally objectionable: Fellini's *La Strada* and Vittoria De Sica's *The Bicycle Thief.*

It could be argued that the church, like the censors, often tended to take a tougher line on sex than violence. Lenny Bruce joked about this when he said he'd prefer his kids to see a stag film than *The Ten Commandments*, "because I don't want them to kill Christ when he comes back."[25]

"The collapse of censorship on the matters of screen sex," wrote Baxter Philips, "was due to increasing pressure put on the censors by public criticism, which endlessly reiterated the theme that nakedness and sexual play harmed few by its example, while the violence of war, shown daily on the television newsreels about Vietnam and Ireland, was a worse influence. How could a censor cut out a pair of breasts for an adult audience when any child could see peasants napalmed to agony on the six o'clock news?"[26]

So where does that leave us now? As far back as 1970, Richard Randall wrote:

> Today the censorship boards are faced with the question of, not whether the camera should play upon a woman's face as she is presumably having intercourse (*Ecstasy*), but whether entire bodies should be shown in intercourse (*A Stranger Knocks*); not whether a heroin needle should be shown entering a man's arm (*The Man with the Golden Arm*), but whether a man's leg should be shown after he has been drawn

and quartered (*Two Thousand Maniacs*); not whether a woman should be portrayed as finding happiness in adultery (*Lady Chatterley's Lover*), but whether she should be shown to have sexual congress with a large dog (*491*).[27]

Randall concludes, "It can almost be said that anything censored as late as the early 1960s would be licensed today, and almost anything censored today wouldn't even have been produced for public exhibition as late as the early sixties."[28]

Thomas Doherty, like Medved, suspects the cure may well be worse than the disease, considering the amount of sludge unleashed on us today in our local video outlets and on the Internet: "Few spectators will not flinch [at such excesses] and find a bit of Breen in themselves, itching to grasp final cut away from the hands of less moral sensibilities."[29]

I doubt we could go back to those dark days even if we wanted to. Idealistic pioneers for any cause always carry aberrations of that cause in their wake, but that doesn't mean it wasn't worth fighting for. We can't throw the baby out with the bathwater even if the water is sometimes sullied. There will always be immature viewers who will commit unpardonable acts when they see them portrayed on a cinema screen, but maybe such people wouldn't be able to differentiate between art and artifice anyway, or would find other catalysts for their perverse proclivities.

At the end of the day, we can't have a nanny state legislating for every eventuality. If something is right, we need to have it in our society, and freedom of speech *is* right — in movies, literature and any other branch of the arts you care to mention.

The problem is that this freedom sometimes morphs into vapidity. When we show everything on screen, in a sense we show nothing. We imagine we're more "realistic" today, but as Mick LaSalle quipped about Julia Roberts' hooker in *Pretty Woman* (1991), a lady who simulates oral sex on her knight in shining armor Richard Gere with an array of colored condoms in tow before he whisks her from the bad end of town to yuppiedom in his Golden Chariot: "She was so cuddly and innocuous she would have made any self-respecting pre–Code actress throw up."[30]

And yet, as Jane Mills reminds us in *The Money Shot*, after this film, Roberts became the first woman for twenty years whose name was big enough to sell a movie. What exactly does that say to us about contemporary standards of filmmaking?

We've won the war on nudity as well, thanks to *The Pawnbroker* and other pivotal films, but has it been a pyrrhic victory? Movie nudity, Olivia

Doyle contended, "is the modern-day equivalent of the casting couch scenario. The only difference is that actresses are now being asked to do their thing for mass audiences instead of solely for the person who's auditioning them."[31] Kim Basinger, who should know, has assured us, "The more flesh you show, the higher up the ladder you go."[32]

Gene Autry alluded to Doyle's point when he joked, "Today you see girls doing on screen what they used to do off the screen to get on screen."[33] Shelley Winters was equally mischievous when asked about disrobing in front of the cameras: "I think nudity on screen is disgusting, shameful and unpatriotic. But if I were 22 and with a great body it would be artistic, tasteful and a progressive religious experience."[34]

It took David Rehak to express the view that it's "just as erotic to watch a woman put on her clothes as it is to take them off."[35] Lauren Hutton made a different kind of point when she surmised that it was arguably more intimate to expose one's mind than one's body.[36] Elle McPherson joked, "I don't have a problem with nudity. I was born naked."[37]

Violence can be trickier than sex when it comes to decisions on censoring it. Does one go by body counts, or the nature of an individual example of brutality? In his book *Censored*, Tom Dewe Mathews notes that in the films *Die Hard II* and *Terminator II* there's an aggregate of over 400 corpses, but these films would not be seen to be as dangerous to impressionable minds as, say, *Henry: Portrait of a Serial Killer* or *The Silence of the Lambs*.[38] George Bernard Shaw liked to say, "One death is a tragedy; a million a statistic." He had a point.

Even children seem desensitized to violence in films today. After a showing of the Arnold Schwarzenegger film *Total Recall* (1990), a twelve-year-old girl told *Entertainment Weekly*, "It's pretty funny to see people being shot in the head."[39]

"At each point where the 'art' film led the way," as one writer inferred, "the exploitation film was bound to follow, and to appeal to an audience which demanded more and more explicit savagery on-screen to get it to leave the television set."[40] In 1997 Ian Grey claimed that every night on prime time U.S. television there were "an average of five acts of simulated violence, and 20–25 violent acts on Saturday morning children's TV."[41]

Grey also believes violence gets an easier ride from the critics than sex. Bodies, he says, "may be shredded (*Die Hard II*), ice-picked (*Basic Instinct*) or shot to ribbons (any big-budget action movie) but God forbid we should see naked bodies making love." Nudity was allowed for women, he argues, but male nakedness was usually limited to "chests and fleeting glimpses of buttocks, with the showing of an actual penis out of the question. What sort of message does this give children?"[42] These words were written in 1997. Things have changed since — not least due to actors like Richard Gere and Mel Gibson apparently delighting in going *au naturel.*

It's interesting to note that one of the last films of the last century, *Blue Streak* (1999), was given a PG-13 rating despite the fact that the villains get away with their crimes.

Does violence on the screen cause it to erupt on the streets? This is an argument that will never be resolved by anyone. *A Clockwork Orange* was blamed for the gang rape of a girl in 1973 in England because the men who did it sang "Singin' in the Rain" as they violated her. This was too close for comfort as far as the censors were concerned, that song having counterpointed a violent scene in Kubrick's movie. The fact that it was made two years before the incident in question didn't enter the equation. It was banned, and Kubrick didn't hide his disgust over that fact. As a result, he said he never wanted to see it playing in England.

And then of course there's the case of John Hinckley, who was alleged to have tried to assassinate Ronald Reagan to "impress" the object of his obsession Jodie Foster as a result of seeing Robert De Niro attempt a presidential assassination in *Taxi Driver*, a film in which Foster co-starred. If we're to demonize (or censor) films like this, we might as well also ban J.D. Salinger's *A Catcher in the Rye* on the grounds that Mark Chapman had it on his person when he shot John Lennon to death in New York in 1980. Chapman originally said the book exposed phoniness and he killed Lennon because he epitomized such phoniness in his own life. In more recent times he's admitted that he killed Lennon simply because he was accessible, his original intention being to shoot either Elizabeth Taylor or Johnny Carson.

Many people linked the horrific killing of the Liverpool toddler Jamie Bulger in 1993 by two ten-year-olds, Jon Venables and Robert Thompson, to the film *Child's Play 3* (featuring an evil doll) which had come out shortly before. The two boys were alleged to have watched it, but David Kerekes found no evidence that either had seen it at all. He writes: "The false allegation that *Child's Play 3* was embroiled in the death of James Bulger has been repeated so often it is accepted as an established fact by the ill-informed, yet it is nothing more than an urban myth."[43] Kerekes believes films have been "the scapegoat for many of society's ills since they first went into production."[44]

6. After the Deluge 191

Journalists discovered that the stepfather of one of the two boys had indeed rented a copy of *Child's Play 3* a few weeks before the killing but there was no evidence to suggest that the boys themselves had watched it. Nonetheless, the press jumped to the conclusion that it was a key factor in their motivation. As one author observed, "Perhaps anything was preferable to having to face up to the fact that society can produce ten-year-old murderers."[45]

More recently, a 14-year-old Kentucky boy named Michael Carneal claimed he went on a killing spree because he was influenced by the Leonardo Di Caprio film *The Basketball Diaries*. Oliver Stone's *Natural Born Killers* was believed to have spawned a copycat murder in Paris in 1994 when a middle-class teenager opened fire on policemen. In 1995, a young woman named Sarah Edmondson and her boyfriend Ben Carrus claimed that the film was the inspiration (if that's the word) behind their killing spree which saw them gratuitously shoot a manager and store clerk. And so on. Many people accept the fact that films influence behavior, particularly the behavior of youths impressionable stages of their adolescence, whereas others argue that the depiction of violence acts as a release valve for such tendencies and thereby lessens it. Jane Mills believes that censorship "merely promotes the bias against understanding where the real roots of violence lie."[46]

In an article in the *Chicago Tribune*, Michael Wilmington asked if it was possible that the violence of the 1960s could be in any way attributable to landmark films like *Psycho, Bonnie and Clyde, Midnight Cowboy* and/or *The Wild Bunch*. Maybe, he surmises, it was more likely to have come from "the Vietnam war, the massive proliferation of firearms, the spread of the criminal syndicate and its satellite drug industry, and the crumbling of national morale after the assassination of four major political leaders: the Kennedy Brothers, Martin Luther King and Malcolm X."[47]

"In its day," he concludes, "*Madame Bovary* was regarded as a dirty book. So were *Ulysses* and *Lolita*. So were Jim Thompson's thrillers. Life itself is often dirty, sexy, violent and unpleasant. And movies will always reflect that — unless they're censored."[48]

Hal Hinson, writing in *The Washington Post*, huffed, "Today, with real-life violence all around us, it's harder to be sure about the cathartic function of art. We're concerned that real violence might overwhelm us, sending us off like the Michael Douglas character in *Falling Down*: half-cocked, defeated and looking for revenge."[49]

The evening news programs, he continues, "are nearly giddy with bulletins of bloody deaths, carjackings, rapes and other tragedies. Why, then, do our movie screens have to be packed with more of the same? Why should we have to deal with degenerate madmen like Frank in *Blue Velvet* or Max Cady in *Cape Fear*? What could we possibly learn from them?[50]

He answers his own question: "Everything or nothing, depending upon what each of us brings to the table."[51]

Chapter Notes

Chapter 1

1. Neil Sinyard, *Directors: The All-Time Greats* (New York: Gallery Books, 1985), p. 118.
2. Lee Grieveson, *Policing Cinema* (Berkeley: University of California Press, 2004), p. 210.
3. Edward de Grazia and Roger Newman, *Banned Films: Movies, Censors and the First Amendment* (New York: R.R. Bowker, 1982), p. 29.
4. Molly Haskell, *From Reverence to Rape: The Treatment of Women in the Movies* (Chicago: University of Chicago Press, 1987), p. 116.
5. *Ibid.*, p. 103.
6. Marjorie Rosen, *Popcorn Venus: Women, Movies and the American Dream* (New York: Avon, 1973), p. 112.
7. *Ibid.*, p. 60.
8. *Ibid.*, pp. 60–1.
9. *Ibid.*, p. 61.
10. Annette Kuhn, *Cinema, Censorship and Sexuality, 1909–1925* (New York: Routledge, 1988), p. 76.
11. *Ibid.*, p. 81.
12. Gregory D. Black, *The Catholic Crusade Against the Movies, 1940–1975* (New York: Cambridge University Press, 1997), p. 15.
13. Tom Hickman, *The Sexual Century* (London: Carlton, 1999), p. 45.
14. James M. Skinner, *The Cross and the Cinema: The Legion of Decency and the National Catholic Office for Motion Pictures, 1933–1970* (Westport, CT: Praeger, 1993), p. 11.
15. David Thomson, *The Whole Equation* (London: Little, Brown, 2005), p. 153.
16. Penny Stallings, *Flesh and Fantasy* (New York: Harper & Row, 1978), p. 120.
17. James Robert Parish, *The Hollywood Book of Scandals* (New York: McGraw-Hill, 2004), p. 18.
18. Booton Hendron, *Mary Pickford and Douglas Fairbanks* (New York: W.W. Norton, 1977), p. 196.
19. Gerald Gardner, *The Censorship Papers: Movie Censorship Letters From the Hays Office* (New York: Dodd, Mead & Co., 1987), xvii.
20. Samuel Marx, *Mayer and Thalberg: The Make-Believe Saints* (New York: Random House, 1975) p. 37.
21. Barry Norman, *Talking Pictures* (London: Arrow, 1991), p. 78.
22. Thomson, *The Whole Equation*, p. 154.
23. Paul F. Boller and Ronald L. Davis, *Hollywood Anecdotes* (London: Macmillan, 1987), p. 215.
24. Kenneth Anger, *Hollywood Babylon* (London: Arrow, 1986), p. 46.
25. Leonard L. Leff and Jerold L. Simmons, *The Dame in the Kimono: Hollywood, Censorship and the Production Code* (Lexington: University Press of Kentucky, 2001), xiv.
26. John C. Lyden, *Film as Religion* (New York: New York University Press, 2003), p. 153.
27. Mick LaSalle, *Complicated Women* (New York: Thomas Dunne Books, 2000), pp. 190–1.
28. Morris L. Ernst, *Censored: The Private Life of the Movies* (New York: Jonathan Cape, 1930), pp. 129–30.
29. John Roeburt, *The Wicked and the Banned* (New York: Macfadden, 1963), p. 76.
30. *The Wit and Wisdom of Movies* (Great Britain: House of Raven Book Services, 2005), p. 114.
31. Cass Warner Spelling and Cork Millner, *Hollywood Be Thy Name* (Lexington: University Press of Kentucky, 1998).
32. Gardner, *The Censorship Papers*, xxi.
33. Hortense Powdermaker, *Hollywood: The Dream Factory* (Boston: Little, Brown, 1951), p. 59.
34. Pat O'Brien, *The Wind at my Back* (New York: Doubleday, 1964), p. 170.
35. *Ibid.*
36. *Congressional Record, Volume 62* (67th Congress, June 29, 1922), p. 9657.
37. Arthur Mayer, *Merely Colossal* (New York: Simon & Schuster, 1953), p. 123.

38. Frank Walsh, *Sin and Censorship* (New Haven: Yale University Press, 1996), p. 51.
39. Haskell, *From Reverence to Rape*, p. 21.
40. David Shipman, *Caught in the Act* (London: Elm Tree Books, 1985), p. 78.
41. Lawrence Kardish, *Reel Plastic Magic* (Boston: Little, Brown, 1972), p. 96.
42. *Ibid.*, p. 98.
43. Jack Vizzard, *See No Evil: Life Inside a Hollywood Censor* (New York: Simon & Schuster, 1970), pp. 38–9.
44. Jeremy Pascall and Clyde Jeavons, *A Pictorial History of Sex in the Movies* (London: Hamlyn, 1976), p. 53.
45. *Ibid.*
46. Haskell, *From Reverence to Rape*, p. 104.
47. Frank M. Laurence, *Hemingway and the Movies* (New York: Da Capo, 1981), p. 52.
48. *Ibid.*, p. 158.
49. Robert Byrne, ed., *The 2,548 Best Things Anybody Ever Said* (New York: Galahad Books, 1996), p. 483.
50. Doug McClelland, *The Unkindest Cuts: The Scissors and the Cinema* (Cranbury, NJ: A.S. Barnes & Co., 1972) p. 53.
51. Gregory D. Black, *Hollywood Censored* (New York: Cambridge University Press, 1994), p. 115.
52. *Ibid.*, p. 126.
53. Jonathan Munby, *Public Enemies, Public Heroes* (Chicago: University of Chicago Press, 1999), p. 192.
54. Patrick McGilligan, *Cagney: The Actor as Auteur* (Cranbury, NJ: A.S. Barnes & Co., 1975), p. 30
55. Sarah J. Smith, *Cinema, Children and Censorship: From Dracula to the Dead End Kids* (London: I.B. Tauris, 2005), p. 152.
56. Stephen Tropiano, *Obscene, Indecent, Immoral and Offensive* (New York: Limelight Editions, 2009), p. 159.
57. Peter Bogdanovich, *Who the Devil Made It* (New York: Alfred A. Knopf, 1997), p. 521.
58. Ian Cameron, *A Pictorial History of Crime* (London: Hamlyn, 1975), p. 26.
59. Hickman, *The Sexual Century*, p. 169.
60. Lea Jacobs, *The Wages of Sin: Cinema and the Fallen Woman* (Berkeley: University of California Press, 1997), p. 150.
61. LaSalle, *Complicated Women*, p. 235.
62. *Ibid.*, p. 236.
63. Murray Schumach, *The Face on the Cutting Room Floor* (New York: Da Capo, 1975), p. 87.
64. Pascall and Jeavons, *A Pictorial History of Sex in the Movies*, p. 68.
65. *Ibid.*
66. *Ibid.*
67. Geoff Tibballs, ed., *The Mammoth Book of Insults* (London: Robinson, 2007), p. 70.
68. Mardy Grothe, *Oxymoronica* (New York: HarperCollins), p. 150.
69. Tibballs, *The Mammoth Book of Insults*, p. 83.
70. John Robert Colombo, ed., *The Wit and Wisdom of the Movie Makers* (London: Hamlyn, 1978), p. 129.
71. *Ibid.*
72. Rosemarie Jarski, *Hollywood Wit* (London: Prion, 2000), p. 69.
73. John Daintith, ed., *Bloomsbury Dictionary of Quotations* (London: Bloomsbury, 1987), p. 124.
74. Mark A. Vieira, *Sin in Soft Focus* (New York: Harry N. Abrams, 1999), p. 107.
75. Les and Barbara Keyser, *Hollywood and the Catholic Church: The Image of Roman Catholicism in American Movies* (Chicago: Loyola University Press, 1984), p. 22.
76. *Ibid.*, pp. 24–5.
77. *Ibid.*, p. 26.
78. Gardner, *The Censorship Papers*, p. 80.
79. *Ibid.*, p. 9.
80. Paul Simpson, ed., *The Rough Guide to Cult Movies* (London: Haymarket Customer Publishing, 2004), p. 157.
81. Theresa Sanders, *Celluloid Saints* (Macon, GA: Mercer University Press, 2002), p. 39.
82. Hickman, *The Sexual Century*, p. 44.
83. Will H. Hays, *The Memoirs of Will H. Hays* (New York: Doubleday, 1955), p. 450.
84. LaSalle, *Complicated Women*, p. 201.
85. Black, *Hollywood Censored*, p. 163.
86. Walsh, *Sin and Censorship*, p. 150.
87. *America 51*, p. 152.
88. Frank Miller, *Censored Hollywood: Sex, Sin and Violence on the Screen* (Atlanta: Turner Publishing, 1994), p. 82.
89. *Ibid.*
90. Kardish, *Reel Plastic Magic*, p. 100.
91. Vieira, *Sin in Soft Focus*, p. 172.
92. Black, *The Catholic Crusade Against the Movies*, p. 240.
93. Harold C. Gardiner, *Catholic Viewpoint on Censorship* (Garden City, NY: Image Books, 1961), p. 194.
94. Thomas Doherty, *Pre-Code Hollywood: Sex, Immorality and Insurrection in American Cinema, 1930–1934* (New York: Columbia University Press, 1999), p. 8.
95. Vizzard, *See No Evil*, p. 51.
96. Doherty, *Pre-Code Hollywood*, p. 56.
97. Smith, *Cinema, Children and Censorship*, p. 60.
98. Vieira, *Sin in Soft Focus*, p. 182.
99. *Ibid.*
100. *Ibid.*
101. Tropiano, *Obscene, Indecent, Immoral and Offensive*, p. 78.

102. *Ibid.*
103. Olga J. Martin, *Hollywood's Movie Commandments* (New York: Arno Press, 1937), p. 33.
104. Tropiano, *Obscene, Indecent, Immoral and Offensive*, p. 79.
105. Alexander Walker, *Sex in the Movies* (Middlesex: Penguin, 1969), p. 192.
106. *Ibid.*
107. Doherty, *Pre-Code Hollywood*, p. 11.
108. Shipman, *Caught in the Act*, p. 17.
109. Walker, *Sex in the Movies*, p. 77.
110. *Ibid.*
111. *Ibid.*
112. Gardner, *The Censorship Papers*, p. 165.
113. Keyser, *Hollywood and the Catholic Church*, p. 39.
114. Richard S. Randall, *Censorship of the Movies* (Madison: University of Wisconsin Press, 1970), p. 168.
115. Barry Norman, *Talking Pictures* (London: Arrow, 1991), p. 5.
116. *Ibid.*
117. Hickman, *The Sexual Century*, p. 50.
118. Colleen McDannell, *Catholics in the Movies* (New York: Oxford University Press, 2008), p. 93.
119. Black, *Hollywood Censored*, p. 39.
120. Vizzard, *See No Evil*, p. 36.
121. *Ibid.*, p. 63.
122. Shipman, *Caught in the Act*, p. 38.
123. Leff and Simmons, *The Dame in the Kimono*, xv.
124. Tony Bilbow and John Gau, *Lights, Camera, Action* (London: Little, Brown, 1995), p. 137.
125. Walsh, *Sin and Censorship*, pp. 72–3.
126. Robert Andrews, ed., *Thematic Dictionary of Quotations* (London: Collins, 1987), p. 36.
127. Schumach, *The Face on the Cutting Room Floor*, p. 43.
128. Black, *The Catholic Crusade Against the Movies*, p. 244.

Chapter 2

1. Marybeth Hamilton, *The Queen of Camp* (London: HarperCollins, 1996), p. 178.
2. Simon Louvish, *Mae West: It Ain't No Sin* (London: Faber & Faber, 2005), p. 134.
3. Walker, *Sex in the Movies*, p. 68.
4. Laura Ward, ed., *Putdowns* (London: Robson, 2004), p. 143.
5. Byrne, ed., *The 2,548 Best Things Anybody Ever Said*, p. 423.
6. Tibballs, ed., *The Mammoth Book of Insults*, p. 102.
7. David Shipman, *Movie Talk* (London: Bloomsbury, 1988), p. 216.
8. Boze Hadleigh, ed., *Hollywood Babble On* (New York: Birch Lane Books, 1994), p. 77.
9. Vieira, *Sin in Soft Focus*, p. 195.
10. Walker, *Sex in the Movies*, p. 74.
11. Hadleigh, ed., *Hollywood Babble On*, p. 181.
12. Maurice Leonard, *Mae West: Empress of Sex* (London: HarperCollins, 1991), p. 113.
13. Vieira, *Sin in Soft Focus*, p. 116.
14. LaSalle, *Complicated Women*, p. 153.
15. *Ibid.*, pp. 153–4.
16. *Ibid.*, p. 154.
17. Leonard, *Empress of Sex*, p. 127.
18. Gardner, *The Censorship Papers*, p. 139.
19. *Ibid.*
20. Kevin Rockett, *Irish Film Censorship* (Dublin: Four Courts Press, 2004), p. 97.
21. Scott and Barbara Siegel, *American Film Comedy from Abbott and Costello to Jerry Zucker* (New York: Prentice Hall, 1994), p. 188.
22. Patrick Robertson, *Film Facts* (London: Aurum Press, 2001), p. 199.
23. Gardner, *The Censorship Papers*, p. 116.
24. *Ibid.*, p. 111.
25. Hedy Lamarr, *Ecstasy and Me* (London: W.H. Allen, 1967), p. 26.
26. *Ibid.*, p. 17.
27. Gardner, *The Censorship Papers*, p. 73.
28. Leff and Simmons, *The Dame in the Kimono*, p. 41.
29. Dawn B. Sova, *Forbidden Films* (London: Checkmark Books, 2001), p. 25
30. *Ibid.*
31. Tony Crawley, ed., *Chambers' Film Quotes* (Edinburgh: W&R Chambers, 1991), p. 64.
32. Jarski, ed., *Hollywood Wit*, p. 212.
33. Doug McClelland, *Hollywood on Hollywood* (Boston: Faber & Faber, 1985), p. 63.
34. Fergus Cashin, *Mae West* (London: Star Publishing, 1982), p. 103.
35. *Ibid.*, p. 102.
36. Schumach, *The Face on the Cutting Room Floor*, p. 221.
37. Walker, *Sex in the Movies*, p. 93.
38. Vizzard, *See No Evil*, p. 42.
39. Leonard, *Empress of Sex*, p. 154.
40. Walker, *Sex in the Movies*, p. 76.
41. Jarski, *Hollywood Wit*, p. 211.
42. *Wit and Wisdom of the Movies*, p. 126.
43. Louvish, *It Ain't No Sin*, p. 301.
44. Graham Greene, *The Pleasure Dome* (Oxford: Oxford University Press, 1980), p. 75.
45. Rosen, *Popcorn Venus*, p. 36.
46. Robert K. Johnston, *Reel Spirituality* (Grand Rapids, MI: Baker Academic, 2000), p. 36.
47. Bilbow and Gau, *Lights, Camera, Action*, p. 18.

48. Leff and Simmons, *The Dame in the Kimono*, pp. 109–10.
49. Warren G. Harris. *Clark Gable: A Biography* (London: Aurum Press, 2002), p. 205
50. De Grazia and Newman, *Banned Films*, p. 53.
51. Carlos Clarens, *Crime Movies: An Illustrated History* (New York: W.W. Norton, 1979), p. 154.
52. Tom Dewe Mathews, *Censored* (London: Chatto & Windus, 1994), p. 76.
53. Colin Jarman, ed., *Dictionary of Poisonous Quotations* (London: Guinness, 1991), p. 134.
54. De Grazia and Newman, *Banned Films*, p. 66.
55. Hadleigh, ed., *Hollywood Babble On*, p. 244.
56. Schumach, *The Face on the Cutting Room Floor*, p. 55.
57. Black, *Hollywood Censored*, p. 293.
58. Pascall and Jeavons, *A Pictorial History of Sex in the Movies*, p. 99.
59. Aubrey Malone, *Hollywood Trivia* (London: Prion, 2004), p. 43.
60. *Ibid.*, p. 44.
61. *Ibid.*, p. 43.
62. Julian Petley, *Censorship: A Beginner's Guide* (Oxford: OneWorld, 2009), p. 65.
63. Miller, *Censored Hollywood*, p. 120.
64. McDannell, ed., *Catholics in the Movies*, p. 94.
65. Haskell, *From Reverence to Rape*, p. 197.
66. Al Diorio, *Barbara Stanwyck* (London: W.H. Allen, 1983), pp. 123–4.
67. *Tidings*, August 11, 1954.
68. John Robert Colombo, *The Wit and Wisdom of Hollywood* (London: Hamlyn, 1979), p. 135.
69. De Grazia and Newman, *Banned Films*, p. 63.
70. McDannell, ed., *Catholics in the Movies*, p. 99.
71. John Griggs, *The Films of Gregory Peck* (London: Columbus Books, 1988), p. 64.
72. Tropiano, *Obscene, Indecent, Immoral and Offensive*, p. 82.
73. Griggs, *The Films of Gregory Peck*, p. 68.
74. *Ibid.*
75. Gardner, *The Censorship Papers*, p. 32.
76. Skinner, *The Cross and the Cinema*, p. 87.
77. Jay Robert Nash and Stanley Ralph Russ, *The Motion Picture Guide* (Chicago: Chicago Cinebooks, 1985), p. 2,440.
78. Schumach, *The Face on the Cutting Room Floor*, p. 164.
79. Skinner, *The Cross and the Cinema*, p. 95.
80. De Grazia and Newman, *Banned Films*, p. 78.
81. *Evening Standard*, 10 November, 1949.

Chapter 3

1. John Huston, *An Open Book* (London: Macmillan, 1981).
2. Sam Kashner, *The Bad and the Beautiful: A Chronicle of Hollywood in the Fifties* (London: Little, Brown, 2002), p. 126.
3. *New York Times*, February 11, 1951.
4. Parish, *The Hollywood Book of Scandals*, p. 117.
5. Laurence Leamer, *As Time Goes By: The Life of Ingrid Bergman* (London: Sphere Books, 1986), p. 259.
6. Tropiano, *Obscene, Indecent, Immoral and Offensive*, p. 88.
7. Adriano Apra, ed., *My Method: Writings and Interviews* (New York: Marsilio Publishers, 1992), p. 51.
8. Tropiano, *Obscene, Indecent, Immoral and Offensive*, p. 88.
9. Black, *The Catholic Crusade Against the Movies*, p. 93.
10. Kardish, *Reel Plastic Magic*, p. 202.
11. James C. Robertson, *The Hidden Cinema* (London: Routledge, 1989), p. 100.
12. Tropiano, *Obscene, Indecent, Immoral and Offensive*, p. 89.
13. Black, *The Catholic Crusade Against the Movies*, p. 101.
14. Federico Fellini, with Charlotte Chandler, *I, Fellini* (London: Bloomsbury, 1994), p. 65.
15. *Ibid.*, p. 64.
16. Jeff Young, *Kazan on Kazan* (London: Faber & Faber, 1999), pp. 83–4.
17. Leff and Simmons, *The Dame in the Kimono*, p. 177.
18. Rudy Behlmer, *Behind the Scenes* (New York: Samuel French, 1990), p. 221.
19. Shipman, *Caught in the Act*, p. 112.
20. Behlmer, *Behind the Scenes*, p. 222.
21. *Ibid.*, p. 223.
22. *Ibid.*, p. 231.
23. Leff and Simmons, *The Dame in the Kimono*, p. 187.
24. *Ibid.*
25. *Ibid.*, p. 181.
26. Brian Neve, *Film and Politics in America: A Social Tradition* (London: Routledge, 1992), p. 206.
27. Charles Higham, *Brando* (London: Grafton Books), 1989, p. 142.
28. Elia Kazan, *A Life* (New York: Alfred A. Knopf, 1988), p. 345.
29. Vizzard, *See No Evil*, p. 177.
30. Marlon Brando, *Songs My Mother Taught Me* (London: Century, 1994), p. 152.
31. Richard Schickel, *Brando: A Life in Our Times* (New York: Atheneum, 1991), p. 67.

Notes — Chapter 3

32. Petley, *Censorship: A Beginner's Guide*, p. 68.
33. Lilli Palmer, *Change Lobsters and Dance: An Autobiography* (New York: Dell, 1975), pp. 165–6.
34. *Empire*, March 2003, p. 145.
35. Anthony Aldgate and James C. Robertson, *Censorship in Theatre and Cinema* (Scotland: Edinburgh University Press, 2005), p. 29.
36. *The Star*, 26 June, 1953.
37. Otto Preminger, *An Autobiography* (New York: Doubleday, 1977), p. 108.
38. Black, *The Catholic Crusade Against the Movies*, p. 123.
39. *Ramparts 4*, September 1965, p. 44.
40. Tropiano, *Obscene, Indecent, Immoral and Offensive*, p. 126.
41. *Ibid.*, p. 123.
42. Bilbow and Gau, *Lights, Camera, Action*, p. 147.
43. Jon Lewis, *Hollywood V. Hard Core* (New York: New York University Press, 2000), p. 108.
44. Bogdanovich, *Who the Devil Made It*, p. 626.
45. Petley, *Censorship: A Beginner's Guide*, p. 68.
46. *The Star*, January 8, 1954.
47. De Grazia and Newman, *Banned Films*, p. 86.
48. *Ibid.*, p. 87.
49. Skinner, *The Cross and the Cinema*, p. 113.
50. Anthony Slide, *Banned in the U.S.A.* (London: I.B. Tauris, 1998), p. 7.
51. Schumach, *The Face on the Cutting Room Floor*, p. 68.
52. *Variety*, June 3, 1953, p. 6.
53. Pascall and Jeavons, *A Pictorial History of Sex in the Movies*, p. 141.
54. Schumach, *The Face on the Cutting Room Floor*, p. 66.
55. *Ibid.*, p. 67.
56. Gardner, *The Censorship Papers*, p. 54.
57. Petley, *Censorship: A Beginner's Guide*, p. 86.
58. Mathews, *Censored*, p. 132.
59. Hickman, *The Sexual Century*, p. 106.
60. *Fifty Years of "Playboy" Cartoons* (San Francisco: Chronicle Books, 2004), p. 4.
61. Vizzard, *See No Evil*, p. 158.
62. McDannell, ed., *Catholics in the Movies*, p. 25.
63. Baxter Philips, *Cut: The Unseen Cinema* (London: Lorrimer, 1975), p. 57.
64. Pascall and Jeavons, *A Pictorial History of Sex in the Movies*, p. 174.
65. De Grazia and Newman, *Banned Films*, p. 91.
66. Gardner, *The Censorship Papers*, p. 170.
67. Kardish, *Reel Plastic Magic*, p. 197.
68. Harry Shapiro, *Shooting Stars: Drugs, Hollywood and the Movies* (London: Serpent's Tail, 2003), p. 96.
69. *Ibid.*, p. 98.
70. *New York Post*, December 18, 1956.
71. Young, *Kazan on Kazan*, p. 226.
72. *Ibid*.
73. Michel Ciment, ed., *Elia Kazan: An American Odyssey* (London: Bloomsbury, 1988), p. 84.
74. *Empire*, March 2003, p. 145.
75. *Hollywood Citizen News*, December 17, 1956.
76. *New York Times*, December 21, 1956.
77. *Ibid.*, December 24, 1956.
78. De Grazia and Newman, *Banned Films*, p. 244.
79. *Time*, December 24, 1956.
80. Eli Wallach, *The Good, The Bad, and Me* (New York: Harcourt, 2005), pp. 174–5.
81. *Ibid.*, p. 176.
82. Jarman, ed., *Dictionary Of Poisonous Quotations*, p. 126.
83. Jeff Young, *Kazan: The Master Director Discusses His Films* (New York: Newmarket Press, 1999), p. 226.
84. Norman, *Talking Pictures*, p. 24.
85. Black, *The Catholic Crusade Against the Movies*, p. 168.
86. *Empire*, March 2003.
87. Lewis, *Hollywood V. Hard Core*, p. 125.
88. Tennessee Williams, *Memoirs* (London: W.H. Allen, 1976), pp. 169–70.
89. Lewis, *Hollywood V. Hard Core*, p. 126.
90. *Hollywood Citizen News*, December 17, 1956.
91. Kazan, *A Life*, p. 564.
92. *Ibid*.
93. Tropiano, *Obscene, Indecent, Immoral and Offensive*, p. 209.
94. Karl Malden, *When Do I Start?* (New York: Simon & Schuster, 1997), pp. 251–2.
95. De Grazia and Newman, *Banned Films*, p. 94.
96. Gardner, *The Censorship Papers*, p. 187.
97. *Ibid.*, p. 188.
98. Skinner, *The Cross and the Cinema*, p. 125.
99. Ben Hecht, *A Child of the Century* (New York: Simon & Schuster, 1954, p. 479.
100. McDannell, ed., *Catholics in the Movies*, p. 26.
101. De Grazia and Newman, *Banned Films*, p. 98.
102. Rosen, *Popcorn Venus*, p. 304.
103. *Ibid.*, p. 305.
104. Rockett, *Irish Film Censorship*, p. 149.

105. Shipman, *Movie Talk*, p. 147.
106. *Ibid.*, p. 148.
107. Guus Luijters, ed., *Marilyn Monroe: In Her Own Words* (London: Omnibus, 1990), p. 111.
108. *New York Times*, August 2, 1998, p. 19.
109. Shipman, *Movie Talk*, p. 11.
110. *Irish Independent*, 16 June, 2009, p. 9.
111. Rosen, *Popcorn Venus*, p. 297.
112. Philips, *Cut: The Unseen Cinema*, p. 60.
113. *Empire*, March 2003.
114. *Variety*, February 10, 1969, p. 1.
115. *Ibid.*, June 19, 1963, p. 5.
116. Pascall and Jeavons, *A Pictorial History of Sex in the Movies*, p. 185.
117. *Ibid.*
118. Walsh, *Sin and Censorship*, p. 291.
119. Jarman, ed., *Dictionary of Poisonous Quotations*, p. 130.
120. Tiballs, ed., *The Mammoth Book of Insults*, p. 88.
121. Skinner, *The Cross and the Cinema*, xiv.
122. Haskell, *From Reverence to Rape*, p. 235.
123. De Grazia and Newman, *Banned Films*, p. 259.
124. Randall, *Censorship of the Movies*, p. 65.
125. Roy Pickard, *James Stewart: The Hollywood Years Facts* (London: Robert Hale, 1992), p. 145.
126. Trevelyan, *What the Censor Saw*, p. 183.
127. Simpson, *The Rough Guide to Cult Movies*, p. 141.
128. Williams, *Memoirs*, p. 176.
129. Sova, *Forbidden Films*, p. 257.
130. David Shipman, ed., *Scorsese on Scorsese* (London: Faber & Faber, 1990), xxv.
131. Bilbow and Gau, *Lights, Camera, Action*, p. 246.
132. Haskell, *From Reverence to Rape*, p. 325.
133. *Ibid.*

Chapter 4

1. Sinyard, *Directors: The All-Time Greats*, p. 57.
2. Pauline Kael, *Deeper Into Movies* (Boston: Little, Brown, 1973), p. 127.
3. *Ibid.*, pp. 129–30.
4. *Ibid.*, p. 131.
5. Paul Coates, *Cinema, Religion and the Romantic Legacy* (Aldershot, England: Ashgate, 2003), p. 18.
6. *Ibid.*, p. 131.
7. Robyn Karney, *Burt Lancaster: A Singular Man* (London: Bloomsbury, 1996), p. 120.
8. Kate Buford, *Burt Lancaster: An American Life* (London: Aurum Press, 2005), p. 205.
9. Gary Fishgall, *Against Type: The Biography of Burt Lancaster* (New York: Scribner, 1995), p. 187.
10. Michael Munn, *Burt Lancaster* (London: Robson, 1995), p. 129.
11. *Ibid.*
12. Buford, *Burt Lancaster: An American Life*, p. 203.
13. *Ibid.*
14. *Ibid.*
15. *Ibid.*, p. 204.
16. Fishgall, *Against Type*, p. 201.
17. Walker, *Sex in the Movies*, p. 193.
18. *Ibid.*, p. 194.
19. John Harkness, *The Academy Awards Handbook: Who Won What When* (New York: Pinnacle Books, 1994), p. 160.
20. *The Wit and Wisdom of Movies*, p. 126.
21. Schumach, *The Face on the Cutting Room Floor*, p. 159.
22. *Ibid.*, p. 215.
23. Doug McClelland, *Starspeak* (Boston: Faber & Faber, 1987), p. 61.
24. Mathews, *Censored*, p. 148.
25. Boze Hadleigh, *Hollywood Bitch* (London: Robson, 1999), p. 128.
26. Charlotte Chandler, *It's Only a Movie* (New York: Simon & Schuster, 2005), p. 259.
27. *Ibid.*, p. 266.
28. Simpson, *Cult Movies*, p. 188.
29. Rockett, *Irish Film Censorship*, p. 129.
30. Doherty, *Pre-Code Hollywood*, pp. 343–4.
31. *Ibid.*, p. 345.
32. *Minutes of the 44th Annual National Conference of Catholic bishops in the U.S.*, October 1962.
33. *Variety*, July 18, 1962, p. 18.
34. Skinner, *The Cross and the Cinema*, p. 143.
35. *Ibid.*, p. 144.
36. *Ibid.*
37. Leff and Simmons, *The Dame in the Kimono*, p. 229.
38. Walsh, *Sin and Censorship*, p. 302.
39. *Ibid.*, p. 244.
40. *Ibid.*, pp. 227–8.
41. Alexander Walker, *Stanley Kubrick Directs* (London: Abacus, 1973).
42. Miller, *Censored Hollywood*, p. 193.
43. *Variety*, June 13, 1962, p. 6.
44. *Time*, June 22, 1962, p. 94.
45. John Lessard, ed., *To Quote a Queer* (Philadelphia: Quirk, 2008), p. 59.
46. Kashner, *The Bad and the Beautiful*, p. 103.
47. Mark Harris, *Scenes From a Revolution* (Edinburgh: Canongate, 2008), p. 208.
48. Hadleigh, *Hollywood Bitch*, p. 216.
49. Robertson, *Film Facts*, p. 199.

50. Gardner, *The Censorship Papers*, p. 191.
51. Walker, *Sex in the Movies*, p. 196.
52. Hadleigh, ed., *Hollywood Babble On*, p. 229.
53. *Ibid.*, p. 243.
54. Shipman, *Movie Talk*, p. 97.
55. *Empire*, March 2003.
56. *The Wit and Wisdom of Movies*, p. 120.
57. *Empire*, March 2003.
58. Brando, *Songs My Mother Taught Me*, p. 121.
59. Jarski, *Hollywood Wit*, p. 211.
60. Hickman, *The Sexual Century*, p. 132.
61. Vizzard, *See No Evil*, p. 304.
62. Skinner, *The Cross and the Cinema*, p. 150.
63. Peter Biskind, *Seeing is Believing* (London: Bloomsbury), p. 343.
64. Vizzard, *See No Evil*, p. 308.
65. Black, *The Catholic Crusade Against the Movies*, p. 221.
66. *The Tablet*, 214, May 21, 1960, p. 23.
67. *Variety*, 4 April, 1965.
68. Marjorie Heins, *Sex, Sin and Blasphemy* (New York: New Press, 1993), p. 104.
69. Vizzard, *See No Evil*, p. 162.
70. *America*, 112, June 26, 1965, p. 895.
71. *Exhibitor*, June 2, 1965.
72. Black, *The Catholic Crusade Against the Movies*, p. 228.
73. *Film Heritage 1*, 1966, p. 1.
74. Petley, *Censorship: A Beginner's Guide*, p. 70.
75. Harris, *Scenes from a Revolution*, p. 265.
76. Walker, *Sex in the Movies*, p. 262.
77. Hadleigh, *Hollywood Bitch*. p. 30.
78. Jonathon Green, ed., *Dictionary of Cynical Quotations* (London: Cassell, 1994), p. 34.
79. Byrne, *The Best 2,548 Things Anybody Ever Said*, p. 276.
80. Skinner, *The Cross and the Cinema*, p. 161.
81. *Hollywood Reporter*, 62nd Anniversary Edition, 1992.
82. Vizzard, *See No Evil*, p. 326.
83. *Ibid.*
84. *Ibid.*, p. 315.
85. De Grazia and Newman, *Banned Films*, p. 290.
86. Walker, *Sex in the Movies* p. 258.
87. Michael Medved, *Hollywood Vs. America: Popular Culture and the War on Traditional Values* (New York: HarperCollins, 1992), p. 282.
88. Harris, *Scenes from a Revolution*, p. 181.
89. *Ibid.*, p. 183.
90. Medved, *Hollywood Vs. America*, p. 283.
91. Vizzard, *See No Evil*, p. 353.
92. *Film Yearbook*, 1989.
93. McClelland, *Starspeak*, p. 62.
94. *The Wit and Wisdom of Movies*, p. 119.
95. Robertson, *Film Facts*, p. 195.
96. Walker, *Sex in the Movies*, p. 265.
97. *New York Times*, April 20, 1967.
98. Sheamus Smith, *Off-Screen* (Dublin: Gill & Macmillan, 2007), pp. 233–4.
99. Mathews, *Censored*, p. 182.
100. Robertson, *Film Facts*, p. 199.
101. *Village Voice*, December 1, 1992.
102. Harris, *Scenes from a Revolution*, p. 257.
103. *Ibid.*, p. 256.
104. Jane Mills, *The Money Shot* (Annandale, NSW: Pluto, 2001), p. 82.
105. *Village Voice*, December 1, 1992.
106. *Ibid.*
107. Jon Grey, *Sex, Stupidity and Greed* (New York: Juno Books, 1997), p. 98.
108. Peter Keough, ed., *Flesh and Blood* (San Francisco: Mercury House, 1995), p. 319.
109. Jerzy Toeplitz, *Hollywood and After* (London: Allen & Unwin, 1974), p. 149.
110. *Time*, December 20, 1971.
111. Peter Biskind, *Easy Riders, Raging Bulls* (London: Bloomsbury, 1998), p. 35.
112. Richard Koszarski, ed., *Hollywood Directors 1941–76* (New York: Oxford University Press, 1977), p. 359.
113. *Ibid.*, pp. 362–3.
114. Sova, *Forbidden Films*, p. 163.
115. Nikolas Schreck, *The Satanic Screen* (London: Creation Books, 2000), p. 137.
116. Tropiano, *Obscene, Indecent, Immoral, Offensive*, p. 251.
117. *Ibid.*
118. Lyden, *Film as Religion*, p. 31.
119. *The Wall Street Journal*, February 24, 1994.
120. Mathews, *Censored*, p. 150.
121. Trevelyan, *What the Censor Saw*, p. 156.
122. *Ibid.*, p. 120.
123. *Ibid.*, p. 209.
124. *Ibid.*, p. 187.
125. Rosen, *Popcorn Venus*, p. 364.
126. Sean French, *Jane Fonda* (London: Pavilion, 1997), p. 68.
127. Rosen, *Popcorn Venus*, p. 364.
128. LaSalle, *Complicated Women*, p. 231.

Chapter 5

1. Justin Smith, *Withnail and Us* (London: I.B. Tauris, 2010), p. 76.
2. Gene Phillips and Rodney Hill, *The Encyclopedia of Stanley Kubrick* (New York: Checkmark Books, 2002), pp. 52–3.
3. *Film in Review*, Jan–Feb, 1995, p. 40.
4. Smith, *Withnail and Us*, p. 82.
5. *Sight and Sound*, February 1972, p. 5.

6. Smith, *Withnail and Us*, p. 79.
7. Simpson, *The Rough Guide to Cult Movies*, p. 44.
8. Haskell, *From Reverence to Rape*, p. 362.
9. Robertson, *Film Facts*, p. 203.
10. Mathews, *Censored*, p. 195.
11. Trevelyan, *What the Censor Saw*, p. 162.
12. John Baxter, *Ken Russell: An Appalling Talent* (London: Michael Joseph, 1973), p. 153.
13. *Ibid.*, p. 188.
14. Shaun Allen, ed., *Dancing Ledge* (London: Quartet, 1984), p. 100.
15. Oliver Reed, *Reed: All About Me* (London: W.H. Allen, 1979), p. 134.
16. *Empire*, March 2003.
17. Joseph Lanza, *Phallic Frenzy* (London: Aurum, 2007), p. 123.
18. *Ibid.*, p. 5.
19. *Ibid.*, p. 122.
20. *Ibid.*, p. 4.
21. *Ibid.*, p. 123.
22. Philips, *Cut: The Unseen Cinema*, p. 93.
23. Lanza, *Phallic Frenzy*, p. 121.
24. Jarski, *Hollywood Wit*, p. 74.
25. Mathews, *Censored*, p. 194.
26. Trevelyan, *What the Censor Saw*, p. 67.
27. Barbara Siegel and Scott Siegel, *Jack Nicholson* (London: Angus & Robertson, 1990), p. 64.
28. Robert Sellers, *Bad Boy Drive* (London: Preface, 2009), pp. 136–7.
29. Haskell, *From Reverence to Rape*, p. 360.
30. Ciaran Carty, *Confessions of a Sewer Rat* (Dublin: New Island, 1995), p. 99.
31. Brando, *Songs My Mother Taught Me*, p. 425.
32. Mathews, *Censored*, pp. 210–1.
33. Sellers, *Bad Boy Drive*, p. 155.
34. *Ibid.*, p. 156
35. Brando, *Songs My Mother Taught Me*, p. 426.
36. *Guardian*, November 18, 1972.
37. Black, *The Catholic Crusade Against the Movies*, p. 237.
38. Haskell, *From Reverence to Rape*, p. 314.
39. Tropiano, *Obscene, Indecent, Immoral, Offensive*, p. 214.
40. Rosen, *Popcorn Venus*, p. 353.
41. Mark Kermode, *The Exorcist* (London: British Film Institute, 1997), p. 110.
42. Keyser, *Hollywood and the Catholic Church*, pp. 204–5.
43. *Ibid.*, p. 205.
44. Pauline Kael, *Reeling* (Boston: Little, Brown, 1976), p. 249.
45. Keyser, *Hollywood and the Catholic Church*, p. 212.
46. John R. May and Michael Bird, eds., *Religion in Film* (Knoxville: University of Tennessee Press, 1982), p. 84.
47. Schreck, *The Satanic Screen*, p. 168.
48. *Ibid.*, p. 169.
49. Mathews, *Censored*, p. 214.
50. Petley, *Censorship: A Beginner's Guide*, pp. 72–3.
51. David Kerekes, *See No Evil* (Manchester: Headpress, 2000), p. 209.
52. McDannell, *Catholics in the Movies*, p. 202.
53. *Ibid.*
54. Shipman, *Movie Talk*, p. 27.
55. Munn, *Gregory Peck*, p. 204.
56. Grey, *Sex, Stupidity and Greed*, p. 65.
57. Shipman, *Caught in the Act*, p. 151.
58. Tropiano, *Obscene, Indecent, Immoral and Offensive*, p. 256.
59. Ben Forest with Mary Kay Mueller, *God Goes to Hollywood* (Lincoln, NE: Writers Club Press, 2000), p. 140.
60. Roy Kinnard and Tim Davis, *Divine Images* (New York: Citadel Press, 1992), p. 195.
61. *Ibid.*
62. *Image: A Journal of the Arts and Religion*, 20, Summer 1998, p. 27.
63. Andrew Yule, *A Life on The Wire* (London: Warner, 1991), p. 214.
64. *Ibid.*, p. 216.
65. Black, *The Catholic Crusade Against the Movies*, p. 239.
66. De Grazia and Newman, *Banned Films*, pp. 148–50.
67. McDannell, *Catholics in the Movies*, p. 321.
68. Sova, *Forbidden Films*, p. 174.
69. Michael Bliss, *The Word Made Flesh* (Lanham, MD: Scarecrow Press, 1998), p. 91.
70. Robin Riley, *Film, Faith and Cultural Conflict* (Westport, CT: Praeger, 2003), p. 38.
71. *Empire*, March 2003.
72. Kinnard and Davis, *Divine Images*, p. 207.
73. *Film Comment*, Sept.–Oct. 1988.
74. Clive Marsh and Gaye Ortiz, *Explorations in Theology and Film* (Hoboken, NJ: Blackhall, 1997), ii.
75. Christopher Deacy, *Screen Christologies* (Cardiff: University of Wales Press, 2001), p. 86.
76. Lawrence Friedman, *The Cinema of Martin Scorsese* (Oxford: Roundhouse, 1997), p. 115.
77. *Ibid.*, p. 113.
78. Deacy, *Screen Christologies*, p. 89.
79. Peter Fraser, *Images of the Passion* (Westport, CT: Praeger, 1998), p. 172.
80. Richard Blake, *Afterimage* (Chicago: Loyola Press, 2000), p. 35.

81. Tropiano, *Obscene, Immoral, Indecent, Offensive*, p. 260.
82. Smith, *Off-Screen*, pp. 220–1.
83. *Ibid.*, p. 221.
84. *Ibid.*, p. 222.
85. Donald Thomas, *Freedom's Frontier: Censorship in Modern Britain* (London: John Murray, 2007), p. 15.
86. *New York Times*, August 13, 1988.
87. *Ibid.*
88. Coates, *Cinema, Religion and the Romantic Legacy*, p. 188.
89. *Ibid.*
90. Fraser, *Images of the Passion*, p. 173.
91. Medved, *Hollywood Vs. America*, p. 46.
92. *Ibid.*, pp. 48–9.
93. *Ibid.*, p. 67
94. *Ibid.*, p. 91.
95. *Ibid.*, p. 322.
96. *Ibid.*
97. Miller, *Censored Hollywood*, p. 257.
98. Pennington, *The History of Sex in American Film*, p. 84.
99. *L.A. Times*, August 27, 1990.
100. Douglas Thompson, *Sharon Stone* (London: Little, Brown, 1994), p. 132.
101. *Empire*, June 1992.
102. Jasmine Birtles, *Chick Wit* (London: Prion, 2004), p. 112.
103. *Parkinson*, BBC, March 11, 2006.
104. Sova, *Forbidden Films*, p. 34.
105. *Entertainment Weekly*, August 26, 1994.
106. Robertson, *Film Facts*, p. 197.
107. Carty, *Confessions of a Sewer Rat*, p. 185.
108. Heins, *Sex, Sin and Blasphemy*, p. 185.
109. Carty, *Confessions of a Sewer Rat*, p. 190.
110. Smith, *Off-Screen*, Preface.
111. *Ibid.*, p. 227.
112. Tripiano, *Obscene: Indecent, Immoral and Offensive*, p. 229.
113. *Ibid.*
114. *New York Times*, July 28, 1980, p. 44.

Chapter 6

1. *Photoplay*, May 1977.
2. Robertson, *Film Facts*, p. 198.
3. *Ibid.*, p. 2.
4. Walsh, *Sin and Censorship*, p. 1.
5. *Ibid.*, p. 2.
6. Pennington, *The History of Sex in American Film*, p. 92.
7. Gardner, *The Censorship Papers*, p. 205.
8. Mills, *The Money Shot*, pp. 132–5.
9. Tibballs, ed., *Mammoth Book of Insults*, p. 97.
10. *Life*, 1984.
11. Haskell, *From Reverence to Rape*, p. 364.
12. Carty, *Confessions of a Sewer Rat*, p. 70.
13. *Ibid.*, p. 44.
14. Ulick O'Connor, *Oliver St. John Gogarty* (London: Granada, 1981).
15. *Irish Times*, February 15, 1943, p. 1.
16. Carty, *Confessions of a Sewer Rat*, p. 41.
17. *Ibid.*, pp. 59–60.
18. *Ibid.*, p. 36.
19. *Ibid.*
20. *Ibid.*
21. Keyser, *Hollywood and the Catholic Church*, p. 62.
22. Medved, *Hollywood Vs. America*, p. 51.
23. *Ibid.*, p. 52.
24. Skinner, *The Cross and the Cinema*, p. 23.
25. Philips, *Cut: The Unseen Cinema*, p. 96.
26. *Ibid.*, pp. 78–9.
27. Randall, *Censorship of the Movies*, p. 228.
28. *Ibid.*
29. Doherty, *Pre-Code Hollywood*, p. 345.
30. LaSalle, *Complicated Women*, p. 236.
31. *The Star*, March 16, 1993, p. 12.
32. *Ibid.*
33. Gene Shalit, ed., *Great Hollywood Wit* (New York: St. Martin's Press, 2002), p. 104.
34. *Ibid.*
35. David Rehak, *Poems from My Bleeding Heart* (Lexington, KY: CreateSpace, 2008), p. 38.
36. Jarski, *Hollywood Wit*, p. 207.
37. Joey Berlin, *Toxic Fame* (Detroit: Invisible Ink, 1996), p. 205.
38. Mathews, *Censored*, p. 260.
39. Medved, *Hollywood V. America*, p. 189.
40. Philips, *Cut: The Unseen Cinema*, p. 65.
41. Grey, *Sex, Stupidity and Greed*, p. 68.
42. *Ibid.*, p. 66.
43. Kerekes, *See No Evil*, p. 328.
44. *Ibid.*, p. 316.
45. Mills, *The Money Shot*, p. 73.
46. *Ibid.*, p. 93.
47. *Chicago Tribune*, June 5, 1994.
48. *Ibid.*
49. *Washington Post*, May 23, 1993.
50. *Ibid.*
51. *Ibid.*

Bibliography

Albee, Edward. *Who's Afraid of Virginia Woolf?* (New York: Atheneum, 1962).

Aldgate, Anthony. *Censorship in Theatre and Cinema* (Scotland: Edinburgh University Press, 2005).

Andrew, Geoff. *Hollywood Gangsters* (New York: Gallery Books, 1985).

Anger, Kenneth. *Hollywood Babylon* (London: Arrow Books, 1986).

Apra, Adriano, ed. *My Method: Writings and Interviews* (New York: Marsilio Publishers, 1992).

Austin, John. *Hollywood's Babylon Women* (New York: SPI Books, 1994).

Bade, Patrick. *Femme Fatale: Images of Evil and Fascinating Women* (New York: Mayflower, 1979).

Bainbridge, Jim, ed. *Show Me the Money: A Century of Great Movie Lines* (Emeryville, CA: Woodford Press, 1999).

Barrios, Richard. *Screened Out* (London: Routledge, 2003).

Baxter, John. *Hollywood in the Thirties* (Stamford, CT: A.S. Barnes, 1968).

———. *Ken Russell: An Appalling Talent* (London: Michael Joseph, 1973).

Behlmer, Rudy. *Behind the Scenes* (New York: Samuel French, 1990).

Bergan, Ronald. *The Life and Times of the Marx Brothers* (London: Greenwood, 1992).

Berlin, Joey. *Toxic Fame: Celebrities Speak on Stardom* (Detroit: Visible Ink, 1996).

Bernstein, Matthew, ed. *Controlling Hollywood* (New York: Pantheon, 1983).

Bilbow, Tony, and John Gau. *Lights, Camera, Action* (London: Little, Brown, 1995).

Biskind, Peter. *Easy Riders, Raging Bulls* (London: Bloomsbury, 1998).

———. *Seeing Is Believing* (London: Bloomsbury, 2001).

Black, Gregory D. *The Catholic Crusade Against the Movies, 1940–1975* (New York: Cambridge University Press, 1997).

———. *Hollywood Censored: Morality Codes, Catholics, and the Movies* (New York: Cambridge University Press, 1994).

Blake, Richard. *Afterimage* (Chicago: Loyola Press, 2000).

Blatty, William Peter. *The Exorcist* (New York: Harper & Row, 1971).

Bliss, Michael. *The Word Made Flesh* (Lanham, MD: Scarecrow, 1998).

Blumer, Herbert. *Movies, Delinquency and Crime* (New York: Macmillan, 1933).

Bogdanovich, Peter. *Who the Devil Made It* (New York: Alfred A. Knopf, 1997).

Boller, Paul F., and Ronald L. Davis. *Hollywood Anecdotes* (London: Macmillan, 1987).

Bowser, Eileen. *The Transformation of Cinema, 1907–1915* (New York: Scribners, 1990).

Brando, Marlon. *Songs My Mother Taught Me* (London: Century, 1994).

Brownlow, Kevin. *Behind the Mask of Innocence* (New York: Alfred A. Knopf, 1990).

Buford, Kate. *Burt Lancaster: An American Life* (London: Aurum, 2008).

Cain, James M. *The Postman Always Rings Twice* (London: Robert Hale, 1971).

Cameron, Ian. *A Pictorial History of Crime Movies* (London: Hamlyn, 1975).

Card, James. *Seductive Cinema* (New York: Alfred A. Knopf, 1994).

Carlson, Julia. *Banned in Ireland* (London: Routledge, 1990).

Carmen, Ira H. *Movies, Censorship and the Law* (Ann Arbor: University of Michigan Press, 1966).

Carty, Ciaran. *Confessions of a Sewer Rat* (Dublin: New Island, 1995).

Cashin, Fergus. *Mae West* (London: Star Publishing, 1982).

Chandler, Charlotte. *It's Only a Movie* (New York: Simon & Schuster, 2005).

———. *Nobody's Perfect: Billy Wilder, A Personal Biography* (New York: Simon & Schuster, 2002).

Ciment, Michel, ed. *Elia Kazan: An American Odyssey* (London: Bloomsbury, 1988).

Clarens, Carlos. *Crime Movies: An Illustrated History* (New York: W.W. Norton, 1979).
Clayton, Marie. *Marilyn Monroe: Unseen Archives* (Bath, England: Parragon, 2005).
Coates, Paul. *Cinema, Religion and the Romantic Legacy* (Aldershot, England: Ashgate, 2003).
Colombo, John Robert. *The Wit and Wisdom of Hollywood* (London: Hamlyn, 1979).
Copjek, Joan K., ed. *Shades of Noir: A Reader* (London: Verso, 1993).
Couvares, Francis G. *Movie Censorship and American Culture* (Washington, DC: Smithsonian Press, 1996).
Crawley, Tony. *Chambers' Film Quotes* (Edinburgh: W & R Chambers, 1999).
Crivello, Kirk. *Fallen Angels* (London: Futura, 1988).
Curtis, Tony, with Barry Paris. *The Autobiography* (London: Heinemann, 1994).
Deacy, Christopher. *Screen Christologies* (Cardiff: University of Wales Press, 2001).
De Beauvoir, Simone. *Brigitte Bardot and the Lolita Syndrome* (London: Andre Deutsch, 1961).
De Grazia, Edward, and Roger K. Newman. *Banned Films: Movies, Censors and the First Amendment* (New York: R.R. Bowker, 1982).
Diorio, Al. *Barbara Stanwyck* (London: W.H. Allen, 1983).
Doherty, Thomas. *Pre-Code Hollywood: Sex, Immorality and Insurrection in American Cinema, 1930–1934* (New York: Columbia University Press, 1999).
Dooley, Roger. *From Scarface to Scarlett* (New York: Harcourt Brace, 1979).
Edmonds, Andy. *Fatty: The Untold Story of Roscoe "Fatty" Arbuckle* (London: Time Warner, 1992).
Edwards, Anne. *The DeMilles: An American Family* (London: Collins, 1988).
Ernst, Morris L. *Censored: The Private Life of the Movies* (New York: Jonathan Cape, 1930).
Essoe, Gabe. *DeMille: The Man and His Pictures* (New York: Castle, 1970).
Eyles, Allen. *That Was Hollywood: The 1930s* (London: B.S. Batsford, 1987).
Facey, Paul F. *The League of Decency: A Sociological Analysis of the Emergence and Development of a Social Pressure Group* (New York: Arno Press, 1974).
Fagan, Jim. *The Hellraisers* (Sydney: Scripts, 1967).
Feldman, Charles. *The National Board of Censorship Review of Motion Pictures, 1909–1922* (New York: Arno Press, 1980).
Fellini, Federico. *I, Fellini* (London: Bloomsbury, 1997).
Field, Andrew. *The Life and Art of Vladimir Nabokov* (London: Futura, 1987).
Finler, Joel. *The Hollywood Story* (New York: Crown, 1988).
Fisher, James Terence. *The Catholic Counterculture in America, 1933–1962* (Chapel Hill: University of North Carolina Press, 1989).
Fishgall, Gary. *Against Type: The Biography of Burt Lancaster* (New York: Scribner, 1995).
Forest, Ben, with Mary Kay Mueller. *God Goes to Hollywood: A Movie Guide for the Modern Mystic* (Lincoln, NE: Writers Club Press, 2000).
Forman, Henry James. *Our Movie-Made Children* (New York: Macmillan, 1933).
Fraser, Peter. *Images of the Passion: The Sacramental Mode in Film* (Westport, CT: Praeger, 1998).
French, Sean. *Jane Fonda* (London: Pavilion, 1997).
Friedman, Lawrence. *The Cinema of Martin Scorsese* (Oxford: Roundhouse, 1997).
Gardiner, Harold. *Catholic Viewpoint on Censorship* (Garden City, NY: Image Books, 1961).
Gardner, Gerald. *The Censorship Papers* (New York: Dodd, Mead & Co., 1987).
Gledhill, Christine, ed. *Home Is Where the Heart Is: Studies in Melodrama and the Woman's Film* (London: British Film Institute, 1987).
Green, Jonathan, and Nicholas J. Karolides. *The Encyclopedia of Censorship* (New York: Facts on File, 1990).
Greene, Graham. *The Pleasure Dome* (Oxford: Oxford University Press, 1980).
Grey, Jon. *Sex, Stupidity and Greed* (New York: Juno Books, 1997).
Grieveson, Lee. *Policing Cinema* (Los Angeles: University of California Press, 2004).
Griggs, John. *The Films of Gregory Peck* (London: Columbus, 1988).
Grothe, Mardy. *Oxymoronica* (London: HarperCollins, 2004).
Hadleigh, Boze. *Hollywood Babble On* (New York: Birch Lane Press, 1994).
_____. *Hollywood Bitch* (London: Robson, 1999).
Hamilton, Marybeth. *The Queen of Camp* (London: HarperCollins, 1996).
Harkness, John. *The Academy Awards Handbook: Who Won What When* (New York: Pinnacle, 1994).
Harris, Mark. *Scenes from a Revolution* (Edinburgh: Canongate, 2008).
Harris, Warren G. *Clark Gable: A Biography* (London: Aurum, 2002).
Hartnell, David. *I'm Not One to Gossip, But* (Auckland, NZ: MacDonald, 1990).
Haskell, Molly. *From Reverence to Rape: The Treatment of Women in the Movies* (Chicago: University of Chicago Press, 1987).

Haun, Harry. *The Movie Quote Book* (New York: Bonanza Books, 1986).
Hayman, Ronald. *Tennessee Williams* (New Haven: Yale University Press, 1993).
Hays, Will H. *The Memoirs of Will H. Hays* (New York: Doubleday, 1955).
Hecht, Ben. *A Child of the Century* (New York: Simon & Schuster, 1954).
Heins, Marjorie. *Sex, Sin and Blasphemy* (New York: New Press, 1993).
Herndon, Booton. *Mary Pickford and Douglas Fairbanks* (New York: W.W. Norton, 1977).
Hickman, Tom. *The Sexual Century* (London: Carlton, 1999).
Higham, Charles. *Brando* (London: Grafton Books, 1989).
_____. *Cecil B. DeMille* (New York: Scribners, 1973).
Hixson, Richard. *Pornography and the Justices* (Carbondale: Southern Illinois University Press, 1996).
Humphries, Joseph, ed. *Jimmy Dean on Jimmy Dean* (London: Plexus, 1990).
Huston, John. *An Open Book* (London: Macmillan, 1981).
Inglis, Ruth. *Freedom of the Movies* (Chicago: University of Chicago Press, 1947).
Izod, John. *Hollywood and the Box Office, 1895–1986* (New York: Columbia University Press, 1988).
Jacobs, Jack. *The Films of Norma Shearer* (New York: Citadel, 1976).
Jacobs, Lea. *The Wages of Sin: Cinema and the Fallen Woman* (Berkeley: University of California Press, 1997).
Jarman, Derek, and Shaun Allen, ed. *Dancing Ledge* (London: Quartet, 1984).
Johnston, Robert K. *Reel Spirituality* (Grand Rapids, MI: Baker Academic, 2000).
Jowett, Garth. *Film: The Democratic Art* (Boston: Little, Brown, 1976).
Kael, Pauline. *Deeper into Movies* (Boston: Little, Brown, 1969).
_____. *I Lost It at the Movies* (Boston: Little, Brown, 1965).
_____. *Reeling* (Boston: Little, Brown, 1977).
Kaplan, Ann, ed. *Women in Film Noir* (London: British Film Institute, 1978).
Kardish, Lawrence. *Reel Plastic Magic* (Boston: Little, Brown, 1972).
Karney, Robyn. *Burt Lancaster: A Singular Man* (London: Bloomsbury, 1996).
Karpf, Stephen. *The Gangster Film, 1930–1940* (New York: Arno Press, 1973).
Kashner, Sam, and Jennifer MacNair. *The Bad and the Beautiful: A Chronicle of Hollywood in the Fifties* (London: Little, Brown, 2002).
Kazan, Elia. *A Life* (New York: Alfred A. Knopf, 1988).

Kent, Nicolas. *Naked Hollywood: Money, Power and the Movies* (London: BBC Books, 1991).
Keough, Peter, ed. *Flesh and Blood* (San Francisco: Mercury House, 1995).
Kerekes, David, and David Slater. *See No Evil* (Manchester: Headpress, 2000).
Kermode, Frank. *The Exorcist* (London: British Film institute, 1997).
Keyser, Les and Barbara. *Hollywood and the Catholic Church: The Image of Roman Catholicism in American Movies* (Chicago: Loyola University Press, 1984).
Kinnard, Roy, and Tim Davis. *Divine Images: A History of Jesus on the Screen* (New York: Citadel, 1992).
Kinsey, Alfred C. *Sexual Behavior in the Human Female* (Philadelphia: W.B. Saunders, 1953).
_____. *Sexual Behavior in the Human Male* (Philadelphia: W.B. Saunders, 1948).
Kobal, John. *Marilyn Monroe: A Life on Film* (London: Hamlyn, 1974).
Kolker, John Philip. *Bernardo Bertolucci* (London: British Film Institute, 1985).
Koszarski, Richard, ed. *Hollywood Directors, 1941–1976* (New York: Oxford University Press, 1977).
Kuhn, Annette. *Cinema, Censorship and Sexuality* (New York: Routledge, 1988).
Lamarr, Hedy. *Ecstasy and Me* (London: W.H. Allen, 1926).
Lanza, Joseph. *Phallic Frenzy* (London: Aurum, 2007).
LaSalle, Mick. *Complicated Women* (New York: Thomas Dunne Books, 2000).
Laurence, Frank M. *Hemingway and the Movies* (New York: Da Capo, 1981).
Leamer, Laurence. *As Time Goes By: The Life of Ingrid Bergman* (London: Sphere Books, 1986).
Leff, Leonard J., and Jerold L. Simmons. *The Dame in the Kimono: Hollywood, Censorship and the Production Code* (Lexington: University Press of Kentucky, 2001).
Leonard, Maurice. *Mae West: Empress of Sex* (London: HarperCollins, 1991).
Lessard, John. *To Quote a Queer* (Philadelphia: Quirk Books, 2008).
Lewis, Jon. *Hollywood V. Hard Core* (New York: New York University Press, 2000).
Lindsay, Vachel. *The Art of the Motion Picture* (New York: Liveright, 1970).
Lloyd, Ann, ed. *Movies of the Forties* (London: Orbis Publishing, 1982).
Loughlin, Gerard. *Alien Sex* (Malden, MA: Blackwell, 2004).
Louvish, Simon. *Cecil B. DeMille and the Golden Calf* (London: Faber & Faber, 2007).
_____. *Mae West: It Ain't No Sin* (London: Faber & Faber, 2005).

Lucaire, Edward. *Celebrity Trivia* (New York: Warner Books, 1980).
Luijters, Guus, ed. *Marilyn Monroe: In Her Own Words* (London: Omnibus Press, 1990).
Lyden, John C. *Film as Religion: Myths, Morals and Ritual* (New York: New York University Press, 2003).
Lyons, Charles. *The New Censors* (New York: Columbia University Press, 1997).
Malden, Karl. *When Do I Start?* (New York: Simon & Schuster, 1997).
Malone, Aubrey. *Hollywood Trivia* (London: Prion, 2004).
Manso, Peter. *Brando* (London: Victor Gollancz, 1995).
Marsh, Clive, with Gaye Ortiz. *Explorations in Theology and Film* (Malden, MA: Blackwell, 1997).
Martin, Olga J. *Hollywood's Movie Commandments* (New York: Arno Press, 1937).
Marx, Samuel. *Mayer and Thalberg: The Make-Believe Saints* (New York: Random House, 1975).
Mathews, Tom Dewe. *Censored* (London: Chatto & Windus, 1994).
May, John, R., ed. *Religion in Film* (Knoxville: University of Tennessee Press, 1982).
Mayer, Arthur. *Merely Colossal* (New York: Simon & Schuster, 1953).
McBride, Joseph. *Hawks on Hawks* (Berkeley: University of California Press, 1982).
McClelland, Doug. *Hollywood on Hollywood* (Boston: Faber & Faber, 1985).
_____. *Starspeak* (Boston: Faber & Faber, 1987).
_____. *The Unkindest Cuts* (Cranbury, NJ: A.S. Brown & Co., 1972).
McDannell, Colleen. *Catholics in the Movies* (New York: Oxford University Press, 2008).
McGilligan, Patrick. *Backstory: Interviews with Screenwriters of Hollywood's Golden Age* (Berkeley: University of California Press, 1986).
_____. *Cagney: The Actor as Auteur* (Cranbury, NJ: A.S. Barnes & Co., 1975).
Medved, Michael. *Hollywood Vs. America: Popular Culture and the War on Traditional Values* (New York: HarperCollins, 1992).
Miller, Frank. *Censored Hollywood: Sex, Sin and Violence on Screen* (Atlanta: Turner Publishing, 1994).
Mills, Jane. *The Money Shot* (Annandale, NSW: Pluto, 2001).
Mueller, Mary Kay, with Ben Forest. *God Goes to Hollywood* (Lincoln, NE: Writers Club Press, 2000).
Munby, Jonathan. *Public Enemies, Public Heroes* (Chicago: University of Chicago Press, 1999).
Munn, Michael. *Burt Lancaster* (London: Robson, 1995).
_____. *Gregory Peck* (London: Robert Hale, 1998).
Nabokov, Vladimir. *Lolita: A Screenplay* (New York: McGraw-Hill, 1974).
Nash, Alanna. *The Colonel* (London: Aurum, 2003).
Nash, Jay Robert, and Stanley Ralph Ross. *The Motion Picture Guide* (Chicago: Chicago Cinebooks, 1985).
Naughton, John. *Movies: A Crash Course* (New York: Simon & Schuster, 1998).
Neve, Brian. *Film and Politics in America: A Social Tradition* (London: Routledge, 1992).
Norman, Barry. *Talking Pictures* (London: Arrow, 1991).
O'Brien, David. *American Catholics and Social Reform* (New York: Oxford University Press, 1968).
O'Brien, Pat. *The Wind at My Back* (New York: Doubleday, 1964).
O'Connor, Ulick. *Oliver St. John Gogarty* (London: Granada, 1981).
Palmer, Lilli. *Change Lobsters and Dance* (New York: Dell, 1975).
Parish, James Robert. *The Hollywood Book of Scandals* (New York: McGraw-Hill, 2004).
Pascall, Jeremy, and Clyde Jeavons. *A Pictorial History of Sex in the Movies* (London: Hamlyn, 1976).
Pennington, Jody W. *The History of Sex in American Film* (Westport, CT: Praeger, 2007).
Petley, Julian. *Censorship: A Beginner's Guide* (Oxford: OneWorld, 2009).
Phelps, Guy. *Film Censorship* (London: Victor Gollancz, 1975).
Philips, Baxter. *Cut: The Unseen Cinema* (London: Lorrimer, 1975).
Phillips, Gene D., and Rodney Hill. *The Encyclopedia of Stanley Kubrick* (New York: Checkmark, 2002).
Pickard, Roy. *James Stewart: The Hollywood Years* (London: Robert Hale, 1992).
Powdermaker, Hortense. *Hollywood: The Dream Factory* (Boston: Little, Brown, 1950).
Preminger, Otto. *An Autobiography* (New York: Doubleday, 1977).
Quigley, Martin. *Decency in Motion Pictures* (New York: Macmillan, 1937).
Quirk, Lawrence J. *The Complete Films of Ingrid Bergman* (New York: Citadel, 1989).
Randall, Richard S. *Censorship of the Movies* (Madison: University of Wisconsin Press, 1968).
Randall, Stephen, ed. *The Playboy Interviews* (Milwaukee: M Press, 2006).
Reed, Oliver. *Reed: All About Me* (London: W.H. Allen, 1979).
Riley, Robin. *Film, Faith and Cultural Conflict* (Westport, CT: Praeger, 2003).

Robertson, James C. *The Hidden Cinema* (London: Routledge, 1989).
Robertson, Patrick. *Film Facts* (London: Aurum, 2001).
Robinson, Edward G. *All My Yesterdays: An Autobiography* (New York: Signet, 1973).
Robinson, Jeffrey. *Brigitte Bardot: Two Lives* (New York: Simon & Schuster, 1994).
Rockett, Kevin. *Irish Film Censorship* (Dublin: Four Courts Press, 2004).
Roeburt, John. *The Wicked and the Banned* (New York: Macfadden, 1963).
Rosen, Marjorie. *Popcorn Venus: Women, Movies and the American Dream* (New York: Avon, 1973).
Rossoe, Eugene. *Born to Lose: The Gangster Film in America* (New York: Oxford University Press, 1978).
Rosten, Leo. *Hollywood: The Movie Colony and the Movie Makers* (New York: Harcourt Brace, 1941).
Russell, Jane. *My Path and My Detours* (New York: Franklin Watts, 1985).
Russo, Vito. *The Celluloid Closet* (New York: Harper & Row, 1987).
Ruth, David. *Inventing the Public Enemy* (Chicago: University of Chicago Press, 1996).
Sanders, Theresa. *Celluloid Saints* (Macon, GA: Mercer University Press, 2002).
Schatz, Thomas. *Hollywood Genres* (New York: McGraw-Hill, 1981).
Schickel, Richard. *Brando: A Life in Our Times* (New York: Atheneum, 1991).
Schreck, Nikolas. *The Satanic Screen* (London: Creation Books, 2000).
Schumach, Murray. *The Face on the Cutting Room Floor* (New York: Da Capo, 1975).
Scorsese, Martin, Ian Christie and David Thompson. *Scorsese on Scorsese* (London: Faber, 1990).
Sellers, Peter. *Bad Boy Drive* (London: Preface, 2009).
Shalit, Gene, ed. *Great Hollywood Wit* (New York: St. Martin's Press, 2002).
Shapiro, Harry. *Shooting Stars* (London: Serpent's Tail, 2003).
Shipman, David. *Caught in the Act* (London: Elm Tree Books, 1985).
_____. *Movie Talk* (London: Bloomsbury, 1988).
Siegel, Scott and Barbara. *American Film Comedy from Abbott and Costello to Jerry Zucker* (New York: Prentice Hall, 1994).
_____. *Jack Nicholson* (London: Angus & Robertson, 1990).
Simpson, Paul, ed. *The Rough Guide to Cult Movies* (London: Haymarket, 2004).
Sinyard, Neil. *Directors: The All-Time Greats* (New York: Gallery Books, 1985).
Skinner, James M. *The Cross and the Cinema: The Legion of Decency and the National Catholic Office for Motion Pictures, 1933–1970* (Westport, CT: Praeger, 1993).
Sklar, Robert. *City Boys: Cagney, Bogart, Garfield* (Princeton, NJ: Princeton University Press, 1992).
Slide, Anthony. *Banned in the U.S.A.* (London: I.B. Tauris, 1998).
Smith, Justin. *Withnail and Us* (London: I.B. Tauris, 2010).
Smith, Sarah J. *Children, Cinema and Censorship: From Dracula to the Dead End Kids* (London: I.B. Tauris, 2005).
Smith, Sheamus. *Off-Screen* (Dublin: Gill & Macmillan, 2007).
Sova, Dawn B. *Forbidden Films* (New York: Checkmark Books, 2001).
Sperling, Cass Warner, and Cork Millner. *Hollywood Be Thy Name* (Lexington: University Press of Kentucky, 1998).
Spoto, Donald. *Dietrich* (London: Corgi, 1992).
Staiger, Janet. *Bad Women: Regulating Sexuality in Early American Cinema* (Minneapolis: University of Minnesota Press, 1995).
Stallings, Penny. *Flesh and Fantasy* (New York: Harper & Row, 1978).
Steen, Mike. *Hollywood Speaks* (New York: Putnam's, 1974).
Sutherland, John. *Offensive Literature: De-Censorship in Britain, 1960–82* (London: Junction Books, 1982).
Tarrant, Graham, ed. *Actors on Actors* (London: Aurum, 2005).
Thomas, Donald. *Freedom's Frontier: Censorship in Modern Britain* (London: John Murray, 2007).
Thompson, Douglas. *Hollywood People* (London: Pan, 1995).
_____. *Sharon Stone* (London: Little, Brown, 1994).
Thomson, David. *Showman: The Life of David O. Selznick* (New York: Alfred A. Knopf, 1992).
_____. *The Whole Equation* (London: Little, Brown, 2005).
Toeplitz, Jerzy. *Hollywood and After* (London: Allen & Unwin, 1974).
Trevelyan, John. *What the Censor Saw* (London: Michael Joseph, 1973).
Tropiano, Stephen. *Obscene, Indecent, Immoral, Offensive* (New York: Limelight Editions, 2009).
Truffaut, François. *Hitchcock* (New York: Simon & Schuster, 1967).
Ullman, Sharon. *Sex Seen: The Emergence of Modern Sexuality in America* (Berkeley: University of California Press, 1997).
Underwood, Peter. *Death in Hollywood* (London: Piatkus, 1992).

Vasey, Ruth. *The World According to Hollywood: 1918–1939* (Madison: University of Wisconsin Press, 1997).

Vermilye, Jerry. *Barbara Stanwyck* (New York: Pyramid, 1975).

Vidal, Gore. *Palimpsest: A Memoir* (New York: Random House, 1995).

Vieira, Mark A. *Sin in Soft Focus* (New York: Harry Abrams, 1999).

Vizzard, Jack. *See No Evil: Life Inside a Hollywood Censor* (New York: Simon & Schuster, 1970).

Walker, Alexander. *Sex in the Movies* (Middlesex: Penguin, 1969).

_____. *Stanley Kubrick Directs* (London: Abacus, 1973).

Wallach, Eli. *The Good, the Bad, and Me* (New York: Harcourt, 2005).

Walsh, Frank. *Sin and Censorship* (New Haven: Yale University Press, 1996).

Ward, Laura, ed. *Putdowns* (London: Robson, 2004).

Wayne, Jane Ellen. *Stanwyck: The Untold Biography* (London: Robson, 1986).

Westin, Alan F. *The Miracle Case* (Tuscaloosa: University of Alabama Press, 1961).

Williams, Tennessee. *Memoirs* (London: W.H. Allen, 1976).

_____. *A Streetcar Named Desire* (New York: New Directions, 1980).

_____. *Suddenly Last Summer* (New York: New Directions, 1958).

Woods, Paul A. *King Pulp: The Wild World of Quentin Tarantino* (London: Plexus, 1996).

Young, Jeff. *Kazan on Kazan* (London: Faber & Faber, 1999).

_____. *Kazan: The Master Discusses His Films* (Scranton, PA: Newmarket Press, 1999).

Yule, Andrew. *A Life on the Wire* (London: Warner, 1991).

Zheutlin, Barbara. *Creative Differences: Profiles of Hollywood Dissidents* (Boston: South End Press, 1978).

Index

Abolition of Film Censorship for Adults 156
The Accused 170
Affleck, Ben 180
Alba, Jessica 183
The Albatross 46
Albee, Edward 138–9
Aldgate, Anthony 85
Aldrich, Robert 124
Alfie 4, 139–40
Algren, Nelson 92–3
All Quiet on the Western Front 24, 27
Allen, Robert 63–4
Allen, Woody 165
Altman, Robert 132, 154
America 53, 62
American Civil Liberties Union 57, 174
An American Life 117
The Amorous Adventures of Moll Flanders 134
Anastasia 80
Anatomy of Murder 107
And God Created Woman 102
Anderson, Robert 98, 100
Angel Heart 170
Angels with Dirty Faces 164
Anger, Kenneth 16
Ann Vickers 53–4
Anna Karenina 57
Antonioni, Michelangelo 138, 185
The Apartment 112, 119–20, 134
Arbuckle, "Fatty" 13–14, 41, 150
Archer, Anne 170
The Asphalt Jungle 75–6, 114
Autry, Gene 189

Baby Doll 93–7, 104–5, 135, 137
Baby Face 26, 30, 51
Back Street 44
The Bad and the Beautiful 76
Baker, Carroll 93–6
Bankhead, Tallulah 21, 44
Bara, Theda 9–11
Barbarella 150
Bardot, Brigitte 104, 105, 107
Barrow, Clyde 38
Barry Mahon Productions 140

Basic Instinct 175–6, 181, 189
Basinger, Kim 189
The Basketball Diaries 191
Bates, Alan 124, 154
Beatty, Warren 124, 143–6
Behlmer, Rudy 82–3
Bell, Rex 22
Belle of the Nineties 57
The Bells of St. Mary's 162
Ben-Hur 127, 135, 171
Bergman, Ingmar 185
Bergman, Ingrid 67–8, 78, 111
Berkeley, Busby 35
Bern, Paul 65
Bertolucci, Bernardo 158–60
The Best Man 135
Betty Blue 170
Beyond the Valley of the Dolls 106
Bibo, Walter 91
The Bicycle Thief 74, 187
The Big Easy 170
The Bigamist 88–9
Binoche, Juliette 181
Binyon, Claude 55
Birkin, Jane 138
The Birth of a Nation 7, 63–4
Biskind, Peter 135
Bisset, Jacqueline 153–4
Bitter Rice 73–4
Black, Gregory D. 12, 38, 79, 85–6
Blackboard Jungle 90
Blackman, Honor 136
Blair, Linda 162–4
Blatty, William 162–3
Bliss, Michael 171
Blonde Venus 44
Blow-Up 138
Blue Streak 190
Blue Velvet 192
Bob & Carol & Ted & Alice 150
Boccaccio '70 129
Bogarde, Dirk 126, 128, 135
Bogart, Humphrey 30–1
Bogdanovich, Peter 31, 151
Boles, John 44

Bonnie & Clyde 143–6, 150, 176, 178, 191
Boorman, John 163
Borgnine, Ernest 92
Bottoms, Timothy 151
Bow, Clara 9, 21–2, 120
Boyd, Rev. Malcolm 109
Boyd, Stephen 127
Brando, Marlon 81–4, 93, 101, 102, 104, 130–1, 147, 157–60
Breakfast at Tiffany's 128–9
Breen, Dermot 142, 157, 179
Breen, Joseph 1–2, 26, 32–3, 36, 38–40, 42–4, 46, 50, 54–7, 59, 63, 65–6, 68, 72–3, 78, 81–3, 85, 89, 91, 135–7, 188
Breillat, Catherine 183
Breslin, Jimmy 144–5
Bridges, Jeff 151
British Board of Film Censors 131, 142, 152
Brooks, Richard 116–8
Brown, Helen Gurley 124
Brown, John Mason 48
Brownlow, Kevin 34
Bruce, Lenny 187
Brynner, Yul 33
Buford, Kate 117
Bulger, Jamie 190
Bundy, Ted 53
Burgess, Anthony 152
Burke, Rev. John 95
Burke, Philip 21
Burstyn, Ellen 151
Burstyn, Joseph 2, 74, 79
Burton, Richard 138, 163
Butch Cassidy and the Sundance Kid 145
Butterfield 8 112, 119–20

Cabot, Bruce 54
Cactus Flower 80
Cagney, James 30–1, 74, 178
Cain, James M. 68, 73
Caine, Michael 139, 167–8
Calhern, Louis 75–6
Caligula 168–9
Call Her Savage 22
Canby, Vincent 142
Cantwell, John 71
Cape Fear 174, 192
Capone, Al 29
Capote, Truman 128–9
The Captive 47
Capucine 128
Cardinale, Claudia 183
Carnal Knowledge 156
Carneal, Michael 191
The Carpetbaggers 132
Carrie 168
Carroll, Madeleine 44
Carrus, Ben 191
Carson, Johnny 190
Carstairs, G.M. 132
Carty, Ciaran 157, 179, 184–6

Cat Ballou 137
Cat on a Hot Tin Roof 127
The Catcher in the Rye 190
Catherine Was Great 60
Catholic Action 114
Catholic Episcopal Committee 33, 38
Catholic Viewpoint on Censorship 38
Catholic World 53
Censored 189
Chandler, Charlotte 80–1
Chaplin, Charlie 13
Chapman, Marc 190
Charlie Bubbles 142, 150
Chicago Tribune 191
Children, Cinema and Censorship 31
The Children's Hour 22, 128
Child's Play 3 190
Christian Film and Television Commission 174, 181
Christie, Julie 135, 154
Cicognani, Archbishop 36
Cinderella 52
Cinema, Censorship and Sexuality 12
Cinema Paradiso 4, 182
Cinema, Religion and the Romantic Legacy 116, 173
The Cincinnati Kid 132
Citizen Kane 44
City Lights 25
Clarke, Mae 30
Cleopatra 9–10
Clift, Montgomery 108
A Clockwork Orange 149, 151, 152–3, 178–9, 190
Coates, Paul 116, 173
The Code and Ratings Administration (CARA) 170, 174, 175
The Coen Brothers 184
Cohn, Harry 38–9, 42, 89
Colbert, Claudette 35, 38
Columbia 21
Confidential 75
Connell, Archbishop Desmond 172
Connery, Sean 136
Cook, Elisha, Jr. 144
The Cook, the Thief, His Wife and Her Lover 174
Cooney, John 104
Cooper, Gary 18, 26–8, 67–8, 139
Coppola, Francis Ford 132
Corliss, Richard 171
Coward, Noel 70
Crash 179
Craven, Wes 180
Crawford, Joan 29, 44, 63
Crimes of Passion 170
Crist, Judith 96, 155
Cromwell, James 54
Cronenburg, David 179
Crosby, Bing 182
The Cross and the Cinema 186–7

Cruising 166–7
Cummings, Dorothy 21
Curtis, Tony 60–1, 118–9

Daily Variety 174
Damage 181
Damaged Goods 8, 9
Dame in the Kimono 16
Damiano, Gerard 161
Dangerfield, Rodney 178
Darling 135
Dassin, Jules 112
Davies, Marion 59
Davis, Bette 44
Davis, Tim 165–6
Day, Doris 106–7
Deacy, Christopher 172
Dead End 44
Dean, James 101–2, 104, 127
Deep Throat 161–2
The Deer Hunter 148
De Grazia, Edward 9, 63, 97
DeMille, Cecil B. 9, 31, 33–6, 76, 95, 113, 118, 162
DeMille, William 34
Denby, David 180
De Niro, Robert 148, 174, 190
De Palma, Brian 167–8, 180
Derek, Bo 183
De Sica, Vittorio 74, 129, 187
D'Estaing, Giscard 164
Destry Rides Again 55–6
The Devils 154–5
Diamond Lil 48, 49–50, 52
DiCaprio, Leonardo 191
Dickinson, Angie 167–8
Die Hard II 189
Dietrich, Marlene 22, 26, 44, 55–6
Dillinger, John 30
Dinner at Eight 44–5
Diorio, Al 68
Disney, Walt 61–2
D.O.A. 88
Dr. Strangelove 124
Dr. Who 130
Doherty, Thomas 39, 41, 124, 188
La dolce vita 113–6, 129
Donat, Robert 44
Donnelly, Gerard 37
Donner, Robert 164–5
Dors, Diana 183
Double Indemnity 68–70, 73, 110, 183
Double Whoopee 25
Dougherty, Cardinal 39–40
Douglas, Kirk 118, 124
Douglas, Michael 141, 170, 175–6, 191
Downey, Robert, Jr. 178
Doyle, Olivia 188–9
The Drag 48
Dressed to Kill 167–8, 180
Duel in the Sun 70–3, 78, 118

Dunaway, Faye 143–6
Dunne, Irene 44, 54

Eastwood, Clint 164, 173
Ecstacy 52, 187
The Ed Sullivan Show 102
Edmondson, Sarah 191
8 and a Half 114
Ekberg, Anita 114, 129
Eliot, Winslow 53
Elmer Gantry 76, 116–8
Eminem 178
Emmanuelle 164
The Entertainer 121
Entertainment Weekly 189
Ephron, Nora 161
Erickson, Leif 98, 100
E.T.: The Extra-Terrestrial 182, 184
Evans, Walter 152
Eve and the Handyman 105
Evening Standard 74
Every Day's a Holiday 60
The Exorcist 162–3, 166
Exorcist II: The Heretic 163–4

Fairbanks, Douglas 13
Faithless 44
Falling Down 191
A Farewell to Arms 26–8
Farr, Felicia, 132–3
Farrow, Mia 111, 147
Faster, Pussycat, Kill, Kill 106
Fatal Attraction 129, 170
Faulkner, William 129
Federal Council of Churches of Christ in America 37, 39
Fellini, Federico 77–81, 113–6, 129, 185, 187
Ferber, Edna 11
Ferman, James 179
Fields, W.C. 47, 59, 60
Film Heritage 137
Films Appeal Board 142
Finch, Peter 154
Finney, Albert 130, 141, 142
Fit to Fight 8
Fitzgerald, Barry 187
The Flowers of St. Francis 78
Fonda, Jane 57, 150, 154
Fontaine, Joan 88–9
A Fool There Was 9
For Whom the Bell Tolls 67–8
Ford, Glenn 90
Ford, John 76
Forever Amber 73
Forman, Henry J. 36
Foster, Jodie 165, 170, 190
491 188
The Four Poster 84
Fowler, Gene 23
The Fox 149
Fox, Megan 183

Frankenstein 24
Fraser, Peter 172, 173
Friday the 13th 184
Friedkin, William 166–7
From Here to Eternity 89–90, 93
From the Terrace 112
From This Day Forward 67
The Front 165
Fry, Christopher 127

Gabin, Jean 105
Gable, Clark 28, 38, 63
Garbo, Greta 55, 57
The Garden of Eden 91
Gardiner, Harold C. 38
Gardner, Gerald 14–15, 35, 41, 50–1, 89–90, 92, 183
Garfield, John 73
Garfunkel, Art 156
Garnett, Tay 73
Gavin, John 73, 121
George, Susan 153
Gere, Richard 188, 190
Gibson, Mel 190
Gilliatt, Penelope 155
Ginsburg, Allen 101
Gish, Lillian 9
Gleiberman, Owen 178–9
Glyn, Elinor 62
God Goes to Hollywood 165
Godard, Jean-Luc 170, 173
The Godfather 159
Goin' to Town 57
Going My Way 110
Goldfinger 136
Goldwyn, Sam 91
Gone, Baby, Gone 180
Gone with the Wind 63, 65, 71, 82
Gordon, Michael 106
Grable, Betty 67
The Graduate 141–2
Graham, Billy 76, 90, 162
Graham, Virginia 74
Grant, Cary 26, 49, 50, 60, 67, 182
Greater London Council 143
The Greatest Story Ever Told 21, 171
Greenaway, Peter 174
Greene, Grahame 59, 64
Grey, Ian 145, 189–90
Grieveson, Lee 8–9
Guccione, Bob 168–9
Guys & Dolls 93

Hail Mary 170, 173
Hair 186
Haley, Bill 90
Halloween 184
Hamilton, Marybeth 46
Harlow, Jean 25, 28, 44, 48, 64–5, 104
Harper's Bazaar 62
Harrelson, Woody 178–9

Harris, Julie 147
Harris, Mildred 13
Harris, Warren 63
Harrison, Rex 84
Harvey, Laurence 108–9, 128
Haskell, Molly 9, 21, 26, 107, 110–1, 153, 156, 160–1, 184
Hawks, Howard 33
Hawn, Goldie 80
Hayes, Archbishop 11
Hayes, Helen 26–8
Haynes-Holmes, John 57
Hays, Will 1, 15–27, 32, 34, 36, 39, 42–3, 47, 49–50, 52, 56–7, 61–2, 67, 70, 122, 149, 182–3
Hays Code 17–23, 27, 35, 37–8, 43–4, 62–3, 110, 132, 140–1, 156–7
Hays Office 17, 25, 29, 31–2, 35, 92, 107, 127, 151
Hayworth, Rita 81
Head, Murray 154,
Hearst, William Randolph 59
Hecht, Ben 100–1
Hefner, Hugh 84, 91, 156
Hegarty, Jerome 172–3
Heins, Marjorie 137
Hellman, Lillian 22
Hell's Angels 25
Hemingway, Ernest 26–8, 67–8
Hemmings, David 138
Henry: Portrait of a Serial Killer 189
Henry and June 175
Hepburn, Audrey 22, 110, 128–9
Hepburn, Katharine 55, 62, 108, 175
Heston, Charlton 127
Heywood, Anne 149
High Noon 114
Higham, Charles 83
Hills, Gillian 138
Hinckley, John 190
Hinson, Hal 191–2
Hitchcock, Alfred 31, 44, 52, 73, 91, 121–4, 144, 167, 168, 180
Hitler, Adolf 26, 67
Hoberman, Joe 143–5
Hoffman, Dustin 141–2, 148, 153
Holden, William 84–5, 181
Hollywood and After 145
Hollywood and the Catholic Church 186
Hollywood Babylon 16
Hollywood Be Thy Name 18
Hollywood Citizen News 50
Hollywood Reporter 139
Hollywood V. Hard Core 97
Home Alone 184
Hope, Bob 88, 182
Hopkins, Miriam 129
Hordern, Michael 128
Horse Feathers 51
Hubert, Isabelle 183
Hud 131

Index

Hudson, Rock 27, 106–7
Hughes, Howard 25, 29, 65, 151
Hughes, Ken 61
Hurry Sundown 150
Huston, John 60, 75–6, 117, 147
Huston, Walter 54, 71
Hutton, Lauren 189

I Am Curious (Yellow) 146–7, 186
I, Fellini 80
I'll Never Forget Whatsisname 142, 150
I'm No Angel 50, 51
The Immoral Mr. Teas 105
In Which We Serve 70
Indiana Jones and the Temple of Doom 170
Institute for Propaganda Analysis 62
International Federation of Catholic Alumnae (IFCA) 21
Invisible Agent 66–7
Irish Independent 5
Irma La Douce 134
Irons, Jeremy 125, 179, 181
Irwin, May 7
It 62
It Ain't No Sin 55–7
It Happened One Night 38

Jackson, Glenda 154
Jaws 121
Jeavons, Claude 33
Jenkins, Billy 156
Joan of Arc 78
Johnson, Ben 151
Johnston, Robert K. 62
Jones, Jennifer 27, 70–2
Jones, Shirley 116
Jones, Terry 165–6
Joy, Jason 29, 149
Joyce, James 142
Juvenal 32

Kael, Pauline 3, 33, 113–4, 150, 160, 162, 166
Kane, Paula 43
Karloff, Boris 24
Kashner, Sam 76
Kauffman, Christine 124
Kaufman, Philip 175
Kazan, Elia 81–3, 93–7, 124, 135, 137
Kazantsakis, Nikos 170–2
Keaton, Buster 14
Keaton, Diane 165
Keeler, Christine 130
Keillor, Garrison 179
Keith, Brian 147
Kelly, Grace 91, 182
Keneally, Patrick 47
Kennedy, Arthur 118
Kennedy, John F. 112, 144–5
Kennedy, Joseph 97
Kerekes, David 190
Kerouac, Jack 101

Kerr, Deborah 89, 98–100
Kerr, John 98–100
Keys of the Kingdom 71
Keyser, Barbara 34–5, 162, 186
Keyser, Les 34–5, 162, 186
Khomeini, Ayatollah 173
Kill Bill 184
The Killing of Sister George 147
A Kind of Loving 154
King, Martin Luther 146, 147, 191
King Creole 102
King Kong 55
The King of Kings 34
Kinnard, Roy 165–6
Kinsey, Alfred 51, 75, 90–1
The Kiss 7
Kiss Me, Stupid 124, 132–5
Klondike Annie 58–9
Klute 57, 154
Knife in the Water 128
Kobal, John 48
Kraus, Karl 138
Kristel, Sylvia 164
Ku Klux Klan 7
Kubrick, Stanley 112, 118–9, 125–7, 145, 152–3, 178, 190
Kuhn, Annette 12

Ladd, Alan 127
Ladies They Talk About 30
Lady Chatterley's Lover 101, 188
Lamarr, Hedy 52
Lancaster, Burt 76, 89, 116–8
Landau, Jon 162
Landi, Elissa 35
Lang, Fritz 66
Lange, Jessica 170
Lanza, Joseph 155
LaSalle, Mick 17, 32, 50, 150, 188
The Last Picture Show 151
The Last Sunset 124
Last Tango in Paris 4, 149, 157–61, 164
The Last Temptation of Christ 170–4
Laughton, Charles, 34–5, 45
Lawrence, D.H. 101, 118–9, 121, 149
Leachman, Cloris 151
Leamer, Lawrence 78
Leaud, Jean Pierre 159
Le Carré, John 27
Leff, Leonard 16, 43–4
Legion of Decency 1, 35–41, 50, 54, 56, 59, 62–3, 65–7, 71, 74, 79–80, 83, 85–8, 92–3, 95–7, 104, 105, 108, 110, 113, 116–8, 121–6, 129–30, 134–5, 137, 142–3, 145–6, 181, 187
Lehman, Ernest 139
Leigh, Janet 73, 121–4
Leigh, Vivien 63, 81–2, 158
Lejeune, Caroline 34
Lemmon, Jack 106, 119, 134
Lennon, John 102, 190
Leonard, Gloria 138

Index

Leonard, Maurice 50
Let's Make Love 120
Levant, Oscar 106
Levin, Ira 147
Lewis, Jon 97
Lewis, Juliette, 176–8
Lewis, Sinclair 53–4
Life 86, 112
Life at the Top 109
The Life of Brian 165–6
Little, Fr. Thomas 106, 132–3, 136–7, 140
Little Caesar 29, 30, 53
Lolita (1962) 104–5, 112, 124–6
Lolita (1997) 125, 180
Lollobrigida, Gina 107, 140, 183
The Lone Ranger 144
Looking for Mr. Goodbar 165
Lord, Fr. Daniel 15, 34, 37, 52, 53, 85–6
Loren, Sophia 107, 131
Lorna 106
Los Angeles Times 83
Losey, Joseph 149
The Lost Weekend 93
Love Is My Profession 105
Lovelace, Linda 161–2
Lumet, Sidney 136–7
Lupino, Ida 88–9
Lyden, John 17, 148
Lynch, David 180
Lynley, Carol 124
Lyon, Sue 125–6, 179

MacDonald, Dwight 107
Machaty, Gustav 52
Macken, Christopher 157
MacLaine, Shirley 22, 119–20, 134
MacMurray, Fred 68–70, 119–20
Madame Bovary 191
Madame Butterfly 67
Madonna 183
Magnani, Anna 77
Magnum Force 164
Mahony, Cardinal Roger 174
Mailer, Norman 89, 157–8
Main Street 11
Maisie's Marriage 11–12
Malcolm X 191
Malden, Karl 94, 96–7
Malle, Louis 181
The Maltese Falcon 16, 38
Mamet, David 57
Man Hunt 66
Man with the Golden Arm 91–3, 187
Mangano, Silvana 73
Mankiewicz, Joseph L. 100–1, 108
Manson, Marilyn 178
March, Frederic 57
Marked Woman 44
Married Love 11
Marshall, Herbert 26
Martin, Dean 132–5

Marty 92
Marvin, Lee 137
The Marx Brothers 51
Mary Poppins 176
Mason, James 125
Mastroianni, Marcello 113–6, 159
Mathews, Tom Dewe 64, 189
May, John 162
McCabe & Mrs. Miller 154
McCann, Madeleine 180
McCarey, Leo 110
McCarthy, Joseph 40
McClafferty, Rev. John 67
McCullers, Carson 147
McDannell, Colleen 91
McDowell, Malcolm 153, 169
McGilligan, Patrick 30
McNamara, Maggie 84–6
McNicholas, Cardinal 33
McPherson, Elle 189
Medved, Michael 141, 173–4, 186, 188
Mencken, H.L. 33
Mercouri, Melina 112
Meyer, Russ 105–6
Midnight Cowboy 148, 191
Miles, Sarah 138
Miller, Henry 151, 175
Mills, Jane 144, 188, 191
Mineo, Sal 127
Minter, Mary Miles 14
The Miracle 2, 7, 74, 76–81, 85, 93, 124
Mirren, Helen 169
The Misfits 103
Mr. Texas 76
Modern Screen 76
The Money Shot 188
Monkey Business 51
Monroe, Marilyn 60–1, 67, 89, 102–4, 107, 112, 120, 128–9, 134, 183
Montand, Yves 120, 129
Montgomery, James 185
Montgomery, Robert 67
Monthly Film Bulletin 166
The Moon Is Blue 84–9, 92
Moore, Owen 13
Mooring, William 71
Morgenstern, Joe 145
Morocco 22
Motion Picture Association of America (MPAA) 88, 92, 137, 140, 153, 168, 174, 179
Motion Picture Herald 15
Motion Picture Producers and Distributors of America (MPPDA) 15, 19, 36, 70
Motion Picture Research Council 53
Motor Psycho 106
Movieguide 181
Mrs. Doubtfire 181
Munby, Jonathan 30
Mundelein, Cardinal 36–7
Muni, Paul 29–30
Munson, Ona 63

Murphy, Stephen 156
The Music Lovers 154
Mussolini, Benito 52
My Little Chickadee 60
Myers, Henry 20
Myra Breckenridge 60–1

Nabokov, Vladimir 104–5, 112, 125–6, 179
The Naked Gun 170
Naldi, Nita 9
Nash, Roy 87
Nathan, George Jean 49
National Board of Film Censors 7
National Catholic Office for Motion Pictures (NCOMP) 136–9, 147, 156–7, 168, 182
National Catholic Welfare Conference 21
National Conference of Catholic Charities 36
Natural Born Killers 176–8, 191
Naughton, John 33
Never on Sunday 112–3
New York 155
New York Censorship Committee 52
New York Society for the Suppression of Vice 46
New York Times 59, 83, 125, 126, 142
Newman, Paul 127, 131
Newsweek 86, 145
Nichols, Mike 138–9
Nicholson, Jack 156, 170
Nielson, Leslie 170
Night After Night 28, 47, 49
A Night at the Opera 51
Night Games 140
Nin, Anaïs 175
9 1/2 Weeks 170
9 Songs 3, 183
Niven, David 85
Norman, Barry 15, 42, 126
Normand, Mabel 14
Novak, Kim 44, 132–4
Nugent, Frank 59
The Nun's Story 110

O'Brien, Edmond 88
O'Brien, Pat 19–20, 186
Observatore Romano 78
Of Human Bondage 44
O'Hara, John 112
O'Hora, Liam 102, 124
Oiltown, USA 76
The Omen 164–5
On the Waterfront 93
An Open Book 75
Open Your Eyes 8
Ordeal 161
Oscar Wilde 128
Oswald, Lee Harvey 145
O'Toole, Peter 169
Our Movie-Made Children 36–7
The Outlaw 18, 65–6, 151

Pacino, Al 166–7
Palance, Jack 144
Parker, Bonnie 38
Parker, Dorothy 11
Parker, Col. Tom 113
Pascall, Jeremy 33
Pasternak, Joe 56
The Pawnbroker 124, 136–7, 139, 141, 188
Payne Fund 53
Peary, Danny 123
Peck, Gregory 70–2, 164
Peckinpah, Sam 144, 153
Penn, Arthur 38, 132, 143–6
Pennington, Jody 175, 183
Penthouse 168–9
Perkins, Anthony 121–2, 168
Petley, Julian 84, 87, 163
Philips, Baxter 91, 105, 187
Pickford, Mary 9, 13
Pike, Dr James 95, 137
Pillow Talk 106–7, 120
Pinter, Harold 55
Playboy 84, 89, 156
Plummer, Christopher 139
Polanski, Roman 128, 147
Policing Cinema 8–9
Pollack, Sidney 173
Pollard, Michael J. 144
Pompidou, Georges 164
Ponti, Carlo 131
Pontifical Council for Social Communication 187
Popcorn Venus 9
Pope John XXIII 114, 136
Pope Pius XII 101
Il popolo 77–8
The Postman Always Rings Twice (1946) 73
The Postman Always Rings Twice (1981) 170
Power, Tyrone 67
Pre-Code Hollywood 41, 124
Preminger, Otto 84–8, 91–3, 107, 149
Presley, Elvis 86, 102–4, 107, 113
Presley, Priscilla 170
Pretty Woman 188
Production Code Administration (PCA) 23–4, 26, 36, 38, 44, 65–7, 71, 80, 83–4, 87–8, 91–3, 97, 129, 139, 142, 146
Production Code Review Board 138
Profumo, John 130
Psycho 73, 121–4, 144, 167, 191
The Public Enemy 29, 30
Putnam, G.P. 125

Queen Christina 22
The Queen of Camp 46
Queen's Work 37
Queer Nation 176
Quiemada 159
Quiet Days in Clichy 151–2
Quigley, Martin 15, 24, 34, 39, 43, 50, 66, 72, 83, 100, 135

Index

Quinn, Anthony 108–9
Il quotidiano 114

Raft, George 49
Rain 29
Rainier, Prince Louis 182
Rampling, Charlotte 183
Ramsey, Dr. 163
Ramsey, JonBenet 179–80
Randall, Richard 187–8
Rappe, Virginia 13
Rathbone, Basil 57
Ray, Nicholas 127
Reagan, Ronald 18, 190
Rear Window 91
Rebel Without a Cause 101, 124, 127
Red Dust 28
Red-Headed Woman 25–6
Redgrave, Vanessa 111, 138, 154–5
Reed, Donna 89
Reed, Oliver 154–5
Reflections in a Golden Eye 147–8
Rehak, David 189
Reid, Beryl 147
Reid, Wallace 14
Remarque, Erich Maria 27
Remick, Lee 107, 129, 164
Rice, John C 7
Rice-Davies, Mandy 130
Riggs, Marion 127
The Roaring Twenties 64
Roberts, Julia 188
Robertson, James C. 79
Robinson, Edward G. 28–9, 68
"Rock Around the Clock" 90
Roeburt, John 17
Rolling Stone 162
Romance 183
Room at the Top 108–10
Roosevelt, Theodore 30
Rosemary's Baby 147–8, 184
Rosen, Marjorie 9, 101, 104–5, 150
Rossellini, Roberto 7, 77–81, 138
Roud, Richard 160
The Rough Guide to Cult Movies 108
Rushdie, Salman 173
Russell, Jane 65–6, 151
Russell, Jeffrey 163
Russell, Ken 154–5
Russell, Rosalind 182

Salamon, Julie 148
Salinger, J.D. 190
Sanctuary 129
Sanda, Dominique 158
The Sandpiper 132
Sanger, Margaret 11
Saratoga 64
Sarris, Andrew 183
The Satanic Verses 173
Scarface 29–30, 145

Scary Movie 184
Schenck, Nicholas 87
Schickel, Richard 83
Schlesinger, John 135, 148–9, 154
Schneider, Maria 157–60
Schneider, Romy 129
Schreck, Nikolas 162–3
Schrembs, Joseph 39
Schumach, Murray 32, 73, 83, 120
Schwarzenneger, Arnold 189
Scorsese, Martin 110, 165, 170–4
Scream 180
Sears, Heather 108–9
Sellers, Peter 134–5
Selznick, David O. 27, 63, 70–2
Sennett, Mack 13
The Sergeant 148–9
The Seven Minutes 106
The Seven Year Itch 120
The Seventh Seal 110
Sex 46–7
Sex and the Single Girl 124
Sex, Sin and Blasphemy 137
Sextette 60, 61
Sexual Behavior in the Human Female 90
Sexual Behavior in the Human Male 75
Shame 144
Shapiro, Harry 92
Shaw, George Bernard 56, 189
She Done Him Wrong 26, 49–53
Shearer, Norma 11
Sheeny, Monsignor Maurice 75
Shelley, Mary 24
Shepherd, Cybill 151, 165
Shipman, David 22, 41, 43, 165
Shooting Stars 92
Shurlock, Geoffrey 45, 85, 93, 120, 127, 132, 134, 136–8, 149
The Sign of the Cross 34–6
Signoret, Simone 108–10
The Silence of the Lambs 189
Simmons, Jean 109, 116–7
Simon, John 107
Simon & Schuster 125
Simpson, O.J. 180
Sin and Censorship 44, 182
Sinatra, Frank 92–3, 112
Sinyard, Neil 113
Skinner, James M. 13, 107, 186–7
Slide, Anthony 87–8
Smiles of a Summer Night 110
Smith, Justin 152
Smith, Sarah J. 31
Smith, Sheamus 172–3, 179
Snow White and the Seven Dwarfs 61–2
Sobchak, Vivian 152
Some Like It Hot 60–1, 106, 134
Something's Got to Give 134
The Song of Bernadette 68, 71, 78
The Sound of Music 139
Sova, Dawn B. 53, 147

Index

Spartacus 118–9, 127
Spellman, Cardinal 67, 77–80, 84–6, 94–7, 106, 137
Spiegel, Sam 108
Spielberg, Steven 121, 170
Splendor in the Grass 124
Springer, John 102
Stanwyck, Barbara 51, 68, 183
The Star 87
Star Wars 184
Steiger, Rod 136–7, 148–9
Stein, Michael Eric 152
Stevens, George 21, 144
Stewart, James 67, 107–8, 141
Stone, Oliver 176–8, 191
Stone, Sharon 175–6
Stopes, Maria 11–12
The Story of Temple Drake 129
La strada 108–9, 187
A Stranger Knocks 187
Stravinsky, Igor 160
Straw Dogs 145, 153
A Streetcar Named Desire 81–4, 104, 130–1, 157–8
Strick, Joseph 142–3
Stromboli 78
Struthers, Sally 183–4
Studio Relations Committee (SRC) 24, 25, 29, 54
Suddenly Last Summer 108
Sullivan, Fr. Patrick 145–6, 168
Summer of '42 153–4
Sumner, John 46
Sunday, Bloody Sunday 154
Sunset Boulevard 181
Sutherland, Halliday 12
Swain, Dominique 125, 179
Swanson, Gloria 181

Taradash, Daniel 89
Tarantino, Quentin 144, 184
A Taste of Honey 128
Taxi Driver 165, 190
Taylor, Elizabeth 108, 119–20, 138, 147, 190
Taylor, Robert 67
Taylor, William Desmond 14, 150
Temple, Shirley 140
The Ten Commandments 95, 187
Terminator II 189
The Texas Chainsaw Massacre 168
These Three 22
They Live by Night 145
This Picture Is Censored 140
Thomas, Donald 173
Thompson, Jim 191
Thompson, Robert 190
Thomson, David 13, 15
Thorson, Jens Jorgen 151
Tidings 68, 70, 71
Tiernan, Fr. 185–6
Time 95–6, 126

The Times 126
The Times-Herald 73
Tiomkin, Dimitri 72
Toeplitz, Jerzy 145
Tom Jones 130
Tornatore, Giuseppe 4
Total Recall 189
Town Without Pity 124
Townsend, Colleen 76
Tracy, Spencer 186
Trevelyan, John 108, 131, 149, 154–6
Trevor, Claire 44
The Trials of Oscar Wilde 128
Tringinant, Jean-Louis 158, 159
Tropiano, Stephen 31, 147–8, 161, 172
True Grit 148
Trumbo, Dalton 118, 124
Turner, Lana 73
Tushingham, Rita 128
Two-Faced Woman 67
Two Thousand Maniacs 188

Ulysses 142
Union of Theological Seminaries 90

Vadim, Roger 150
Valenti, Jack 140–1, 174
Valentino, Rudolph 182
Van Doren, Mamie 183
Van Dusen, Henry Pitney 90
Variety 38, 126
Venables, Jon 190
Verhoeven, Paul 175–6
Victim 126
Vidal, Gore 60, 127, 135, 169
Village Voice 143–4
Visconti, Luchino 129
The Vixen 9
Vizzard, Jack 23, 91, 136, 137, 139–41
Voight, Jon 148
Von Sydow, Max 21

A Walk on the Wild Side 128
Walker, Alexander 40–1, 48, 56, 57, 119, 138, 142, 155
Walker, Robert 68
Wall Street Journal 148
Wallach, Eli 94, 96
Walsh, Frank 44, 182
Walston, Ray 132–5
Wanger, Walter 78
Warner, Henry 18–19, 39
Warner, Jack 18–19, 42, 127, 141
Washington Post 191
Wayne, John 76, 148
Weber, Lois 7–8
Welch, Raquel 60, 183
Weld, Tuesday 125
Welles, Orson 129
West, Mae 1–2, 26, 28, 46–61, 64, 66, 102, 164

Index

Westminster City Council 179
Whale, James 24
When Willie Comes Marching Home 76
Where Are My Children? 8
Whistle Down the Wind 124
White Heat 74, 114
Whitehouse, Mary 130, 155
Whitney, Dwight 48
Who's Afraid of Virginia Woolf? 138–9, 141
The Wild Bunch 145, 191
Wild Gals of the Naked West 105
The Wild One 104
Wilde, Oscar 128, 182
Wilder, Billy 61, 68–70, 85, 104, 106, 110, 112, 119, 129, 132–5
Williams, Esther 28
Williams, Tennessee 46, 82–4, 93–5, 108
Wilmington, Michael 191
Wilson, Pres. Woodrow 71
Wingate, James 25, 27, 36, 50, 53, 54

Winner, Michael 142
Winters, Shelley 189
A Woman Rebels 62
Wood, Natalie 124
Wood, Sam 68
Wuthering Heights 70
Wray, Fay 55
Wyler, William 22, 127, 128

Yeaman, Elizabeth 50
Yeats, W.B. 65
Yevtushenko, Vevgeny 147
York, Susannah 147

Zanuck, Darryl F. 33, 73, 85
Zarachi, Meir 5
Zaring, E. Robb 57
Zetterling, Mai 140
Zinnemann, Fred 89